The Medieval Kirk, Cemetery and Hospice
at Kirk Ness, North Berwick

The Scottish Seabird Centre Excavations
1999–2006

Old St Andrew's Church at Kirk Ness, as fancifully depicted in 1591 in the pamphlet 'Newes from Scotland', at the time of the Nortyh Berwick witch trials (By permission of University of Glasgow Library, Special Collections)

The Medieval Kirk, Cemetery and Hospice at Kirk Ness, North Berwick

The Scottish Seabird Centre Excavations 1999–2006

Thomas Addyman, Tanja Romankiewicz, Kenneth Macfadyen, Alasdair Ross and Nicholas Uglow

With specialist contributions by John Borland, Stewart Brown, Stuart Campbell, Ruby Cerón-Carrasco, Carol Christiansen, Simon Colebrook, Rosemary Cramp, Michael Donnelly, Julie Franklin, George Haggarty, Derek Hamilton, Derek Hall, Sarah-Jane Haston, David Henderson, Nick Holmes, Fraser Hunter, Stephen Lancaster, Dawn McLaren, Nicola Russell, Scott Timpany, Lore Troalen and Catherine Smith

OXBOW BOOKS

Oxford and Oakville

Published by
Oxbow Books, Oxford, UK

© Oxbow Books and the authors 2013

ISBN 978-1-84217-663-4

A CIP record for this book is available from the British Library

Typeset by M.C. Bishop at The Armatura Press

Printed by Berforts Information Press, Oxford

This book is available direct from

Oxbow Books, Oxford, UK
(Phone: 01865-241249; Fax: 01865-794449)

and

The David Brown Book Company

PO Box 511, Oakville, CT 06779, USA
(Phone: 860-945-9329; Fax: 860-945-9468)

or from our website

www.oxbowbooks.com

A project supported by the Scottish Seabird Centre, Historic Scotland, The Charles Hayward Foundation, The Russell Trust, The Manifold Trust, The Catherine Mackichan Charitable Trust, and The Strathmartine Trust.

Cover: Perspective view of Kirk Ness and the settlement of North Berwick as it may have appeared in the 14th century, looking south (© David Simon).

Contents

List of Figures in Text

List of Tables in Text

Contents of CD

Acknowledgements

For the duration of this long and complex project, since early 1999, a host of people have been involved in one way or another.

Particular thanks to Tom Brock OBE, Chief Executive of the Scottish Seabird Centre for supporting the archaeological project at all stages; and to Lillian Kelly, former Development Manager. The project owes an especial debt to Charlie Marshall, present Fundraising and Business Development Manager, who very effectively raised funds for the post-excavation and publication stages and has helped to drive the project through to the completion of the present volume. We wish to thank all the staff of the Scottish Seabird Centre generally, who, in a very friendly way, have been highly supportive of the project at all stages.

Many thanks are due to Sir Hew Hamilton-Dalrymple, Bt. for his assistance at various points throughout the project and for sharing his knowledge of his family's contribution to the history of the site.

Mark Collard and John Lawson, CECAS, as archaeological advisors to East Lothian Council, were involved with the earlier stages of this project.

The involvement of East Lothian Council Archaeology Service with the project was important to its success. Bridget Simpson, Heritage Officer, was unfailing in her support and good humour throughout the works, and was a principal driver for the responsible completion of the archaeological aspects of the developer-funded project, and a particular debt is acknowledged. Andy Robertson's support as Archaeology Officer, following on from Bridget Simpson's, is also gratefully acknowledged, as is that of Stephanie Leith, Heritage Officer.

During the excavation site works we gratefully acknowledge the support of Simpson & Brown Architects, particularly of Stewart Brown, Richard Shorter and Sue Whittle; of the site contractors, MJ Gleeson Group PLC (Tom Anderson, site agent), and of Scott Castle of MPM Capita (formerly MPM Adams).

The completion of this project would not have been possible without the support, in many ways, by Historic Scotland. In particular a very great thank you is due to Olwyn Owen, Senior Inspector of Ancient Monuments, whose personal support for and interest in the project has been constant and generous throughout. During challenges with the tunnel excavation her intervention proved critical, as was that of her colleague, Patrick Ashmore, Chief Inspector of Ancient Monuments, this proving key to the successful conclusion of the fieldwork; their assistance and recognition of the importance of the site is gratefully acknowledged.

Dr Noel Fojut, then Head of Archaeology Programmes & Grants Advice, Historic Scotland, was instrumental in subsequent support for the project and, in particular, the successful development of a comprehensive programme of post-excavation work and publication. Rod McCullough, succeeding as Head of Archaeology Programmes & Grants Advice, had the unenviable task of pushing the publication through to completion, an operation he conducted very effectively in difficult circumstances, and with good humour – this very much appreciated by the authors.

The project was given much practical assistance by the staff of the East Lothian Council Museums and Libraries Services who have been unfailing in their willingness to be of assistance in researching their collections and archives, for providing temporary curation of finds from the site, and for making their facilities available for artefact illustration. In particular we wish to thank Kate Maynard, Principal Museums Officer, Craig Statham, Archivist; and Paul Zochowski, now of the East Lothian Council Planning Department, and Katherine Weldon and Sheila Asante who both provided much assistance in the museum stores.

Thanks are also due to the unfailingly helpful staff of the National Library of Scotland and of the Royal Commission on the Ancient and Historical Monuments of Scotland.

The excavation stage was funded by the Scottish Seabird Centre and its supporters. The church survey and the St Andrew's Kirk & Anchor Green Environmental Improvement Project, which included some excavation and additional recording, were funded by Historic Scotland. This stage of works was also funded in part by Scottish Enterprise Edinburgh and Lothian (SEEL), contact Colin Beveridge, as part of their North Berwick Harbour: Environmental Improvements project. Historic Scotland also very generously provided emergency funding for the excavation of the tunnel area once the complexity and significance of the remains there became evident; without their timely support the completion of this important stage of the project would certainly not have been possible.

We gratefully acknowledge the very generous financial assistance at the post-excavation and publication stage by Historic Scotland, The Charles Hayward Foundation, Margaret Guido Charitable Trust, The Russell Trust, The Manifold Trust, The Catherine Mackichan Bursary Trust, and The Strathmartine Trust.

The authors wish to express their appreciation of the support and interest throughout the project of the people of North Berwick. Many individuals came forward during the site works and at a number of public presentations by Tom Addyman of the results of the works with very helpful information about the site, with their reminiscences of James Richardson's excavation, and extensive knowledge of the history of North Berwick more generally. Joy Dodd's contribution was of particular help in this respect, with her extensive knowledge of early church and burgh records; her transcriptions of the Kirk Session minutes are included within the text (all abbreviations have been silently expanded).

The authors very much appreciate the contribution of Dr James Marple for sharing the fruits of his own extensive documentary research into the site and the earlier history of North Berwick generally. David McAdam, Geologist, very kindly provided a copy of his 2004 geological report on St Andrew's Church.

In addition to the authors, Tom Addyman and Kenneth Macfadyen, the site staff during excavations and recording at the site included Florence Boisserie, Shelley Brown, David Connolly, Malcolm Corney, Mike Donnelly, Tom Macfadyen, Sarah Phillips, David Reay, Owen Rybald, and John Terry.

We are greatly indebted to the specialists who contributed to this volume. In addition to those cited on the title page we wish to acknowledge the advice at various stages of other archaeological colleagues and specialists. These include Stephen Carter; David Caldwell; Chris Tabraham; Morag Cross, who kindly pursued some particular avenues of historical research; Gary Stratton, Alice Blackwell and Martin Goldberg for their input and advice on Early Medieval section; Tim Holden for discussion about early kiln structures; Anne Crone for permitting sight of the draft manuscript of her forthcoming Auldhame publication; Professor Rosemary Cramp and John Borland for input on stone; Professor Richard Oram; Julie Franklin wishes to thank Alison Cameron, then of Aberdeen City Council Archaeological Unit, for information about the bone pin from St Nicholas Church.

Many thanks to Chris Lowe for his review of Chapter 3, and Peter Addyman who very kindly provided editorial review of the text and for his support throughout.

The illustrations were prepared by Kenneth Macfadyen, Marion O'Neill (monuments and finds), and David Simon and Alan Braby (reconstruction drawings); Tom Parnell photographed the small finds. Derek Hall provided photographic imagery of early pottery from the site. We are indebted to John Dalrymple-Hamilton OBE for permission to reproduce an excerpt of Forrest's 1804 plan of the North Berwick Estate, and to Mrs. Lorna Burton for permission to reproduce images of the 1951 excavation taken by her father, Jack Stewart. The RCAHMS were generous in the terms by which images in their collection were reproduced, with thanks to Neil Fraser and his team.

The authors particularly wish to thank Julie Gardiner and the editorial staff at Oxbow for their patience and understanding in seeing this work through publication.

All responsibility for interpretation and conclusions, errors or omissions, remains entirely with the authors.

Preface

We shall not cease from exploration
And the end of all our exploring
Will be to arrive where we started
And know the place for the first time.
T. S. Eliot

North Berwick is a very special place – rightly famed for the beauty of its beaches, the charm of its High Street and harbour, the allure of the islands in the Forth, and the green shimmy of its coastal golf courses. A joy for those of us lucky enough to live here, North Berwick has also been a draw for visitors ever since the Prince of Wales first arrived by train in 1859 on the new railway line. He was followed by prime ministers and bishops, and well-to-do ladies and gentlemen, as North Berwick became the choice holiday destination of the wealthy in society – the Biarritz of the North. And from about 1900, when the outdoor pool was built, thousands more visitors began to flock to the town for holidays and day-trips – and they have kept coming, not least from Edinburgh and its surrounds. Any North Berwick resident will tell you of the countless people that have said to them: 'Oh, you live in North Berwick – we used to go on holiday there!'

But North Berwick was a special place long before today, and long before the Prince of Wales visited in 1859. A thousand and more years earlier, our forebears also appreciated the advantages of this spot and made their homes here. The remains of the 12th-century St Andrew's Kirk on Anchor Green have been known about for many years and were exposed by one of North Berwick's most famous sons, the archaeologist Dr James Richardson, in 1951–2. North Berwick has also long been known as the site of a wealthy nunnery in the medieval period, whose remains still stand as a romantic ruin in the grounds of The Abbey old people's home on Abbey Road. Its well-known claim to be the point of departure for the pilgrim ferry to St Andrews via Earlsferry was underlined by the famous discovery in 1893 of a medieval mould for pilgrim's badges. But despite all these clues, and many others, the story of early North

Berwick has remained frustratingly shadowy – until now.

It gives me enormous pleasure to welcome this publication of the excavations at Kirk Ness 1999–2006. As is so often the case today, all of the recent archaeological work has been carried out in connection with development – in this instance, the building, landscaping and extension of the Scottish Seabird Centre. But Tom Addyman and his team have done so much more in this book than reported the results of their various recent digs. Against the background of some important new discoveries, in this volume they have brought together and re-examined all the evidence for early North Berwick – archaeological, historical, documentary, pictorial and cartographic. They have opened a fascinating window on the history of our very special town, and have explained it in an engaging and highly readable account.

On Anchor Green, Tom and his team have unearthed confirmation at last of the early occupation of Kirk Ness, in the shape of domestic occupation and agricultural processing from as early as the late 5th to 6th centuries – in the period of early Northumbrian or Anglian penetration into East Lothian. This tantalising glimpse has also given us the North Berwick great auk, a corn-drying kiln from as early as the 7th–9th centuries, butchered seal bones, and a myriad of other fascinating and more mundane insights into the lives of our forebears. The evidence for medieval North Berwick is also amplified and revisited, with the discovery of remains perhaps associated with the recorded 12th-century hospice for poor people and pilgrims; re-interpretation of the ruined footprint of St Andrews Kirk; and we come face to face with some of our ancestors in the human remains recovered from Anchor Green, including one unfortunate young man who was fatally stabbed four times in the back in the 12th or 13th centuries. Finally, we revisit later Kirk Ness and its ever-changing uses following the demise of the old kirk, right up to the present day, from quarry and boatyard, to Rocket Patrol and Seabird Centre.

The archaeology of Scotland's historic towns is often surprising – and North Berwick is no exception. Towns have always had to change and adapt to remain vital and viable, and past changes and adaptations are written into our townscapes and lie beneath the streets and within the fabric of the buildings which host our daily business. This is why a town's visual and historic qualities can satisfy part of society's need for cultural and physical roots. Understanding and appreciating the urban historic environment is not only of passing interest, but also about the present character and shape of towns, their intrinsic qualities and the differences between them. And it is about the future, for the decisions made today will be our legacy to succeeding generations of town-dwellers. Sustaining the heritage of towns and cities is about using resources wisely. At heart, it is about the careful recycling of urban land and buildings, about managing change to enhance, rather than diminish, the character of towns. There can be few better examples of this than in the success, at every level, of the Scottish Seabird Centre – which is but the latest chapter in the long and important story of Kirk Ness.

It seems particularly fitting that this excellent book is published in 2013. Dr James Richardson, who was appointed Scotland's first Inspector of Ancient Monuments in 1914 and first excavated the historic kirk on Anchor Green in 1951–2, was also instrumental in setting up North Berwick Museum in the fine old school building in 1957. The Museum was sadly forced to close in 2002, but it has just been beautifully refurbished by East Lothian Council and reopened in July as the Coastal Communities Museum. The Museum now has an even more interesting story to tell …

On behalf of Historic Scotland, I am delighted to congratulate Tom and all those who have contributed to this fine volume, which is also a fitting tribute to Dr Richardson's memory.

Olwyn Owen
Historic Scotland, August 2013

1. Introduction

Kirk Ness, a rocky promontory formerly connected to the East Lothian shore by a tide-washed spit of beach sand, has in many ways always been a focal point within the settlement and Royal Burgh of North Berwick. Over time, and under the patronage of the nunnery of North Berwick, Kirk Ness developed into the principal harbour and ferrying point on the pilgrimage route from the south to the shrine of St Andrew, at St Andrews in Fife. Here, too, was located the medieval parish and burgh church, similarly dedicated to St Andrew.

After the Reformation the church continued in use until its dramatic destruction by winter storms in the middle of the 17th century. Though some burial activity carried on thereafter, the site was progressively abandoned and, by the beginning of the 19th century, the church had all but disappeared. From that time onwards the harbour area saw successive reclamation and redevelopment. With North Berwick's transformation into a seaside watering place in the middle and later 19th century, Kirk Ness became a hub for recreational activities and remains so today. This continuing role was recently enhanced by the construction of the Scottish Seabird Centre, opened on 21 May 2000 by HRH The Prince Charles, Duke of Rothesay.

The choice of Kirk Ness as the site for the Scottish Seabird Centre necessitated a series of development-related archaeological interventions required as part of the general planning process and carried out between 1999 and 2006 by Addyman Archaeology and its predecessors. The development of the building itself, the associated landscape improvements, and subsequent works, primarily impacted on the central and north-eastern areas of the promontory and, particularly, the area formerly occupied by the medieval church and part of its cemetery.

Excavation revealed a complex and important sequence of archaeological remains. Confirmed for the first time at Kirk Ness were a prehistoric component and a long sequence of early medieval activity, the latter long-suspected. This was in addition to many remains relating to the better attested later medieval and post-medieval history of the site. The archaeological work also included

intensive building recording and archaeological assessment of the adjacent ruins of the medieval church, which were subject to a separate programme of consolidation and repair.

This publication

The logic of this volume requires some explanation. Its primary purpose is to offer a comprehensive account of the archaeological works undertaken at the site between 1999 and 2006, of the findings made, and of the results of post-excavation analysis of materials recovered. The intention is to satisfy the contractual obligations relating to the work and conditions imposed, in particular, by the Planning Authority, East Lothian Council, and by Historic Scotland, and to disseminate knowledge of the important archaeological remains encountered.

However, the various archaeological interventions were very disparate in nature and it proved almost impractical to describe these without presenting a comprehensive overview of the wider site, extending to much of the Kirk Ness promontory and harbour area. This provided a distinct geographical unit whose archaeology and history was clearly definable. All parties agreed that this approach was highly desirable and the publication plan for the project was evolved along these lines. A particular exercise that lay out-with the original scope of the site works was to attempt to better understand the progress and results of a major, but unreported excavation, carried out at the church site under the auspices of the late Dr James Richardson in 1951–2.

Kirk Ness was always, and still is, a principal focus of the town life of North Berwick and, moreover, is part of its *raison d'etre* – an anchorage and harbour, and crossing point to Fife (indeed a ferry boat is the theme of the burgh's coat of arms). With the construction of the Scottish Seabird Centre it is today one of the premier visitor destinations in south-east Scotland. So varied is the interest of the Kirk Ness site, both to the academic community and to the community of North Berwick and beyond, that this volume, in addition, seeks to address

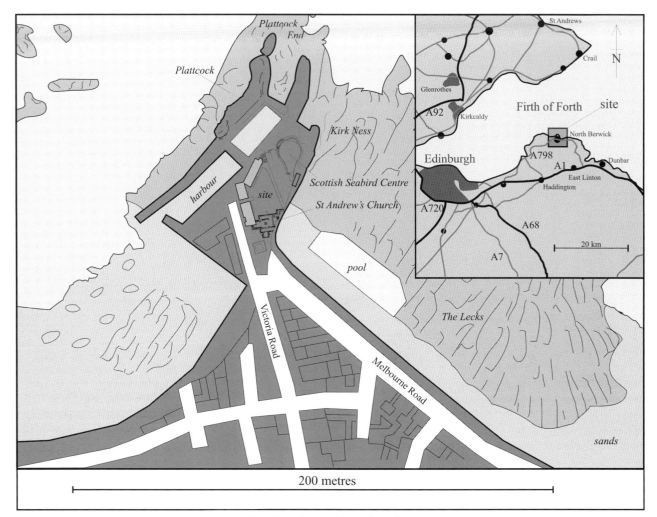

Fig. 1.1: General location plan

aspects of its wider history, including some of the numerous incidents of particular topical interest, and features of its more recent evolution. It was also hoped that this, and the generous provision of good illustrations, would broaden the appeal of the work.

Chapter 1 introduces the Kirk Ness site, its topography and geology. There follows an account of the various and often convoluted archaeological interventions required for the development of the Scottish Seabird Centre and the associated conservation, repair and presentation of the Old Church site.

Chapter 2 records the limited but now certain archaeological presence of a prehistoric (Iron Age) component of the Kirk Ness site.

Chapter 3 examines a complex series of early historic remains encountered at the site, particularly within the tunnel excavation area at its north end. Here, first the archaeological findings and their complex sequence are introduced and explained. A synthesis is given of the results of a sequence of radiocarbon dates and Bayesian modelling by which the stratigraphy and chronology were more properly understood; an understanding that developed considerably after the excavation phase. The latter part of the chapter discusses a possible historical

context within which this account of the archaeology can, perhaps, be better understood – both in relation to the local tradition of an early Christian presence at Kirk Ness and within the regional geo-political sphere.

In contrast, Chapter 4, which addresses the medieval and early post-medieval history of the site, begins with a review of its known history. This is followed by consideration of antiquarian sources and early cartographic material, and then presents an account of James Richardson's important excavations of 1951–2. The evolution of the church is then reassessed. A section describes past and more recent exposure of human remains at the site including the formal excavation of an area of the cemetery to the north of the church. The medieval period is also represented by remains of a more domestic character made in the area of the tunnel excavation. Historic finds from the church site are brought together and described in context for the first time.

Chapter 5 considers the history of the Kirk Ness site following the demise of St Andrew's Church in the middle part of the 17th century and provides an overview of successive developments around the periphery of the early site – including the eroding shoreline to the east, the expansion of facilities around the harbour area, the early

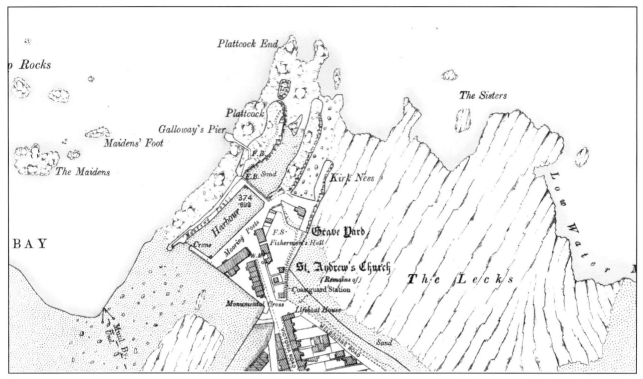

Fig. 1.2: Detail of the Ordnance Survey (25in:mile), first revision of 1893/4: detail from Haddingtonshire sheet II. It shows many more buildings on the Kirk Ness than the earlier plans, including the 'Coastguard Station'. It also shows the boatyard, on ground levelled with spoil from the harbour deepening excavations in the 1860s (Reproduced by permission of the Trustees of the National Library of Scotland.)

establishment of recreational facilities, and more recent regeneration including the creation of the present Scottish Seabird Centre.

Chapter 6, the conclusion, presents an overview of the project works, of the discoveries made, and of the wider site. It also suggests some possible priorities for future research at the site. The appendices, in text and on the accompanying CD, report in more detail the results of a variety of post-excavation analyses undertaken on finds from the site by commissioned specialists.

Topography

The East Lothian coast is defined by its rocky cliffs and crags, long beaches and dune systems, beyond which lies a fertile hinterland, the coastal plain that extends along the south side of the Firth of Forth. North Berwick lies at the mouth of the Forth estuary, but still within the compass of the firth, protected from the open North Sea by the southern coastline of Fife to the north (Figure 1.1).

The surrounding land forms a broad projection into the Forth, extending from Gullane Point in the west to Tyne Mouth and St Baldred's Cradle in the east. This is partnered on the north side of the firth by a similar, though somewhat lesser, projection of the Fife coast, stretching from Shell Bay to the west of Earlsferry to Sauchar Point, east of Elie. At North Berwick, the principal settlement on the East Lothian side, the Kirk Ness headland extends northwards from the shore between two

bays – North Berwick Bay to the west and Milsey Bay to the east. At Earlsferry there is a similar peninsula, Chapel Ness. The latter forms a counterpart to Kirk Ness, the pairing at the shortest crossing point at the mouth of the firth, a distance of some 18km.

The broad protrusion of the wider East Lothian coastline in this area is emphasised by two large bays, Aberlady Bay to the east, and to the west Tyne Mouth and Belhaven Bay, these cutting deep into the land. The valley of the River Tyne running from south-east to west and the low-lying lands surrounding the Mill Burn and Peffer Burn in the east form a low, broad stretch of land, lying only about 20m above sea level. The ground rises again to the south, but also to the north, to form a low ridge on the widest part of the projection on which North Berwick lies.

North Berwick Law, the town's conical landmark rising 187m above the coastal plain, is also the highest point of north-central East Lothian. Together with Traprain Law to the south and the Bass Rock to the northeast these volcanic plugs rise high against the west–east glacial drift. Both Traprain Law and North Berwick Law are crowned by prehistoric fortifications.

Kirk Ness itself is a low-lying rocky promontory, long connected to the mainland by a narrow sand neck, a seawashed tombola. This, once the site of a causeway or bridge, was only formally reconnected to the town at the beginning of the 19th century, with the northwards extension of what is now Victoria Road, formerly Shore

Fig. 1.3: Aerial view of Kirk Ness, c.1950 looking NNW. The swimming pool can be seen to top right; below this is the Harbour Pavilion, of 1930, which occupies the site of the existing Scottish Seabird Centre (© RCAHMS Aerofilms Collections. Licensor www.rcahms.gov.uk)

Street, to the harbour. In common with the town itself Kirk Ness has been repeatedly subjected to catastrophic windblown events that inundated the headland under layers of sand. Elsewhere the destructive action of winter storms has dramatically eroded the former extent of the peninsula, particularly on its eastern side.

Geology

The underlying geology of the surrounding area was formed around 327–342 million years ago in the Carboniferous period and is of a Basaltic Tuff, an igneous bedrock formed from semi-mobile to mobile and highly gaseous silica-poor magma rising to the surface where sudden pressure relief caused explosive volcanic eruptions, producing fragmentary pyroclastic material and ash.

This bedrock is overlain with superficial deposits of Devensian-Diamicton till formed up to 2 million years ago by ice age glaciers scouring the landscape and depositing moraines of till with outwash sand and gravel from seasonal and post-glacial melt waters. Along the coastline

beneath North Berwick exists a band of Flandrian age raised marine deposits overlying the Basaltic Tuff bedrock; this was formed in shallow seas 2 million years ago in the Quaternary period. These contain mainly siliciclastic sediments deposited as mud, silt sand and gravel.

To the south of North Berwick the Basaltic Tuff is broken by the large volcanic plug that makes up North Berwick Law. This is composed from Phonolite, an igneous bedrock formed 327–354 million years ago. A further outcrop is noted as the North Berwick Abbey Plug on St Baldred's Road, formed from Monchiquite igneous bedrock 256–327 million years ago.

These geological conditions of this coastline area appear to have been advantageous for early human activities in the area. The Aeolian deposits upon which the golf links have been built to the east and west of the town of North Berwick have produced occupation deposits, internments and artefacts ranging from the Neolithic to the 6th century AD.

The Kirk Ness promontory itself comprises a series of linear outcrops of rock running SW– NE into the sea (Figure 1.2). These relate to the spreading of the earth's tectonic plates and intrusions of liquid lava into fissures formed by the spreading. The excavated sites at Kirk Ness mainly lie on a linear outcrop of Trachybasalt, igneous bedrock whose rocks were formed from mobile magma poor in silica, rising to the surface and erupting as fluid lava from fissures. Immediately to the west of this is a linear outcrop of Plagioclase Olivine Clinopyroxene Macrophyric Basalt igneous bedrock, a rock formed from silica-poor magma intruding into the earth's crust and cooling to form intrusions. The latter range from large course crystalline, often gabbroic, plutons at depth, to smaller fine to medium crystalline, often basaltic dykes and sills. The next outcrop of rock is composed of Mugearite, an igneous bedrock also formed from eruptions of fluid lava. The promontory is finished with a linear outcrop of Plagioclase Macrophyric Basaltic igneous bedrock before sloping down into the sea. A feature of the foreshore immediately to the east of the Kirk Ness peninsula is a volcanic outcrop of tufa known as 'the red leck' (sources – http://mapapps.bgs.ac.uk/geologyofbritain, and Cruft *et. al.* 2006, 1–10).

The site

The site proposed for the construction of the Scottish Seabird Centre occupies a parcel of land on the eastern side of Kirk Ness, the former site of the Harbour Pavilion (NGR: NT 55422 85627). Much of the earlier topography of the north-west and west parts of the promontory is now obscured by historic and more recent development including, from north to south, the site of a lido or outdoor swimming pool (now a boat park), the harbour, associated harbour buildings, and a small residential area that fronts on the northern end of Victoria Road on its western side, the latter now connecting Kirk Ness to the town (Figure 1.3). The surviving remains of St Andrew's Old Kirk, a Scheduled Ancient Monument, and its associated burial ground, Anchor Green (formerly Auld Kirk Green), are located immediately to the south and south-west of the Scottish Seabird Centre development site (NGR: NT 55402 85555). Immediately north of the Scottish Seabird Centre site is a paved esplanade; a sea wall bounds these to the east and north-east. Rocky headlands extend out to the north-east, the northernmost of which, the Plattcock, terminates at Plattcock End.

Historical introduction

The earliest known medieval parish church at North Berwick, at Kirk Ness, was dedicated to St Andrew. It is now called the 'old kirk' and has already been the subject of a number of excellent detailed investigations by both historians and archaeologists. All of these reports have focused, to different extents, on hagiography relating to an even earlier and still rather obscure local saint called St Baldred who, it is said, lived in the area in the mid-8th century AD (Arnold 1882–5, I, 48). Unfortunately, there

is very little surviving information relating to St Baldred and his mission apart from a couple of references in English sources and later hagiography from the Aberdeen Breviary. Yet, his figure overshadows the history of both the church of St Andrew and North Berwick to a considerable extent.

The archaeological investigations of the site between 1999 and 2006 resulted in the discovery that a major component of the site belonged to the early medieval (pre-*c*.900) period. In this context it is increasingly tempting to suggest that there may have been an earlier Christian presence upon the site that was then overlaid by the medieval parish church dedicated to St Andrew.

The narrative history of the old parish church as presented in this publication is inevitably based upon secondary sources since there are essentially no surviving Scottish documentary records from the pre-1100 period. This situation does not improve much for the period 1100–*c*.1550 because the North Berwick burgh records for that period have not survived. This leaves the cartulary of the medieval Cistercian nunnery of North Berwick as virtually the sole source for material relating to the old kirk because its revenues belonged to the convent. Post-*c*.1560 and the Reformation this ecclesiastic record can be increasingly supplemented by both the surviving burgh records (NAS, B56) and by assorted papers from the records of the different families, like the Dalrymples, who held the barony of North Berwick.

Archaeological works in 1999–2006

The recent archaeological involvements at Kirk Ness related to the construction of the Scottish Seabird Centre, the provision of associated services and the improvement of its immediate surroundings, particularly at Anchor Green, the site of North Berwick's medieval church and graveyard. This section summarises the stages and progress of these archaeological involvements (Figure 1.4). A more detailed account of each stage of the works is contained in the individual Data Structure Reports cited in the bibliography under Addyman and Macfadyen respectively. Copies are lodged with the East Lothian Council Archaeology Service's SMR in Haddington, and at the RCAHMS search room, Edinburgh, where the site archive is also deposited.

The Scottish Seabird Centre site (1999)

The first stage of work related to the excavation of the footprint of the proposed Scottish Seabird Centre building, the site of which bounded the north-east perimeter of Anchor Green. This area had, until recently, been occupied by the Harbour Pavilion (demolished 1998), effectively a brown-field site for which the proposed new building represented a major initiative towards the regeneration of the harbour area.

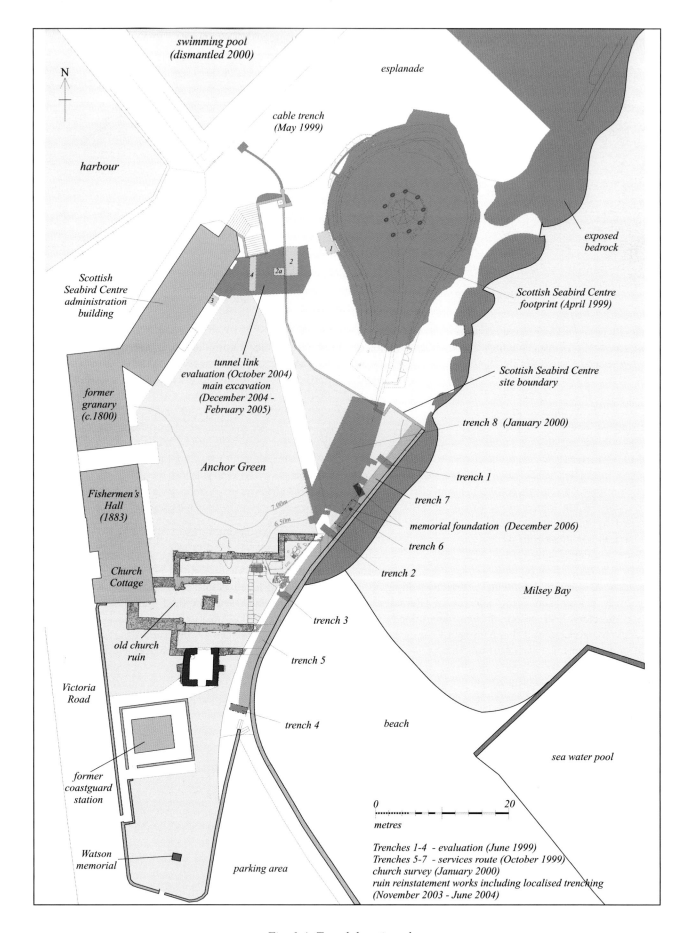

Fig. 1.4: Trench location plan

Fig. 1.5: General view of the Scottish Seabird Centre construction area, looking NW

By means of a Desk-Based Assessment (see below), it was understood that the site had until *c.*1862 consisted of a sea-washed coastal inlet bounded by bedrock ridges. At that stage the inlet was in-filled and a stone-walled boatyard constructed, some standing remains of which survive. This compound was subsequently replaced by the Harbour Pavilion, built in 1930–1.

Excavation for the lower level of the new building had begun in early 1999. This prompted a meeting on 14 April of interested parties and those concerned with potential archaeological issues at the site. Present were Mark Collard and John Lawson of the City of Edinburgh Council Archaeology Service, on behalf of East Lothian Council; Olwyn Owen, Inspector of Ancient Monuments, Historic Scotland; Scott Castle of MPM Capita (formerly MPM Adams), project managers; Richard Shorter, Simpson & Brown Architects; Thomas Addyman of Addyman & Kay; and Tom Anderson of Gleeson's, the site contractors, and others. It was determined that a strategy for archaeological recording of the part-excavated site be formulated for immediate implementation. Addyman & Kay were then commissioned to undertake an assessment of exposed archaeological remains on the site; this took place on 14–16 April 1999.

The excavation area consisted of a trapezoidal area measuring some 80m (N–S) by a maximum of 40m (E–W). This site was bounded on the east by a bedrock outcrop forming an irregular ridge running approximately north–south, culminating as a sea-girt promontory. Beyond this lies Milsey Bay's beach, and thereafter the sea. On the west side of this ridge the land had been artificially in-filled in the 19th century to create a level terrace; parts of a second, parallel bedrock ridge are still visible bounding the west side of the site area.

Within these boundaries, the footprint of the proposed Scottish Seabird Centre itself occupied an area that was approximately pear-shaped in plan, the outline of this structure narrowing towards its southern margin, and measuring some 33m (N–S) by 23m (E–W) overall.

In early 1999 in advance of an archaeological presence on the site the footprint and foundations of the structure had been excavated down to some 2m (at the southern end) to 2.5m (to the north) below the existing surface (Figure 1.5).

A general clean-up included dressing back of all vertical sections and the removal of disturbed overburden to expose the upper surfaces of any archaeological deposit surviving below. By these means, a considered assessment of the extent, nature and survival of archaeological material was made. Deeper excavations were made into the areas of proposed foundation trenching, these with the aim of assessing the nature of lower deposits present elsewhere on the site. To this end, a south-east to north-west aligned sondage 7m long by 2m wide was excavated by JCB, to a depth of around 2m below the surrounding levelled surface (Figure 1.6). This revealed the buried sand bed of the tidal inlet that had existed in this area before reclamation took place; from here were recovered miscellaneous 18th and 19th century finds. The sequence of the subsequent landfill deposition was recorded; the latter also produced a varied sample of predominantly 19th century finds including a dump of black glass bottles of mid-19th century date.

No deposits or residual material was identified that might have related to the site of known archaeological sensitivity immediately to the south and southwest, namely the burial ground at Anchor Green. The assessment thus concluded that the area of early settlement activity lay just beyond the south and west perimeter of the development site; construction of the Scottish Seabird Centre was therefore permitted to proceed with no further archaeological requirements.

Further works in 1999–2000

Between April 1999 and March 2000, Addyman Associates was commissioned to undertake a series of further evaluations, watching briefs and more extensive excavations. While these formed separate and distinct phases of investigation, all were necessitated as a result of the programme of building and landscaping work associated with the construction of the Scottish Seabird Centre. Together these interventions permitted an integrated appraisal of archaeological deposits present within the core area of the site at Kirk Ness, centred on Anchor Green.

DESK-BASED ASSESSMENT

A Desk-Based Assessment (DBA) was undertaken of readily available documentary source material relating to the site in order to better predict its archaeological potential. Although the initial priority of the DBA was to identify source material directly relating to the areas already impacted, so that on-site assessment of archaeological remains could be rapidly achieved, the study was subsequently extended to consider the surrounding area, to take in the existing harbour and swimming pool, and the site, ruins and immediate surroundings of St Andrew's Old Church, located just to the south of the Scottish Seabird Centre site. Consequently, the results of this assessment were available to inform the later phases of archaeological work and have been integrated into this report.

SERVICES TRENCH TO THE NORTH-WEST OF THE SCOTTISH SEABIRD CENTRE SITE

In May 1999 the laying of a temporary electrical supply for the site works during the construction of the Scottish Seabird Centre, required the excavation of a trench from the north-west sector of the Scottish Seabird Centre construction site to a connection with the mains cable at the south corner of the open-air swimming pool some 15m to the west-north-west. The proposed trench was excavated by hand to a depth of 0.60m and a width of about 0.3m. The truncated upper surface of whin bedrock was encountered directly below the existing concrete surfacing in most areas; no significant finds were made. It is probable that this levelling of the bedrock occurred in the early 1860s, when this area was reclaimed (Figure 1.7).

EVALUATION BEHIND THE SEA WALL (TRENCHES 1–4)

Four evaluation trenches were excavated in June 1999 along the sea wall bounding the east side of the ruin of St Andrew's Old Church and its former churchyard, in advance of construction works – the proposed laying of services. Consideration was given to the most pragmatic and direct route for the connection of services, running in from the town to the south to the Scottish Seabird Centre site, and one that was judged to be least likely to disturb significant *in situ* archaeological remains. The most obvious potential route lay along the east boundary of the site, immediately against the rear side of the existing masonry-built sea wall and for the most part beneath an existing footpath.

Agreement upon the proposed route was closely co-ordinated with Historic Scotland, who have responsibility for the Scheduled Ancient Monument of the church ruin itself, and CECAS, advisors to East Lothian Council, for the non-scheduled parts of the site. Following this consultation it was agreed that four evaluation trenches be located along the proposed services trench line in order to identify the eastern edge of archaeologically sensitive deposits (the erosion-truncated eastern end of the church itself, and its associated graveyard) and to determine whether there was enough room between this and the rear side of the sea wall to avoid disturbance of significant remains. The evaluation also provided the opportunity to characterise the nature of the archaeological site at Kirk Ness on its east side, and to determine the extent of its survival in relation to historic coastal erosion and subsequent disturbance, the latter including the extent of Dr James S. Richardson's investigation in the early 1950s.

Within the four trenches the eastern limit of *in situ* archaeological deposits was defined following the excavation of multiple dumpings of fill of very varied character infilling the void behind the newly constructed sea wall of *c.*1857 (Figure 1.8). This edge represented the extent of coastal erosion up to the mid-19th century. A charnel pit was located in Trench 2, adjacent to the original north transept; this contained the remains of 30 inhumation burials, considered to have been the product of excavations of the church site in the early 1950s by Dr Richardson. Three *in situ* inhumation burials were also identified 0.3m below the existing surface but were left undisturbed. A fire-pit was revealed and sampled in Trench 4, this subsequently dated to the pre-Roman Iron Age (see Chapter 2).

The trenches demonstrated that there was likely sufficient space (approximately 1m) between the rear of the sea wall and the surviving archaeology to insert the services route.

SERVICES TRENCH BEHIND THE SEA WALL (TRENCHES 5–7)

Work in October 1999 involved an archaeological monitoring exercise over the mechanical excavation of a 1.5–2.0m wide services trench along the rear side of the mid-19th century sea wall bounding the east side of the church ruin and Anchor Green (Figure 1.9). This was a requirement of both Historic Scotland and CECAS as archaeological advisors to East Lothian Council, in light of the results of the evaluation trenching exercise reported in the previous section. The trench ran from a little to the south-east of the surviving church porch to the north-east corner of Anchor Green, at the point where the sea wall ran across into the Scottish Seabird Centre site proper. From thereon the first stage of works had demonstrated that no significant earlier archaeology survived.

During the period 1–22 October 1999 the trench was mechanically excavated to a depth of about 1.0–1.2m.

Fig. 1.6: Sondage through fill deposits dating to the early 1860s, revealing the bed of the former foreshore beneath

Fig. 1.7: Northern part of the services trench to the NW of the Scottish Seabird Centre site, bedrock revealed, looking SW

Fig. 1.8: Trench 1 showing the extent of undisturbed deposits (unexcavated), looking NE

Fig. 1.9: General excavation of the services trench behind the sea wall (trench 5), looking south

Fig. 1.10: Exposure of in situ cemetery deposits behind the sea wall in the area of trench 6, looking south

All excavation works were closely monitored and in most areas only mid-19th century backfill behind the sea wall was encountered. At one point, just to the north of the church ruin (beyond the north transept) an area of the former graveyard extended well into the excavation trench. This area was formally excavated by hand down to the trench formation level; here a number of *in situ* burials were recorded and exhumed. For ease of description the mechanically excavated trench to the south of this area was arbitrarily designated 'Trench 5,' the area of *in situ* deposits was designated 'Trench 6' and the remainder of the excavation area beyond to the north, 'Trench 7'.

TRENCH 5

Trench 5 ran along the rear face of the sea wall for approximately 30m, from the area of the steps upto the Anchor Green path to the south-east of the former church porch, to the area of evaluation Trench 2. For the entirety of the length of the trench only mid-19th century and later deposits were impacted and in only two areas were *in situ* archaeological levels actually exposed.

The first exposure was at the eastern terminus of the ruined exterior wall of the south aisle of the church. Here a mass of human charnel had been deposited over what appeared to be a level of rubble fill (as opposed to *in situ* archaeology); the latter was found to contain a fragment of 18th or 19th century pan-tile. This deposit of charnel

had apparently been placed in no particular order, and had perhaps been gathered together at that point during the construction of the sea wall in the middle of the 19th century. Despite its proximity to the ruined wall of the church none of its fabric was actually exposed and no direct relationship with the adjacent deposits was established. The surrounding matrix was of beach sand. The deposit of charnel was overlain by a number of general fill levels.

The second exposure of archaeological deposits was in the area of Trench 2, where the vertically-cut side of the graveyard deposits was traced further to the north for a short distance beyond the north section of the trench.

TRENCH 6

Between 1.2m and 5.5m beyond the north side of Trench 2 a bulk of undisturbed archaeological deposits was found to extend into the area of the services trench at a relatively low level, at 0.6–0.8m below the existing surface (Figure 1.10). The exposure was overlain by the 19th century and mid-20th century fill deposits recorded elsewhere. Beyond 4.4m to the north of Trench 2 a mass of loose charnel had been deposited upon the surface of the archaeological levels, evidently further material gathered together during the construction of the sea wall.

The general matrix of what, until the construction of the sea wall, had been eroding graveyard deposits consisted of a medium-brown, slightly humic gritty silt. In a number of areas this contained concentrations of stones

Fig. 1.11: Exposure of deeply stratified deposits in the NW section of trench 7

(whin) and there was some quantity of smaller stones throughout. The deposit had been cut by a number of inhumation burials, the majority of which had been partly or largely eroded away by the sea to the east. Skeletal material was readily apparent within most of the burial cuts. The decision was consequently taken to fully excavate the remains in advance of the service trenching operation. Five burials were fully excavated within the Trench 6 area and two more were identified but left *in situ* as they would not be further impacted by trenching.

TRENCH 7

'Trench 7' included the northern parts of the services excavation, running north-north-east/north-east from the north side of Trench 6 for a further distance of 14m. The excavation varied in width between 0.70m and 1.4m but was generally 1m wide. Mid-way along its length, Trench 7 cut across the backfilled evaluation Trench 1. At its north-east end the excavation terminated at an existing brick wall/foundation of a demolished toilet block associated with the former Harbour Pavilion dance hall (this appears in Figure 1.3).

Beneath the topsoil, mostly removed by a prior surface strip, the upper 0.8–1.1m of deposits across the trench consisted of the same mixed sandy backfill behind the sea wall as recorded in Trench 1. Along much of the length of the north-west (up-slope) section of Trench 7 pre-existing *in situ* archaeological deposits were revealed at the base of the section, these slightly cut into by the excavator at points. The upper surface of these, which evidently represented the surface as exposed by coastal erosion before the construction of the sea wall in *c.*1857, had formerly sloped down steeply to the south-east and generally disappeared at steep inclination at the base of the excavated trench. These deposits represented the surviving maximum extent of *in situ* archaeological deposition and were recorded in section.

The upper levels further to the south-west consisted of a narrow layer of light sands that partly overlay a darker sand layer, these perhaps respectively representing wind-blown sand over a buried topsoil horizon. These in turn overlay a

mix of beach gravels and stone, revealed at the base of the trench; a bedrock protrusion rose up through this at one point, suggesting the gravels lay at the base of the sequence.

Further north-east the gravelly material was evidently overlain by a band of light coloured mottled wind-blown sands that continued as an irregular layer within much of the remainder of the trench section further north-east. Beneath this level, further north-east and continuing below the limit of excavation at the base of the trench, was an irregular deposit of a darker, stonier sand seen within the south-west part of the trench. At a similar stratigraphic level further to the north-east, the wind-blown sand was revealed to overlie some darker but similar sands, that in turn overlay a mixed level of beach gravels crushed shell and stones, this possibly a continuation of the similar material encountered further to the south-west, as already described. A small sondage made into this deposit revealed a further level of dark sands extending below the limit of excavation (Figure 1.11).

No direct evidence for human activity was revealed within this sequence of deposits in Trench 7. The absence of evidence for burial activity within this section was particularly notable, possibly suggesting this area lay at the fringe of or partly out-with the area occupied by the cemetery.

AREA TO THE NORTH OF THE CHURCH (TRENCH 8)

The final stage of construction work involved landscaping to allow for the provision of an approach path to the Scottish Seabird Centre itself, a process that required a significant reduction in the ground level over an open area of some 120m² lying between the south entrance of the Scottish Seabird Centre and the north side of the ruined north transept of St Andrew's church. The entirety of this zone was located within Anchor Green, an area which, from historic maps, bore testing (*pers. comm.* S. Carter) and the previous works conducted on the site, clearly formed part of the burial ground of St. Andrew's Church. An open area excavation was thus undertaken in January and February 2000.

Fig. 1.12: Trench 8, general view looking NNE, showing exposure of inhumation burials

The work was preceded by a topographic survey of the entire area of Anchor Green to the north of the church. Following mechanical removal of topsoil and cleaning, excavation was carried out by spit and natural level in order to identify *in situ* archaeological remains which, when encountered, were then recorded and reduced to the depth required for construction.

In the southern parts of the excavation archaeological deposits were found almost immediately below existing topsoil, where landscaping work in the mid-1950s had reduced the ground level. Here a particular concentration of burials was encountered; a total of 21 inhumations and two dog skeletons were exhumed. A number of further grave cuts were also identified. This group of inhumations was generally judged to date to the later use of the church site, perhaps both of late pre- and early post-Reformation date (Figure 1.12).

Various episodes of post-graveyard activity were identified that included landfills, a substantial ditch, and the brick bottoming of a path laid out in the mid-1950s. A sondage within the northern part of the excavation area revealed the overall depth of deposition which overlay a sequence of coastal-derived geological layers.

OSTEOLOGICAL ANALYSIS

An extensive osteological assessment of all exhumed skeletal material was completed by David Henderson, a notable result of which was the identification of the violent death by stabbing of a young male individual.

CHURCH SURVEY

As a separate exercise Historic Scotland directly commissioned an archaeological and analytical survey of the existing ruin of St Andrew's Old Church, this leading to a stand-alone report. The results of the survey work are integrated into Chapter 4.

ST ANDREW'S KIRK & ANCHOR GREEN ENVIRONMENTAL IMPROVEMENT PROJECT (2003–4)

Proposed environmental improvements within the Scheduled area of the medieval church ruin were developed in close cooperation with Historic Scotland, principally represented at this stage by Olwyn Owen. Archaeological interventions associated with these works (which are described in Chapter 4) were carried out in stages.

Small evaluation tests were made at a number of points about the site in advance of works. These were located at the foot of ruined walls in order to investigate their sub-structure, and at a number of points within the grassed areas. The latter were required to identify the upper surface of archaeological deposits in order to inform the design process. These works were undertaken by Kenneth Macfadyen between the end of October and the end of November 2003.

General monitoring of the ruin consolidation and repair programme continued thereafter until May 2004. This stage included formalisation and recording of a number of pits left by the removal of an iron-fenced enclosure in the north transept area. Here details of the

Fig. 1.13: General view of the tunnel area excavation in progress: working shot, looking E

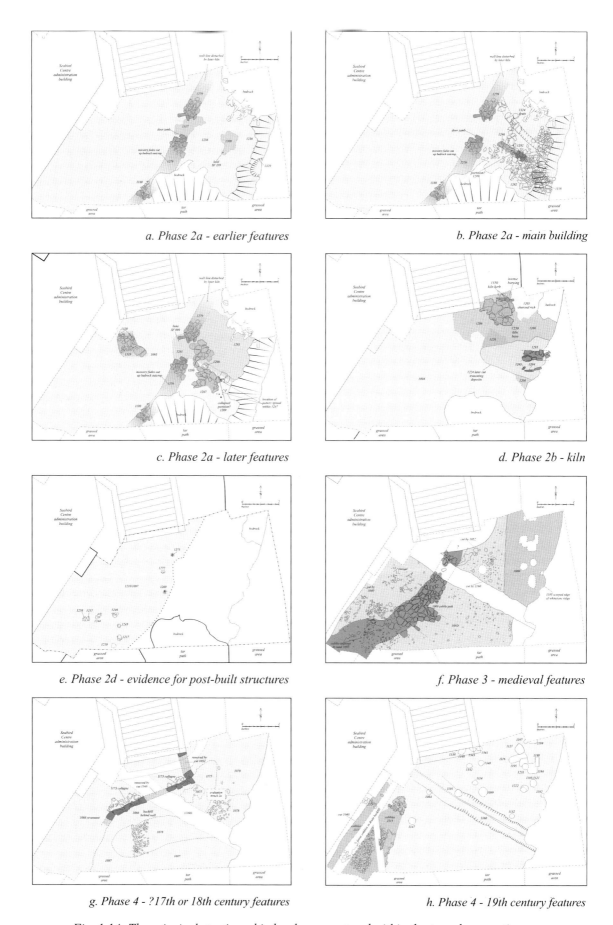

a. Phase 2a - earlier features

b. Phase 2a - main building

c. Phase 2a - later features

d. Phase 2b - kiln

e. Phase 2d - evidence for post-built structures

f. Phase 3 - medieval features

g. Phase 4 - ?17th or 18th century features

h. Phase 4 - 19th century features

Fig. 1.14: The principal stratigraphic levels encountered within the tunnel excavation area

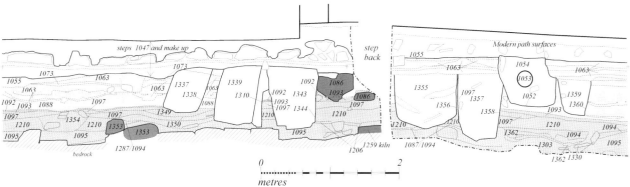

Fig. 1.15: Tunnel excavation: sample section showing the complexity of stratification along the northern limit of excavation

interior wall faces of the transept were revealed, including interior plasterwork. *In situ* inhumation burials were revealed at the north-east corner of the font plinth during its consolidation but were not disturbed further. The works permitted further appraisal of the evolutionary history of the church (see also DES 2000, 27–8). A final stage of monitoring took place in June 2004 in response to the re-turfing of the site.

TUNNEL AREA – EVALUATION (2004)

In October 2004 Addyman Associates were contracted by the Scottish Seabird Centre to carry out an archaeological evaluation in advance of the construction of an underground tunnel link at the extreme north end of Anchor Green, to extend between the basement level of the Scottish Seabird Centre and the basement chambers below the Centre's existing administration building to the west. The evaluation area lay at the head of the straight flight of northwards-descending concrete steps that connects Anchor Green to the asphalted road and parking areas adjacent to the harbour. The evaluation was required as a condition of Planning on the advice of the East Lothian Council Heritage Officer, Bridget Simpson.

Four evaluation trenches were excavated in November 2004; these revealed the presence of significant archaeological remains and deeply stratified deposits, although little artefactual material was recovered. It was concluded that, beneath a complex series of more recent deposits and features, there existed a medieval occupation surface and associated deposits that, in turn, overlay remains that were likely to be considerably earlier. With regard to the latter, the possibility that the site contained an Anglian/early Christian or even prehistoric component was suggested, an interpretation in line with limited individual discoveries previously made at Anchor Green, including Addyman Associates' work in 1999–2000. As anticipated deposits were found to terminate abruptly to the north-east, at the edge of the Scottish Seabird Centre construction area; this also marked the line of the historic boundary of the site, in existence since at least the mid-19th century.

TUNNEL AREA – MAIN EXCAVATION (2004–5)

A mitigation phase excavation followed on rapidly from the October 2004 evaluation. This necessitated the complete excavation of the western and central parts of the proposed tunnel area. The approach to the mitigation was agreed in consultation with and to the requirements of East Lothian Council and to an agreed project design. The excavation was undertaken at very short notice, under difficult contractual circumstances, and in weather that was very often poor – low temperatures and strong winds.

The area to be affected by the proposed works – the mitigation excavation area – was approximately trapezoidal in plan, measuring *c.*5–6m in width and, along its south side, up to 18m in length. The depth of the proposed cut for the tunnel – up to 4m – would self-evidently impact and wholly destroy all underlying deposits. It was known from the Scottish Seabird Centre site excavation in 1999 and from the October 2004 evaluation that significant archaeological deposits terminated at the eastern side of the underlying whinstone ridge; to the west they had been cut by the footings of the 19th century building that had occupied the site of the existing administration building.

The mitigation phase was undertaken during the period 14–24 and 29–30 December 2004 and 1 January–15 February 2005 (Figure 1.13). The duration of the excavation was extended twice as the complexity and extent of significant archaeological remains was successively revealed.

Because of the increasingly evident importance of the site the extension of the project was generously supported by Historic Scotland who provided financial assistance in addition to the original budget – a grant towards the completion of the site works. The involvement of Olwyn Owen, Senior Inspector of Ancient Monuments, and Patrick Ashmore, Chief Inspector of Ancient Monuments, proved key to the successful conclusion of the fieldwork. In spite of the extreme constraints of the project, Bridget Simpson, Heritage Officer, East Lothian Council, insisted that proper archaeological standards were to be maintained and that the entire site be completely excavated.

From previous excavation of the footprint of the Scottish Seabird Centre in 2000, and from outcrops still visible at the surface at the north end of the site it is clear that the western part of the excavation area occupied the surviving width of the top of a broad ridge of whinstone bedrock running south-west to north-east through the site area (the central of the three bedrock ridges that form the underlying geology of Kirk Ness). The Scottish Seabird Centre and administration building occupy sites on lower ground on either side of the ridge; the latter built up against and partly cut in to its west side.

The surviving archaeological remains proved to be extremely complex, the earlier deposits in particular having apparently suffered from long exposure and extensive bioturbation before eventually being sealed beneath later deposition. Mid-level and upper deposits had been extensively disturbed by 20th century services and other modern feature cuts. Figure 1.14 provides an overall graphic representation of the principal archaeological levels encountered. The more significant of these are discussed in more detail in the relevant chapters. Figure 1.15 is an illustration of the complexity of the stratigraphy encountered and the extent to which secondary intrusions had impacted pre-existing deposition.

The tunnel excavation area provided the most detailed stratigraphic data for any part of the wider site area. Four principal early medieval horizons were encountered, each of which revealing evidence for domestic occupation (Figure 1.14, a–e). These were overlain and sealed by a horizon of medieval date (f), again comprising evidence for occupation of a more domestic nature and in stark contrast to excavated areas further south which primarily related to the use of the church and the associated cemetery. This horizon was in turn overlain by wind-blown sand deposits followed by a further sequence of features, structures and other evidence of activity, from the 17th or 18th centuries through to modern times (g–h). A particular constraint on the excavation was the presence of a network of services of comparatively recent date (not illustrated).

In spite of the intensity of the occupation represented, over a duration of some 1,500 years, only very limited artefactual material was recovered from the tunnel excavation area. However, from the earlier levels were recovered significant assemblages of faunal material and marine shell. Deposits from the site were also extensively sampled and a series of post-excavation analyses of these was undertaken.

POST-EXCAVATION PROCESS

Partly on account of funding-related delay the post-excavation process proved to be a protracted operation, managed by Tanja Romankiewicz and generously supported by Historic Scotland, and by the Scottish Seabird Centre through a number of grants made by charitable foundations.

Of particular significance has been a programme of radiocarbon dates, these funded by Historic Scotland and carried out by SUERC. Long after the completion of archaeological site works these had a considerable impact upon the phasing and interpretation of the archaeology of the site. Radiocarbon samples from both terrestrial and marine samples were also included as part of a research project into the marine reservoir effect, a study carried out by Nicola Russell at SUERC.

MEMORIAL AT ANCHOR GREEN (2006)

On 21 December 2006 Addyman Archaeology undertook a joint archaeological evaluation and watching brief in relation to two installations at Anchor Green in the grassed area by the sea wall a short distance to the north-east of the north transept of the medieval church ruin. The more significant involved preparations in advance of the erection of a large upright memorial stone dedicated to personnel of the Royal Air Force, Coastal Command, casualties of the Second World War in the Atlantic. The installation of the memorial was coordinated by Group Captain Bob Kemp of Coastal Command; it was unveiled on 4 May 2007 (Figure 1.16).

Additional work undertaken at the same time involved the installation of a lamp-post, sited in close proximity to the memorial. The excavation of a foundation pit for the post, undertaken by East Lothian Council (contact Mike Omand), was subject to archaeological monitoring. The archaeological works were undertaken by Kenneth Macfadyen and Florence Boisserie according to the provisions of a Written Scheme of Investigation agreed in advance with Bridget Simpson, Heritage Officer, East Lothian Council.

Fig. 1.16: The Coastal Command memorial as newly installed, May 2007

The footing trench for the memorial measured 1.70m north–south by 0.70m east–west and excavated to a maximum depth of 0.55m. Though the edge of *in situ* archaeological deposits was identified at the up-slope end of the trench no evidence for burial cuts was identified and no significant archaeological finds were made within the limited area excavated. From the overlying fill was recovered some redeposited cemetery charnel and a single shard of medieval pottery.

2. Iron Age

Tanja Romankiewicz and Thomas Addyman

The archaeological evidence

The earliest dated feature demonstrating human activity on site was a discrete pit, *416*, situated in the south-east area of Kirk Ness. It was encountered within evaluation trench 4 between the remains of the 16th century church porch to the north-west and the existing sea wall to the east (Figures 1.4, 2.1–2.3). The relatively shallow (but truncated) feature, 0.2m deep, was discovered below the 19th century overburden relating to the sea wall. Underneath this *c*.0.8m thick build-up lay a further layer of windblown sand, *417*, into which the pit *416* was cut.

The pit contained a series of sub-round fire-blackened cobbles, *415*, within a matrix of charcoal, *420*, the latter being about 0.1m in thickness with the stones protruding out into the upper fill. The firing event appears to have been extinguished by a deliberately thrown-in layer of sand, *414*. The pit was then abandoned and left open, as a further layer of wind-blown sand containing considerable amount of lensing appears to have gradually filled up the pit and sealed it, *413*.

The feature lay isolated at the northern corner of Trench 4, excavated in 1999. It appears to have been eroding at the time of the construction of the sea wall,

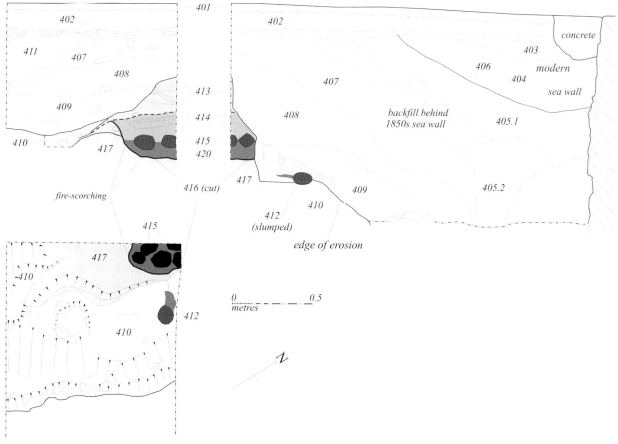

Fig. 2.1:Trench 4 – sections (above) and plan of the fire pit.

Several heat-affected pebbles were recovered from the burnt fill of the pit, strongly supporting the evidence for an Iron Age firing- or cooking-pit, which suggests evidence for a domestic occupation in this period. However, the pit appears to be isolated, since no further features could be associated with it at the time of excavation, or in any subsequent investigation at the site. The fact that there appears to be only one burning layer present suggests that the pit represents only a single event. It also seems unlikely that it was situated within a house or an otherwise covered area as it filled up gradually with wind-blown sand shortly after its abandonment, which suggests it was exposed to the elements.

Discussion

Cooking pits are often found to have been the central feature of later prehistoric roundhouses forming the focus around which life revolved in the house (eg. Pope 2007). The particular cooking technique involved heating or roasting fist-size stones over a heat source, this a method to store the instant heat from the fire for longer and allowing more even distribution of the heat to ensure a gradual cooking process. The heated stones may also have been thrown into a tank or comparable container to heat up water in which food could be boiled (Moore and Wilson 1999, 227). The difference in temperature between the heat of the fire and the cold water often caused the stones to crack; however, those found in the pit at Kirk Ness are not fire-cracked, only charred from the fire. Despite apparently using a similar technique of heating stones in a fire, the pit at Kirk Ness seems to simply represent a single event, most likely for food preparation, perhaps during or after fishing activity at the shore.

The firing pit itself holds very little information about the use of the wider site in the pre-Roman Iron Age, and the absence of any other prehistoric features on the promontory – at least as recovered during excavation – is perhaps significant in itself. With the prehistoric hillfort at North Berwick Law in viewing distance of the site, one might well expect that the prominent headland, which presented landing opportunities for boats at Kirk Ness, might have attracted prehistoric activities that would have left more archaeologically tangible remains (cf. Hall and Bowler 1997, 660). However, as prehistoric activity may have focused more directly on the shoreline, it is possible that much may have been lost to erosion.

The other significant discovery in relation to the discrete pit feature was the considerable depth of the layer of wind-blown sand, *413*, that completely sealed and overlay it. Clean sand layers were repeatedly recognised in subsequent excavation phases which suggests that the site had been subject to major recurring wind-blown sand depositions that may have made occupation periodically impossible. The distribution of these layers, concentrating on the central and eastern parts of the peninsula and

Fig. 2.2: Trench 4 – the fire pit as revealed, looking NW, with church porch behind

causing parts of the pit content to collapse down slope. The full extent and size of the pit thus could not be established. The sand layers sealing the pit correlate stratigraphically to the wind-blown sand found to underlie much of the 12th century church, thus an indicator of the pit's early date.

A sample taken from the *420* burnt layer yielded small fragments of heather stems (*Calluna vulgaris*), one of which dated roughly to the pre-Roman Iron Age (SUERC-27987: 2000±35 BP; 100 cal BC–cal AD 80 at 95.4%). The burnt deposit also contained seaweed (*unspecified*), sedge (*Carex* sp.) and carbonised weed seeds of spearwort/buttercup (*Ranunculus* sp.) and grass (*Gramineae* spp.). The residue was initially interpreted as deriving from burnt turf material, perhaps even from peat, which would have complicated radiocarbon dating, as the material could be much older than the burning event itself. However, as the date of the burning event supports the stratigraphic position of the pit within the overall sequence, the dates seem more likely to correspond to the use of the pit. It can thus be assumed that the heather and probably the seaweed were used directly as a source of fuel or, if they derived from turfs, that the organic component was still relatively fresh when burnt.

Fig. 2.3: Detail of the fire pit, looking NW

their general slope from west to east, implies that this was caused by prevailing easterly or south-easterly winds, with the sand most likely deriving from the eastern beach and dune landscape in the Marine Park/Castle Hill area. The evidence from the pit indicates that the prehistoric activity was abandoned before this wind-blown event. With subsequent recorded activity at the site from around the 5th century, the site may have been without permanent use for several hundred years.

3. Kirk Ness in the Early Medieval Period

Thomas Addyman, Tanja Romankiewicz and Alasdair Ross

Introduction

The most significant concentration of features, deposits and structural remains pre-dating the later medieval occupation of the site was encountered in 2004–5 at deep level within the Scottish Seabird Centre tunnel excavation at the northern end of Anchor Green. These represent at least two major episodes of activity – *phases 2a* and *2b* – with a number of possible sub-phases, and agricultural activity – phase 2c and 2d (Figure 3.1). While other possible remains were found at a similarly deep stratigraphic level elsewhere, principally behind the sea wall bounding the east side of the site, none of these produced diagnostic finds or otherwise datable material and therefore cannot be directly associated.

The tunnel excavation revealed a complicated sequence of archaeological features and deposits representing periods of occupation and extended episodes of abandonment during which extensive bioturbation, erosion, and much disturbance occurred. Such factors severely affected the survival of the remains, many of which were very ephemeral or hard to define. This greatly hampered the understanding of the stratigraphy encountered. In spite of these taphonomic limitations an important sequence of radiocarbon dates assigned these remains to the early medieval period, a dating that was compatible with the limited range of finds recovered. The confirmation of an early medieval occupation at Kirk Ness is of considerable significance as an addition to the limited corpus of sites identified and examined archaeologically for this period in south-east Scotland/northern Northumbria.

Phase 2a: early structure (5th–early 7th centuries)

The earliest built structure within the tunnel excavation area, lying immediately to the west-south-west of the present Scottish Seabird Centre building, comprised a substantial wall footing running diagonally across the trench, aligned north-north-east to south-south-west,

1279. It contained a 1m wide gap, interpreted as a probable entrance. While the northern side of this entrance was somewhat disturbed, the southern side retained a solitary block that was vertically set, evidently part of a deliberately formed jamb. The footing was built without mortar or obvious bonding material, of medium-sized whin rubble stones and a rubble core consisting of smaller material; whether there had originally been a bonding material such as clay was no longer apparent. The remains were generally relatively disturbed, with some facings dislodged or missing. The footing incorporated bedrock outcrops at its southern and northern ends, and where not placed directly onto bedrock the stones were set on top of a coarse matrix of degraded rock, *1236.* A possible continuation of the stone setting, *1180,* beyond the southern bedrock outcrop may or may not be associated with this structure, it being on a slightly different alignment.

At between 0.7m and 0.85m in width the stone footings could have supported substantial walling above. The feature was interpreted as the lowest surviving foundation courses of the west exterior wall of a roofed structure. Remains of paving and spreads that accumulated against the eastern side of this wall were interpreted as internal floor surfaces, or preparation for such surfaces, and associated deposits; no such deposits were revealed on its western side (Figure 3.2).

Because of the limited trench area the full extent of this structure could not be established. The wall remains were also very ephemeral or non-existent in the areas where bedrock was exposed, and the building may well have extended beyond the limits of the excavated area. At the northern end of the trench the walling had been disturbed by a later kiln structure (Phase 2b, discussed below). Further to the east the ground had eroded away where there was a steep scarp above the former shoreline, this generally representing the eastern extent of the *in situ* archaeology.

The building occupied a lower-lying area between two bedrock outcrops. The lower deposits within this hollow enclosed by the wall consisted of a light orange–brown

Phase	Activity	East part of site	West part of site	Radiocarbon dates 95% probability
Phase 1	**Pre-Roman Iron Age (c.100 BC – 80 AD)**			
Phase 2	**Early Medieval (5th – 9th century)**			
Phase 2a *The early building*	construction and early floor deposits : first occupation of the building	Contexts: *1236, 1180/1279, 1309, 1317, 1326, 1327, 1329, 1333, 1334* Small finds: *SF119 lead object*	-	*1309*: cal AD 410-610 *1317*: cal AD 420-620
	first pavement and drain : second occupation of the building	Contexts: *1282, 1289, 1290, 1291, 1292, 1293, 1294, 1299, 1302, 1304, 1305, 1318, 1322, 1323, 1324, 1325*	-	-
	period of abandonment or agricultural use	Contexts: *1281, 1287, 1300, 1301, 1303* Small finds: *SF153 pounder, SF157 peck-marked stone, fired clay /pottery and flint flake*	Contexts: *1095, 1096, 1319, 1320, 1321*	*1281*: cal AD 770-990 [?from contaminated material] *1287*: cal AD 420-670 amplitude
	second pavement : third and final occupation of the building	Contexts: *1280, 1288* Small finds: *SF100 burnisher*	-	-
	final abandonment / demolition	Contexts: *1260, 1261, 1278*	-	-
Phase 2b: *The corn-drying kiln*	construction and period of use	Contexts: *1226, 1227, 1259, 1284, 1285, 1295, 1330*	Contexts: *1094*	*1226*: cal AD 540-870 amplitude
	catastrophic combustion / abandonment	Contexts: *1205, 1206*	-	-
Phase 2c: *agricultural use / wasteland*			Contexts: *1097, 1210* (redeposited)	*1097*: cal AD 430-650 and cal AD 640-780
Phase 2d: *Post-built structures and later disturbance*	rectangular post-built structure and arc of post holes	Contexts: *1217, 1219, 1243, 1244, 1246, 1257, 1258, 1264, and 1269, 1272, 1275*	-	-
Phase 3	**Medieval - (12th century onwards)**			

Fig. 3.1: General phasing and radiocarbon dates for early medieval period

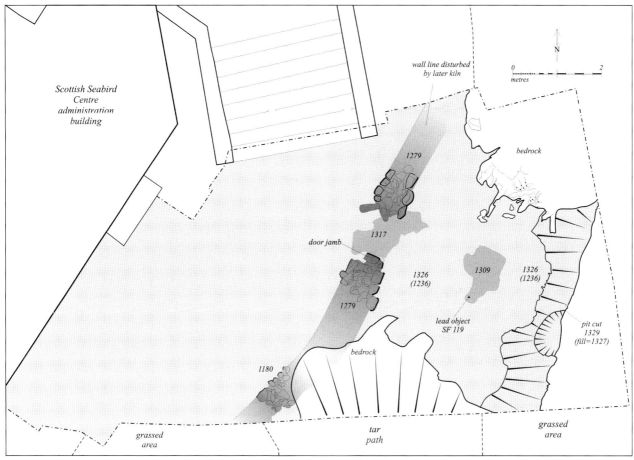

Fig. 3.2: Plan of early features relating to phase 2a

clayey sand, which incorporated shells (primarily limpets), bedrock chips and pebbles and some finer sands, *1326*. The initial interpretation was that this matrix was undisturbed natural, but it is possible that the material had been redeposited from the adjacent foreshore to level out the hollow between the bedrock outcrops. The overlying sequence of paved floor surfaces suggests continuing attempts to level the ground above the bedrock. However, no cultural material was identified in association with this lowest deposit.

First occupation of the early building

Features within the footprint of the early building

The earliest features associated with this building had been cut into the *1326* matrix. These included pit *1329*, which may be directly associated with the construction or the primary use of the structure. The pit contained a mixed fill, *1327*. The presence within this of mammal and bird bone suggests it to be culturally-derived midden-like material; the deposit in particular yielded a comparatively large quantity of shag bones (see Smith, *infra*). Other early features consisted simply of shallow hollows and discrete patches of periwinkle shells dumped together with clayey material. These deposits had apparently formed part of an original (or first surviving) earthen floor, perhaps even associated with the construction of the building.

From one of these patches, a charcoal-rich dump, *1309*, was recovered a small lozenge-shaped lead object SF 119, possibly a net sinker (Figures 3.3–3.4); a similar object was found at Coppergate in York, there associated with Anglian material (McLaren and Hunter, Appendix B).

The material associated with *1309* was dated to the 5th–6th centuries AD (juvenile cattle skull fragment, SUERC-28294: 1550 ± 40 BP; cal AD 410–610 at 95%). A very similar date from a charred hulled barley grain (SUERC-28295: 1525 ± 40 BP; cal AD 420–620 at 95%) was obtained from a grey sandy silt spread, *1317*, an apparent dump forming part of a compacted surface in the entrance area of the early building (for dates see Appendix N, Figure N.1). From within this spread was also recovered a distal right humerus bone of a great auk (*Alca impennis*) – see vignette (Figures 3.5–3.7, and Smith, Appendix J). Because there was no direct physical overlap, the relationship of the *1317* 'surface' within the entrance area to the early deposits within the building could not be fully clarified. Since all these earlier deposits were overlain by later paving (*1282* and *1280,* see below), it is possible to suggest grouping them within the broader stratigraphic sequence. In the entrance area, however, the overlying paving was partially lost or disturbed and the stratigraphy was less clear than within the interior of the

Fig. 3.3: Photograph of deposit 1309 *under excavation*

Fig. 3.4: Small finds recovered from phase 2 deposits: clockwise from left – possible pounder (SF153), pecked-marked stone (SF157), siltstone burnisher (SF100), lead object (SF119), reworked flint flake (–) (see specialist reports)

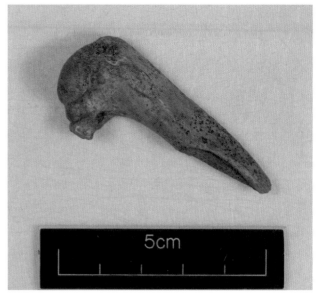

Fig. 3.5: Part of a humerus of a great auk (SF56) recovered from Kirk Ness excavations, context 1307, phase 2a

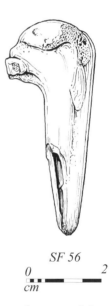

SF 56

Fig 3.6: Drawing of great auk bone, SF56, by Marion O'Neil

building; the dumping of *1317* within this area may potentially relate to later activity – see *1302* described below. The early date obtained from the former nonetheless confirms its relatively early place in the overall site sequence and, even if not precisely coeval, the marginal difference between the two date ranges of *1309* and *1317* imply that their deposition was near-contemporary. From the Bayesian modelling it can be postulated with 95% confidence that the activity within the early structure started between AD 410 and 590 (and between AD 485–565 at 68% probability – see Hamilton, Appendix N), thus the early structure could be firmly assigned to a (late) 5th–6th century date (Figure N.6).

Although the exact size and particular function of this

building remains obscure, the deposits encountered within the interior contained ash residues, animal bone and shells suggestive of domestic occupation. Animal bone analysis from these early contexts identified skull fragments from an adult grey seal with further bones from newborn grey seal pups. However, only small quantities of seal bones were recovered from phase 2 overall, and cannot therefore be taken as certain evidence for large-scale exploitation (cf. Smith, Appendix J); the presence of newborn seal pup bones suggests Autumnal activity (October/November).

The abundance of charcoal fragments from these contexts implies that wood had been the main fuel used in this period, this in contrast to the earlier apparent use of

The North Berwick Great Auk

Of particular topical interest was the recovery from early medieval deposits at the site of a wide variety of bird bones, the presence of most likely to be associated with their deliberate exploitation, principally as a food source. The birds represented were both domestic and wild and, not unsurprisingly, the wild birds included many seabird species. Present were domestic fowl (*Gallus gallus*) and domestic/greylag goose (*Anser anser*). Wild birds included cormorant (*Phalacrocorax carbo*), shag (*Phalacrocorax aristotelis*), probable mallard (*Anas* cf. *playrhynchos*) and eider ducks (*cf. Somateria molissima*), probable herring gull (*Larus* cf. *argentatus*), raven (*Corvus corax*) and starling (*Sturnus vulgaris*) – see Smith, Appendix J.

In addition to these finds one bone of a great auk (*Alca impennis*), a distal right humerus (Figures 3.5 and 3.6), was recovered from an early floor spread within the entrance area of the early building, layer *1317*, which was radiocarbon dated to the 5th–7th centuries AD. This species was a favoured food source and, being flightless, was comparatively easy to catch (Figure 3.7). Human predation led to the inexorable decline of the species, ensuring that by the middle of the 19th century it had become persecuted and exploited into extinction.

The auk was a 1 metre tall, flightless, penguin-like seabird whose range at one time extended from the north-eastern United States across the Atlantic to the British Isles, France and Northern Spain. Because of its value for both food and also as a source of oil it was hunted down relentlessly until it became the most eagerly wanted taxidermy specimen and its eggs prized collectors' trophies. Unable to escape hunters on its stubby wings, the auk was wiped out systematically from its breeding grounds in one of the saddest examples of human avarice. It was last seen in British waters in July 1840 when one was taken on St Kilda. In little more than a decade, fishermen hunted down the remaining few and the last one was seen on the Grand Banks of Newfoundland in 1852.

turf or heather, and seaweed, present in the Iron Age phase of the site (*cf.* Haston and Timpany, Appendix L). The fragment size of the charcoal, of up to 3cm, suggests that, although the charcoal was scattered, these deposits had seen relatively little mechanical reworking (by trampling or burrowing, for example) after initial deposition. Charred cereal grain of oat and hulled barley was found throughout these early deposits, but in low quantities and rather scattered, and would thus not indicate an area of concentrated cereal processing. The early date of the grain from the *1317* spread within the entrance area strongly suggests that the grain in the early deposits was not intrusive through bioturbation from later kiln use in this area. The poor preservation of some of the grain may support the interpretation of the spreads as trample.

Second phase of occupation of the early building

Apart from the early earthen surfacing deposits described above, two further levels of paving and several episodes of dumping were identified within the early building. Overall these suggest repeated occupation, abandonment and subsequent re-use.

The earliest 'pavement'

The early deposits just described were overlain first by a preparation of laid stones, these predominantly flattish pieces of whin, within a silty matrix, *1322*. Seemingly not a pavement itself, the feature appears to have been intended in part as a revetment to level up the ground to the east, close to the steep edge of the bedrock outcrop.

Fig. 3.7: Artist's visualisation of the hunting of great auks off the East Lothian shore, drawn by Alan Braby

Fig 3.10: The pivot stone 1290 *as retrieved showing the wear of the pivot hole*

Fig. 3.8: The pivot stone 1290 *in situ*

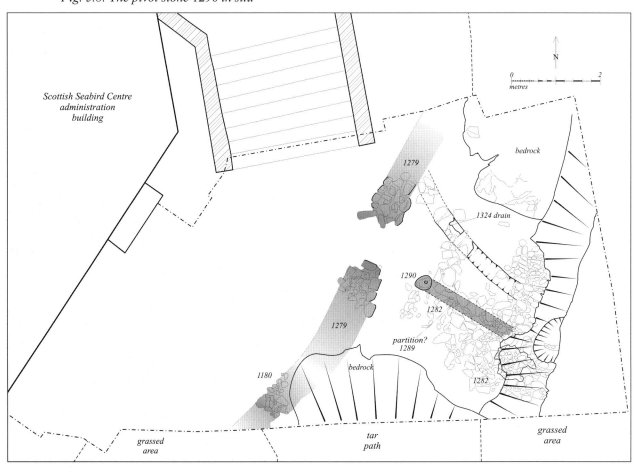

Fig. 3.9: The pivot stone 1290 *in situ*

Fig. 3.11: The drain 1324 *under excavation*

This packing had formed the make-up beneath a much more extensive level of somewhat rudimentary paving, *1282*, composed of medium-sized flat whin slabs, the interstices well-fitted with some smaller cobbles (Figure. 3.8). It had been formed to a relatively level surface that extended southeast from the *1279* walling, and continued eastwards to the edge of the scarp, but did not survive over the entire area. The paving also seems to have incorporated some of the upper parts of the bedrock outcrops. At one point beyond the eastern edge of the *1282* paving was a further localised area of similarly well-laid 'flooring', this consisting of irregular cobbles of somewhat smaller scale, *1318*. The site stratigraphy suggested that *1318* was originally part of the same paving episode as *1282*. The recorded extent of this combined area of surfacing measured 1.8m east–west by about 3.0m north–south, an overall area of about 5.5m². However, its original extent was not entirely clear because of later truncation and the restricted trench area.

Within the area of the *1282* paving and respected by it were the partial remains of what was interpreted as a further wall footing, *1289* (Figure 3.9). Of about 0.4m average width, the footing line was represented by an alignment of deeper-set small boulders. It lay in perpendicular relationship to the *1279* wall (i.e. running WNW–ESE) and was aligned with the southern margin of the entrance within that wall. It was interpreted as an internal partition within the early building, a suggestion supported by the evidence of a surviving pivot stone set at its north-eastern end, *1290* (Figures 3.8–3.10). A small

whin boulder, this stone in particular appeared to be incorporated into the early pavement. A well-formed pivot hole in its upper surface, showing some abrasion internally, would have received the wooden pintle of a door. The internal entrance thus implied, between this stone and the main wall of the structure to the north-west, had presumably connected a chamber to the north-east with another to the south-west.

Thin and relatively discreet spreads of midden material had accumulated on top of the *1282* paving. This sequence contained *1304* and *1305* – discreet thin deposits of silty clay and mottled humic silt in the south-east part of the trench – and a further trample of fine silty material in the entrance area, *1302*. These are interpreted as culturally-derived material, possibly deliberately dumped, relating to the use of the building in its second phase.

Protected from the worst homogenising effects of bioturbation was a further sequence of individual lenses preserved underneath one or two larger stones in the area of the *1289* partition on its northern side – *1291*, *1292*, and *1294*. These, respectively deposits of silty clay with charcoal flecks, shelly gravel, a charcoal-rich humic silt, and a patch of compacted ash, were interpreted as remnants of a sequence of flooring/occupation deposits. Unfortunately the very localised survival did not allow for further understanding of their former extent, but provided an indication of what may have existed more generally and the extent to which subsequent bioturbation had occurred.

Stone-lined drain

Within the northern compartment of the early structure were revealed the remains of a drainage channel, *1324* (Figure 3.11). Given the extensive subsequent bioturbation, general disturbance and truncation (eg by the much later cut of *1224*), this feature was only recognised at a late stage of the excavation and it was not possible to determine with certainty from which level it had been cut.

The surviving remains of the *1324* drain channel measured some 0.30m in width and varied in depth between 0.12m and 0.25m. Its course ran south-east from the area of the northern extent of the *1279* walling and formed a gentle arc continuing eastwards to the east edge of the site, terminating a little on the north side of the *1289* partition. The channel had evidently drained out in this direction. At its north-west end the channel preserved evidence for capping with coarse whin slabs, a number of which were found partly slumped into the channel, *1325*.

The feature was initially thought to relate to the function of a later kiln, the latter described within *phase 2b*, below; the base of the kiln was found to directly overlie the drain at its north-west end. However, further east it was also overlain in one area by some of the sequence of lenses, *1291, 1292, 1293, 1294,* and *1299*, already described, and thus more certainly associated with the

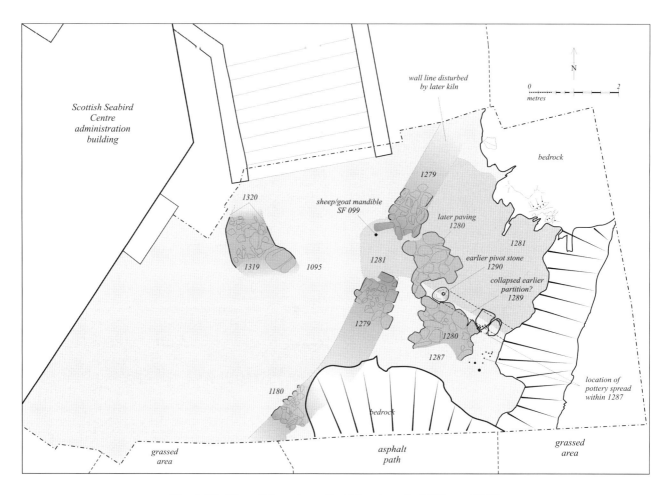

Fig. 3.12: Plan of the extent of midden deposits 1281 *and* 1287

earlier structure – it had possibly been formed at the time of the construction of the *1282* paving.

The presence of such a drain might suggest the function of this part of the structure to have been a byre, although not necessarily so, given that it was located within the base of the natural hollow between the two bedrock outcrops, a point where ground water might naturally tend to accumulate.

The channel was partly in-filled with distinguishable layers of humic sediments, these interleaved with ashy lenses, *1323*.

Re-use or abandonment of the early building

The *1282* paving (and associated flooring deposits) was evidently no longer in use when a major dumping of winkle shells, *1303*, was spread across its area, covering most of its southern parts and extending further southwards, up over part of the bedrock outcrop at the southern limit of excavation (Figure 3.12). The *1303* deposit incorporated a localised shallow spread of light greenish–brown clay, 2–3cm thick, *1300*. Overlying the *1303/1300* deposit was a further substantial layer of midden-like material, *1287*. The latter primarily consisted of humic silt with some charcoal, shell and animal bones that evidently accumulated on top of it. The *1287*

midden make-up seems to have partially overlain the remains of the early partition, *1289*, which suggests that it (and the internal entrance) had also fallen out of use by this time.

An homogeneous midden matrix of similar character to *1287* was found to overlie the earlier paving to the north of the *1289* partition wall, this identified as *1281*. It covered the entire area of the bedrock within the east and northeastern parts of the interior of the building and continued through the entrance area of wall *1279* to lens out beyond to the west. Where the two contexts appeared to overlap, the field observation was that *1281* overlaid *1287*. In contrast to the comparatively clean *1303* midden spread, the overlying humic infill of *1281* and *1287* appears to represent a more gradual accumulation of midden-like material and soil (Figure 3.12).

From a concentrated area within the *1287* deposit were recovered 72 small fragments and crumbs of fired clay, tentatively interpreted as pottery (Figures 3.13–3.14). As all fragments appeared to be of similar material and firing they were judged to have had a common origin, although whether as parts of a single vessel remains uncertain on account of their fragmented nature; it is also possible that the material may simply represent accidentally fired daub (see Hall Appendix C on CD). Very similar material was recovered from at least two

Fig. 3.13: Concentrated deposit within 1287 *midden of 72 small fragments and crumbs of fired clay under excavation, tentatively interpreted as pottery*

further discrete and spatially separated patches within the same context. The distribution suggests that these fragments could also represent the remains of several similar items, rather than having derived from a single object. The find-spots of the pottery fragments do not form a coherent line or pattern, thus it is unlikely that they were deposited *in situ*, but brought in as fragments as part of the sequential midden infilling. Several individual fragments of this fired clay were also recovered from the wider area of the early building, two further fragments from the underlying *1302* deposit, and 20 fragments from the similar *1281* deposit further north-east. Given that the majority of fragments were from *1287*, it is most likely that the deposition of the material originated within this layer. The occurrence of stray fragments within the upper and lower contexts are likely the result of bioturbation or later reworking. In particular the matrix of the upper layer, *1281*, had certainly seen some localised later disturbance.

From within the *1287* midden deposit were also recovered possible coarse stone tools (possible pounder SF153 and peck-marked stone SF157) and a small reworked flint flake (see Donnelly, Appendix A on CD, and Figure 3.4). The deposit also revealed a concentrated localised cluster of pieces of rounded and angular whinstone, *1301*, whose purpose, if any, remained unexplained.

The general matrix of *1281* contained animal and fish bone, limpets and oysters; there was also a significant animal and fish bone as well as shell component within *1287*. These together could be interpreted as having derived from household waste, a suggestion supported by the identification of evidence for butchery of cattle, sheep/goats and pigs in the form of small cut fragments, including articular ends. The boned meat had been chopped to fairly small sizes, apparently to fit cooking pots, this particularly illustrated by a group of chopped cattle epiphyses (SF170) from *1287*. The range of fragments points towards a self-subsistent existence,

Fig. 3.14: Selection of the early ceramic material as recovered from context 1287; *photograph by Derek Hall*

whereby all available foodstuffs, including the bones, were utilised. The bird bones within *1281* and *1287* show no butchery tool marks, which suggests they were cooked whole until the meat could be easily removed from the carcass. Within the lower parts of the *1287* midden a partial skeleton of a very young, neonatal dog was found, although its deposition was possibly a later intrusion. A further dog bone, a proximal femur from an adult, was found in *1281* (see Smith, Appendix J).

In summary, the similarity between the composition and contents of *1281* and *1287* suggests that, together, they represent the deposition of a household midden, and that they accumulated at broadly the same time. The homogeneity of this midden material, with a general absence of internal lensing, suggests some, or even considerable, reworking; whether this occurred because of the presence of livestock is less certain but may be one possibility.

The humic nature of the matrix of *1287* suggests that topsoil may have accumulated during a period of abandonment, reworked within the midden material. Another possibility may be a degraded turf component – this possibly from the collapse of the walls of the structure itself. This assumes that large parts of the early building

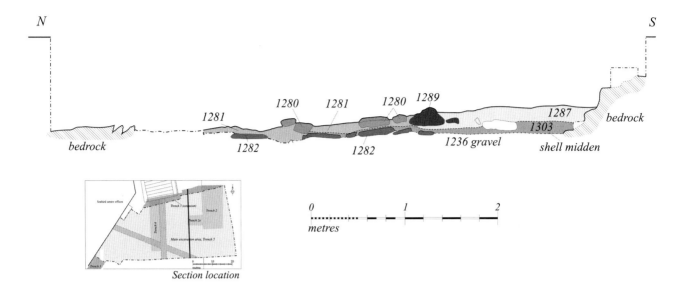

Fig. 3.15: West-facing section across deposits within the interior of the early structure, including levels 1281 *and* 1287

had been of turf construction with the stone walls (*1279* and, possibly, *1180*) forming the foundation course for a thick turf wall that supported the roof structure. The latter may possibly have also employed turf as roofing material. The substantial thickness of the stone wall footings, 0.7–0.85m, would not be inappropriate for the construction of a turf-built wall. For a single stone wall these remains may have been over-dimensioned for what seems to have been a relatively modest structure otherwise (although its original extent clearly remained undefined). A turf construction might also better accord with the relatively mundane character of the limited evidence for material culture associated with the structure. At this early date, a full stone-walled building would, in all likelihood, be associated with a higher status or ecclesiastical use, of which there is little direct evidence so far identified archaeologically. If the upper midden material within the building is thus interpreted as representing, in part, the collapse of a turf wall or roof, this would further support the archaeological evidence generally for the building's abandonment and collapse, and that it was perhaps even left open subsequently.

Taphonomic problems of the midden infill of the early structure

The general relationship between the *1287* and *1281* deposits was not entirely clear, as they derived from separate areas within the building, with no clear physical relationship conclusively demonstrated (Figure 3.15). The two contexts were equated in the field primarily because of similarities in composition and because of the recovery of the fired clay fragments from both of them. They were thus both selected for radiocarbon dating to scientifically confirm their contemporaneity. The samples from *1287* returned a 5th–7th century AD date (four sample amplitude cal AD 420–670; with the higher probability modelled between the middle of the 6th and middle of

the 7th century AD; see Appendix N for details). However the sample of sheep/goat mandible from context *1281* produced a significantly younger date of cal AD 770–990 (at 95% SUERC-28291; 1150±40 BP). Testing the date for *1281* statistically does not demonstrate it to be contemporary with either the underlying *1287* or with the overlying *1226* deposit. In all likelihood, the single date for *1281* may have been derived from intrusive material. This is not entirely surprising, given the evidence for localised disturbances at the edges of *1281*, as indicated by the recovery of a large ungulate rib that shows evidence for sawn marks, perhaps suggestive of butchery practice of later periods. This midden infill also contained a single fragment of human charnel, though not identified as such during excavation; it is possible that this was also intrusive.

The date from the *1281* deposit was obtained from the left mandible of a sheep or goat (SF99). This displayed little post-depositional wear and in all likelihood seemed contemporary with its accumulation (Figure 3.12).

The Bayesian analysis identified the date from *1281* as a statistical outlier. The likely explanation is that the dated sample was inadvertently retrieved from a contaminated area. A large feature cut, *1224*, the extent and purpose of which was not fully understood, had been made through from above and destroyed or disturbed most of the deposits and structures associated with the remains of a kiln (see below) which post-dates the early structure but immediately overlies the northern end of its surviving walling. This area also corresponded to the southern parts of the underlying *1281* and thus the later cut *1224* may have also disturbed these to some extent. The fill within the *1224* cut was of a mid-brown matrix very similar to that of *1281/1287*, making it difficult to differentiate one from the other during excavation. Since the straight southern edge of the *1224* cut coincides closely with the line of the internal partitioning of the early building, *1289*, it is possible that the cut partly destroyed this stone wall as well. The disturbance may also have continued further west, this perhaps explaining the damage to the northern jamb of the entrance to the early structure. It was from the latter area that the mandible within *1281* was recovered that produced the outlier in the dating sequence. While this date cannot be safely associated with the infilling of the early structure, it might relate to the period when the later kiln structure was abandoned and the large cut for *1224* was made and in-filled, thus between the late 8th to the late 10th centuries.

If it is accepted that the date for *1281* had been inadvertently obtained from later intrusive material, this interpretation would not be at odds with the field observation that *1281* and *1287* are part of the same infilling event. The presence of the midden material within the abandoned structure likely implies an associated focus for occupation in close proximity, perhaps in the immediate vicinity a little further to the south. The dating of the midden infill suggests the abandonment of the early building occurred in the 6th–7th centuries AD.

Third and final phase of occupation of the early building

After the early structure had been in-filled with the midden material, and had possibly fallen into disrepair, a third and final phase of use occurred, the principal evidence for which was the installation of a new area of paving within the interior, *1280*. The paving slabs were partially set into the underlying humic material of *1281* and *1287* and found to be up to 10–15cm thick in places; in other areas the stones were set into a bedding matrix of shell sand, *1288*. From this interface of midden and paving a rectangular siltstone burnisher (SF100) was found associated with the matrix of *1280*, but recorded for *1281* (Figure 3.4).

The new *1280* paving formed a less regular surface than the earlier *1282* paving, it being degraded and robbed in places. It consisted of roughly flat cobbles and irregular whin flags. Pressed or trampled into the joints

Fig. 3.16: The collapsed rubble 1260 from the early structure under excavation, looking SE

between the stones was found a large number of winkle shells, the only notable finds material. Because of the poor survival and the lack of diagnostic finds, it remained unclear how long the final stage of occupation of the building lasted or what function it served. Given the evidence for the derelict partition wall, overlain by the substantial midden infill, it has to be assumed that the new paving was associated with at least some repair and possibly rebuilding of the previously abandoned and collapsed structure.

Abandonment

On top of the *1280* paving were found large rounded beach boulders and other angular stones, *1260*, apparent collapse deriving from a rubble wall, perhaps from the *1279* walling itself, following the final abandonment of the structure after the final phase of its occupation (Figure 3.16). This rubble was intermixed with a gravely deposit, *1261*, and individual lenses of gravels and shells, *1278*. The matrix of the destruction deposit contained no material that could be interpreted as roofing nor any charred wooden remains from building timbers. There is thus no indication from these deposits for how the upper parts of the building would have been constructed or whether the building was roofless at the time of collapse.

The quantity of stone found within the final collapse horizon of the building suggests that the early building was quite a substantial stone-built structure at this stage. Such solid stone wall construction seems at odds with the rather mundane artefact assemblage and absence of other archaeological remains that might suggest a high status use. The simplest explanation may be that the Kirk Ness headland did not offer sufficient amount of turf divots for construction, and that the rubble stone used for the walls was much more easily obtained from the whinstone ridges of the promontory.

In summary, the evidence perhaps suggests that the building finally fell out of use or was beyond repair and subsequently abandoned and demolished. Given that part of its footprint to the north west was reused as the site of a later kiln in Phase 2b, it seems likely that the building was deliberately demolished, the ground levelled (and perhaps the better, more angular building stones salvaged for new construction) to prepare the area for the use of the kiln. This scenario would date the final destruction of the early building to about the early to mid-7th century AD at the earliest (this based on the Bayesian model dates for contexts *1287* and *1226*).

Phase 2b: the corn-drying kiln (mid-7th–early 9th centuries)

The archaeological remains

An area of flat sandstone slabs, *1259*, showing evidence of burning and somewhat degraded and very friable,

Fig. 3.17: The red stones of the kiln base as revealed (top), looking N

was discovered immediately to the north of the remains of the early building (Figure 3.17). The stone setting was found to partly overlie the north part of wall *1279*, its construction evidently having disturbed the earlier structural remains. Of reddish hue these slabs were recognisable as blocks of the local *leck-stone* deriving from the foreshore outcrops immediately east of Kirk Ness. With the necessity to further extend the excava-

tion perimeter in this area, more remains of this feature were revealed to the north and east, the stone setting ultimately found to extend to an area of 1.9m east–west by 1.5m north–south. Also revealed by the trench extension was an alignment of three slabs set on edge, *1330*, forming a kerb towards the northern recorded extent of the feature. No other structural features were found that were directly related with the *1259* slabs and *1330* orthostats (Figure 3.18).

A cache of burnt grain, *1226*, was found immediately to the south of the centre of the slab setting, recovered at the south-western edge of a matrix of orange peat ash, *1206*, and a dark, charcoal-rich soil containing burnt turf or peat and clay, *1205* (Figure 3.19). The burning deposits, *1206* and *1205*, were found to extend southwards by some 2m from the northern trench edge, at which point they had been cut by the large, shallow intrusive feature, *1224*, previously noted; this marked their surviving southern extent. Their full eastern and western extent could not be established as they both lensed out and appeared to have been disturbed by later activities.

An early kiln structure

The evidence of burning associated with the flat stones and the kerb setting at its north side, the quantities of grain, and the overlying ash and burning deposits were all

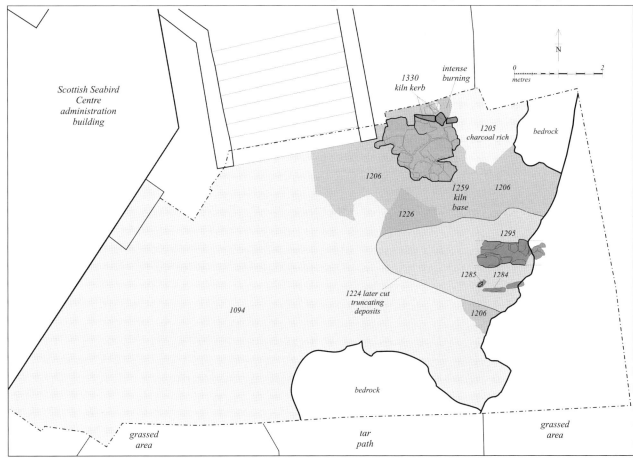

Fig. 3.18: Plan of the 1259/1330 *kiln and associated deposits*

Fig. 3.19: The spread of orange peat-ash, 1206, charcoal-rich soil, 1205, and concentration of burnt grain, 1226; looking E

consistent with the identification of the stone setting itself as the remains of a kiln base. The kerb stones to the north had been interpreted in the field as the remains of a flue, extending either further north or east. However, when compared with evidence of similar features examined elsewhere (such as those at Hoddom, discussed below) the upright stones seem more likely to have formed the northern *edge* of a kiln base, and that these and the basal stones had formed the lining of a shallow hollow that was intended to have a clay and turf superstructure. The high clay and turf (or possibly peat) ash content within *1205* and *1206* might indicate that the kiln superstructure incorporated turf divots, these most likely derived from the glacial tills of the hinterland to the south and west (note – in Appendix M Lancaster comments on similar sources for turf within *1095* and *1210* soils from local till-derived and poorly drained topsoils that can be quite peaty). The clay component may have been part of a capping or a wattle-and-daub construction. It may also be possible that turf or peat were used as kiln fuel, although heather stems within the burnt deposits had been identified as such in the environmental analysis of the kiln material (see below, and Haston and Timpany, Appendix L).

The quantities of ash and burning suggest that the Kirk Ness kiln came to a catastrophic end in a single conflagration event, after a period of apparently intensive and repeated use – the degradation of the sandstone slabs of the kiln base indicates frequent firing of the kiln. Bayesian modelling of the radiocarbon dates obtained from the cache of burnt barley from *1226* found near the kiln base confirmed its frequent use. The dates suggest a period of protracted use for the kiln, concentrating on the 7th up to the start of the 8th century AD (amplitude of dates from *1226*: cal AD 540–870 at 95% probability, thus possibly extending into the early 9th century AD; compare also with dates from *1281*, this most likely contaminated by material introduced by the cut of the later feature *1224*; see Appendix N). The date range from *1226* does not indicate an exact date of abandonment, but that

it is likely that burnt grain accumulated during the use of the kiln and that the samples were taken from this accumulated material. Given the position of the cache immediately to the south-west of the kiln base as surviving, it seems likely that it represents subsequent rake-outs from the kiln after each drying interval.

The environmental evidence from the kiln

The dominant grain type recorded in the samples associated with the kiln was barley, followed by lesser numbers of oat grain. As these samples contained little in the way of weed seeds it is suggested that the dried grain was relatively clean with the majority of the barley grain having been removed from their hulls (Haston and Timpany, Appendix L). As no embryonic growth was recognised on the barley, the grain was apparently ungerminated before drying. This observation means that the grain had not been malted prior to the drying, thus excluding the possibility of brewing-related activity.

The charred grain from the upper fill of the *1324* drain (apparent contamination of this earlier feature), and from other associated features, was similarly dominated by barley and thus likely to represent a spread of material from the kiln. This also applies to the large quantities of grain recovered from a shell midden, *1227*, dumped immediately above the kiln area. The latter suggests that the kiln was abandoned after the conflagration event and that the area was subsequently used for disposing domestic waste that also contained burnt and unburnt animal bone, fish bone and other shellfish such as oyster and mussel. The abrasion of the charred grains within the midden was again an indicator of the amount of bioturbation on the site. The recovery of frequent remains of heather stems, leaves and charred florets (flower heads) may be indicative of the material used as kiln fuel (Haston and Timpany, Appendix L). The possibility that a further, or replacement, kiln existed in the vicinity – either not surviving or out-with the excavation area – may also be considered.

Structures possibly associated with the use of the kiln

Although no other structural features could be directly linked with the kiln floor and its northern kerb, further stone settings were found to the south-east of the kiln base that clearly did not form part of the underlying early building (Figure 3.18). These included a linear setting of upright stone slabs, *1284*; running east–west; this was on a similar alignment to the kerb of the kiln base, and of comparable size. Also notable was that one of the stones was of the same red *leck-stone* as employed for the kiln construction. To the immediate north-west of these slabs was a group of small stones, apparently forming post-packing for a square socket of 10–12cm, *1285*. A roughly rectangular area of flat, horizontally lain unworked stone blocks lay further to the north and closer to the kiln base, *1295*. This appeared roughly parallel to the *1284* orthostat setting.

Although within the extent of the earlier building, it seems unlikely that these stone features were part of its structure. Some of the stones that were seemingly part of the *1295* setting, and one orthostat associated with *1284*, were found to sit within the infill related to the earlier drain, thus post-dating its use. If it is assumed that the drain was contemporary with the earlier use of the building, the stone settings cannot have been part of the early structure.

By their relative positions to the kiln base and their stratigraphic relationship these features could be interpreted as settings for internal partitioning as part of the wider kiln structure. If the *1284* stones formed the kerb stones marking the southern extent of the kiln floor, the latter would have covered an area extending to about 3.7m across (north–south).

Taphonomy, dating and the scale of the kiln use

The cache of barley provided a modelled date range for the ongoing use of the kiln that peaked in the 7th up to the start of the 8th century AD (see Hamilton, Appendix N.). As suggested by the Bayesian modelling, this date range reflects the protracted use of the kiln, not simply its date of abandonment. Based on these dates one can postulate that the kiln was used during the 7th century, and probably fell out of use in the 8th or 9th century, although the later date seems less likely.

The presence of a kiln on a settlement site is very unusual for the 7th century. More unusually the evidence from Kirk Ness suggests a stone-built base and turf superstructure that conveys an impression of permanent infrastructure for large-scale processing of grain. The investment in a substantial structure dedicated to grain drying would seem beyond the usual requirement for drying of small quantities for everyday use within a small settlement; at this early period it is usually assumed to have happened in a drying pan over the hearth fire (*cf.* Holden 2006a, 108). If the southern stone setting can be associated with the kiln base as preserved to the north, the extent of some 4m for the kiln floor would render the corn-drying a large-scale process, beyond the needs of a typical early medieval settlement (*cf. ibid.*). However, this association of the stone setting with the kiln base must remain unconfirmed.

Corn-drying on a scale beyond simple self-subsistence?

The eventual final collapse, or possible demolition, of the early stone structure, seemingly of 7th century date, and the re-use of its site for the construction of a kiln indicates continuing occupation into the 8th, possibly even into the 9th century. The size and structural evidence of the kiln, and the type and amount of charred grain recovered, appear to suggest the production of barley for bread making on a scale larger than for simple domestic requirements. The surviving remains of the kiln base at Kirk Ness – between 1.5m and 3.7m wide – are of comparable dimension to the kiln floor in the kiln barn structures 6 and 7 at Hoddom, Dumfriesshire. Excavations at this early monastic site exposed at total of 14 kiln structures, with a date range contemporary with the evidence from Kirk Ness. The evidence at Hoddom was interpreted as the large-scale processing of grain as part of a 'specialised cereal handling centre' (Holden 2006b, 155).

The Hoddom kiln structures, and structures 6.2 and 7.1 in particular, were in total about 4m long with a separate firebox to the south. The kerb setting at Hoddom, lining the northern edge of the kiln floor of structure 6, for example, could be paralleled by the evidence of the three edge-set slabs at Kirk Ness, also placed on the north side of the kiln base. If the stone setting further south is accepted as marking the full extent of the kiln floor at Kirk Ness, its dimensions of some 4m east–west would be comparable with the Hoddom structure. However, the Kirk Ness kiln is far less well preserved. There are no surviving remains of a firebox, though an area of intense burning at the northern trench edge, north of the kerb, possibly indicated its former position (Figure 3.18). The apparent lack of a flue feature at the Kirk Ness kiln might also be explained by the evidence from Hoddom, where kiln flues were apparently absent from the archaeological remains (e.g. structure 7, Lowe 2006, 65).

The parallels between the Hoddom structure 6 and 7 kilns and the Kirk Ness kiln evidence may suggest that a similar constructional form, the *kiln barn*, was also in use at Kirk Ness. Both comparable kilns at Hoddom appear to be of similar date to Kirk Ness, based on their respective radiocarbon dates (cal AD 650–870 at 95% for Kirk Ness (as modelled from all terrestrial samples, see Hamilton Appendix N), cal AD 650–950 for Hoddom structure 6; cal AD 650–950 for Hoddom structure 7, *cf.* Dalland in Lowe 2006, 165f).

A kiln-barn structure at Kirk Ness would imply a relatively large-scale processing of cereal grain, but still nothing of the scale found at Hoddom, a major monastic foundation of the period (Lowe 2006, 195; Holden 2006a, 108). At Kirk Ness only one kiln was recovered and the grain as preserved suggested food production only. No evidence for malting indicative of brewing was recovered at Kirk Ness.

On the whole, the survival of archaeological remains at Kirk Ness is admittedly less than ideal, and the presence of a kiln-barn cannot be confirmed. Given the proximity of the kiln base to the very northern edge of the bedrock outcrop, the northern extent of the practicably habitable area, it seems that the kiln structure, of whatever superstructure it may have been, was placed deliberately on the margin of the settled area, perhaps at the furthest distance away from the permanently inhabited buildings; one would assume in order to minimise the risk of spreading fire (*cf.* Holden 2006a, 102). As evidence suggests, this may have been a wise choice; the kiln appears to have been combusted catastrophically and its use was subsequently abandoned. The exposed situation at the outer edge of the headland may not have been the most ideal situation for the operation of a kiln (Tim Holden, *pers. comm.*).

Despite the suggested parallels and potential of the archaeological remains at Kirk Ness, realistically, the recovered evidence is too ephemeral, and the areas investigated too confined, to confirm any of this with certainty. It would also be highly speculative to link this directly with any historic association of the site with supposed ecclesiastical or monastic occupation in the 7th century AD. In the absence of more comprehensive archaeological evidence our understanding of the occupation of Kirk Ness in the early medieval period relies primarily on documentary evidence and the historical and archaeological context provided by nearby sites such as Tyningham, Auldhame, Eldbotle and Dunbar (see below).

The abandonment of the kiln after the catastrophic conflagration

After the conflagration event, it appears that this part of the excavated area was completely abandoned and ultimately sealed under a relatively thick make-up deposit of clay, *1080/1092*, that was assigned a later medieval date, perhaps of the 13th–14th centuries (see Chapter 4). The burnt layers associated directly with the conflagration of the kiln, *1205* and *1206*, were directly overlain by this very compact matrix; however, as will be described, the laying down of the clay deposit seems to have been preceded by deliberate levelling and truncation of pre-existing levels – this apparently removed any accumulated soil layers over the kiln feature. Only in discrete places did the stratigraphy suggest that the upper parts of agricultural soils to the west of the kiln had originally encroached and overlain the abandoned kiln area (see below). Reworking, re-deposition and bioturbation of this soil complex, which incorporated weathered and fragmented bone material, suggests that the area was left uninhabited following abandonment of the kiln, and initially used for light agricultural purposes such as grazing (see below and Appendix M).

Phase 2c: the use of the open area to the west of the early building

The area outside the early building to the west preserved a substantial thickness of soil, which had apparently accumulated in front of the building's western entrance and was bounded by the *1279/1180* wall footings. During excavation it was initially assumed that wall *1279* was cut into these soil layers, but no cut was subsequently observed. While it is possible that the material accumulated against the walls of the early structure, thus post-dating them, this could not be proven; it is alternatively possible that evidence for a cut, had it existed, may have been eradicated by later reworking of the soil (Figure 3.18). If the soil build-up post-dated the building of the early structure this would imply that the latter had been formed with wholly upstanding walls and had not been any form of semi-sunken structure, such as the *grubenhaus* type of construction found at Ratho (Smith 1995, 104–8) of probable 7th century date (*ibid.*, 110), and commonly found on Anglian sites throughout the country (Lowe 1999, 18–19).

Characterisation of the soil build-up

The soil make-up to the west of the early building consisted of three different layers, two being more substantial levels of humic soil – *1095* below and *1210* above, these in all likelihood cultivated – separated by a thin ash layer, *1094*. The lower soil, *1095*, was a deep (15–25cm) but relatively homogeneous dark brown silt that was almost devoid of finds. This material directly overlay bedrock outcrops in the area, identified here as *1096*, and an apparently natural deposit of reddish sand and degraded bedrock to the west, *1236*. The *1210* soil level consisted of a mid-brown loamy silt matrix; this was identified by thin section analysis as a possible garden soil (Lancaster, Appendix M). Its uppermost part, which contained a high quantity of animal bone and identified at the time of excavation as a separate context, *1097*, yielded datable material (see Figure 1.15 – darker band of deposits).

The nature and composition of (1095) – evidence for early cultivation in the 5th–6th centuries?

The morphology of the deposits outside the early building, in the western parts of the tunnel excavation area, was tested by thin section analysis (see Lancaster, Appendix M). This showed that the character of the lower material, *1095*, was that of a buried natural soil that was most likely already present on site before the first human activity or, just possibly, deliberately imported for the purpose of cultivation. This natural soil was then reworked and enriched with culturally-derived material, charcoal in particular. The make-up showed signs of disturbance by plough or, more likely, spade.

The soil composition suggests a high turf content, consisting of burnt and unburnt material. The turf most likely derived from glacial tills, as found in the hinterland, to the west and south of North Berwick (Macaulay Institute 1982, see Appendix M). It could not be established whether the burnt elements within represented an *in situ* event or burnt material brought into this area from

Fig. 3.20: Part of the 1094 *ash layer overlying soil level* 1095*; a section of the overlying* 1210/1097 *remains to left, with later cobbling on top (*1069*); excavated to underlying bedrock to right; view looking E*

elsewhere. The latter seems more likely as no source of direct burning was identified within the excavated extent of *1095*.

The few bone fragments recovered from *1095* mainly comprised cattle, with some red deer and horse, marine fowl and marine mammal. Part of the flipper of a seal (distal metapodial SF9, Smith, Appendix J) from this context had been cut with a knife near the articulation, apparently to remove the flesh. Evidence of such butchery marks on the seal bones in *1095* may not simply represent food consumption. The seal's skin may have been cured, and the underlying fat processed for its oil. Seal oil was traditionally used in *cruisie* lamps for lighting, especially in the Northern Isles (Fenton 1978, 525, *cf.* Smith, Appendix J). The presence of bones from young seals or pups, presumably in their first white coats, suggests that these were killed for their fur. That there may be a direct association between the midden material in *1095* and the earlier use (or clearing out?) of the adjacent early building is perhaps suggested by the recovery of seal bones from within the structure (from deposits *1303* and *1309*).

It is interesting to note generally that the seal bones from Kirk Ness all concentrate in the early occupation levels of the site, in Phases 2a (as described above) and 2c (in *1206* and within redeposited material from *1097* and *1210*). Based simply on this distribution of seal bones the beginning of the cultivation of the *1095* midden soil may be coeval with the original use of the early building, in Phase 2a.

A higher quantity of shell and bone was noted in the upper zone of *1095*, at its interface with the *1094* ashy layer. Thin-section analysis suggested that these bones and shells were deposited relatively shortly before this level was buried and sealed by *1094*. The comparatively good condition of the bone within this layer suggests that, immediately prior to the deposition of *1094*, the *1095* soil had not been subject to disruptive processes such as digging or ploughing (Lancaster, Appendix M). It seems that cultivation of the *1095* soils had been temporarily abandoned, and that an episode of midden dumping had been allowed to take place, this then followed by the deposition of the ashy material.

Intermediate ashy layer (1094) – repeated rake-out from the firing of the kiln?

The thin and colourful ashy layer, *1094*, was laminated in character, suggestive of a series of small depositional events in the form of mineral ash, probably derived from peat or turf fuel (Figure 3.20). The lamination seems to have originated from a series of depositions representing several burning events, not an individual conflagration.

Early field observations had assumed a relationship between the two ash-rich layers, *1094* and *1206*, the orange turf and peat ash found overlying the kiln structure and associated with its final abandonment. The latter was indeed very similar in colour and texture (Figure 3.21), but its composition suggests that it originated from a single conflagration event rather than a periodic or sequential deposition as suggested by the lamination within *1094*.

Nonetheless the *1094* ash may have derived from the use of the kiln. Given the relatively large quantities of ash represented and the frequency of deposition indicated by its lamination it seems plausible that *1094* represents the raked-out ashes from the firing of the kiln, rather than part of its destruction deposit. The distribution of the raked out ashes, to the south of the kiln base, would correspond well with the location of the *1226* charred barley cache, also located to the south of the remaining kiln base, and similarly interpreted as the grain residue from raking out the kiln fill. The full extent of *1094* could not, unfortunately, be plotted as it survived only in patches and was not present within a section coinciding with the kiln structure and related destruction deposits.

Later soil build-up (1210) – abandonment of the area, wasteland or light grazing?

The *1094* ash was sealed by another humic cultivation soil, *1210*, of which the upper part was composed, in large part, of uncomposted household waste containing large quantities of bone (*1097*). Although subject to surface abrasion, butchery marks were observed on some of the bones, suggesting that the meat had been cut off the

Fig. 3.21: Excavated west-facing section through the 1206/1205 deposits, these overlying the kiln base (to centre left), looking E

bone prior to cooking (e.g. shaft of sheep/goat calcaneum, SF78). Layer *1210* generally had been interpreted as an imported soil, similar to *1095* in its biological reworking, but with no sign of more disruptive disturbance such as ploughing or digging. The *1210* soil seems to have developed without such disruption and presented more of the character of an established pasture or wasteland (Lancaster, Appendix M).

The whole complex of soil build-up in this area contained no evidence for a major natural dumping event such as a large windblown episode; the latter was clearly a factor in the make-up of deposits at the site as discussed in the preceding section, and subsequently.

The only radiocarbon dates from this area were obtained from *1097*, the animal bone-rich uppermost layer in this soil sequence outside the building. The two dates obtained span a comparably large time period (*1097*: SUERC-28293: 1490±40 BP; cal AD 430–650 95%, and SUERC-28292: 1320±40 BP; cal AD 640–780 at 95%). This date range could represent the accumulation of midden over a relatively long period of time, at least from the middle of the 5th century, possibly until the late 8th century. Given that the dates for *1097* were obtained from the latest context of the soil sequence and have a significant date range stretching over up to four centuries, it seems much more likely that this represents material redeposited from a midden source elsewhere. The highly fragmented and weathered condition of the bone within *1097* would certainly support this interpretation. The context as a whole was also fairly homogenous and showed little evidence for post-depositional mixing with underlying or overlying deposits, again supporting the latter interpretation of introducing re-deposited material. The Bayesian modelling dismisses the two dates from *1097* as not statistically consistent, also implying

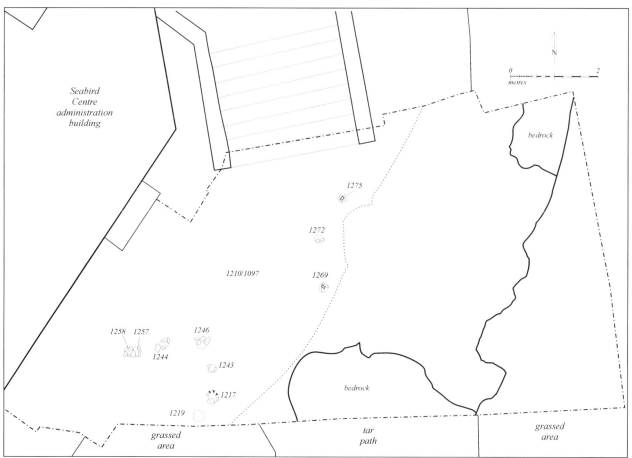

Fig. 3.22: Plan of post-setting groups within the upper levels of the 1097/1210 cultivation soils

that the dated material is either reworked, or intrusive. The dates therefore only represent a *terminus post quem* for the deposition of the midden. The radiocarbon dating and the quantity of food residues present together suggest that there was extended domestic activity on site at a period between AD 430 and 780, from which this midden was derived.

A stone-setting within the lower levels of the cultivation soils

A sondage along the north-western edge of the trench revealed a group of set stones associated with the *1095* soil built-up, which was otherwise notable for the absence of associated features. These stones, *1319*, formed an irregular alignment roughly orientated north-west to south-east (Figure 3.12). The stones lay within a shallow cut, *1320*, into *1095*. The whole feature was poorly preserved and relatively fragmented, defined only by a few larger stones at its south-eastern extent. Otherwise it consisted of multiple smaller stone fragments, small slabs and spalled pieces of whin. The fill of cut *1320* surrounding the *1319* stones was similar to *1095*, but contained a notably higher concentration of animal bone. The preservation of these bones, primarily cattle, was fairly good with butchery marks suggesting the use of a cleaver or axe (Smith, Appendix J). A discrete concentration of seashell, *1321*, was also dumped within the cut at the eastern edge of the sondage, together with guillemot bones, apparently exploited as a food resource as well.

Although the survival of the stone feature was very ephemeral, the most likely interpretation for its function would be that of the remains of a rough cobbled surface. The larger stones may represent degraded remains of a kerb. The construction of this surface seems to have been associated with a dump of household waste. The stone setting was apparently sealed by the *1094* ash deposits, and subsequently by the upper garden soil *1210*.

The use of the early building and the area to the west for agricultural purposes?

The relatively high turf component within *1095* and a similarly humic character of the midden-like matrix of *1281* and *1287* within the early building deserve some further exploration. The *1281/1287* material represents the infill of the early building at around the 6th–7th centuries, and together with the cultivation of *1095*, the lowest ploughsoil in front of the early building, the similarities might permit some speculation regarding their contemporaneity. This in turn might help to shed some light on the use of the early building,

It seems that the infilling of the building with turf and midden material occurred after a winkle-rich clayey layer was spread across the earliest paved floor. As already discussed above, the infilling with *1281/1287* apparently lasted for a prolonged period, enough time to generate

0.10–0.15m depth of humic material that was much more layered originally than the generally surviving homogenised character suggested. Such evidence of infilling and bioturbation seems curious if the material was simply dumped into an abandoned structure; one possibility may be that the structure had seen reuse as a byre or pen, with animals causing the mixing of the material inside the building; the general absence of a stratified sequence of interior occupation deposits may be significant in this respect. The humic component of the upper infill material may relate to the presence of animals, but it is notable that the numerous shells within the same matrix showed little evidence of fracture or crushing that might be expected as a result of trample. A natural build-up of topsoil within and upon the upper midden-like infill might also account for the humic content.

Deposits *1281/1287* (inside the structure) and *1095* (outside to the west) display similarly high turf components, this perhaps suggesting material from within the structure (particularly if in part deriving from the presence of animals) may have been cleared out from time to time through the western entrance and spread onto the cultivated land in front of the building. Since both sequences thinned out towards the entrance of the early building, their direct relationship is unclear and was unfortunately not recorded in section.

If it is assumed that the evidence for midden dumps associated with *1287* inside the early structure indicates a period of abandonment of the dwelling use, then this might explain why a cultivation soil was allowed to build up in front of the building's western entrance – it seems unlikely that this entrance was still in regular use while a substantial depth of soil and midden was cultivated directly in front of it. The stone setting *1319* within the *1095* soil might have represented an area of hard standing or even part of a path leading up to the entrance, allowing access across the field.

Overall, the character of the open area to the west of, and contemporary with, the early building is that of introduced midden material from domestic refuse and small-scale industrial waste, apparently in part from seal processing. This matrix may have been intermixed with humic material/dung derived from animal bedding, or possibly from turves deriving from previous constructions, in order to create fertile cultivation soils. The ash layer overlying *1095* perhaps represents raked-out hearth ashes from subsequent firing events, most likely associated with the later kiln. All this indicates at least some domestic occupation on the wider site, even though possibly episodic, during this longer general period of apparent agricultural use.

Phase 2d: post-built structures within the upper levels of the cultivation soils

In the area to the southwest of the kiln a group of three post-holes arranged in a flat arc, was recorded as cutting

Fig. 3.23: The group of post-settings to the SW, looking E

through the *1210* garden soil – *1269, 1272* and *1275* (Figure 3.23). Each contained a setting of flat vertically-positioned post-packing stones. A further group of eight post-holes *1257, 1258, 1264, 1244, 1246, 1243, 1217* and *1219*, also cut into *1210*, were of similar depth, dimension and character as the others. This group lay further to the south-west of the kiln, towards the southern edge of the excavated area, and formed a clear angled alignment (Figures 3.22 and 3.23). However, no other structural or depositional evidence could be associated with these sets of post-holes, related upper deposits having evidently been truncated. The limited evidence of food debris recovered from the post-hole fills, comprising only shells and unburnt animal bone, did not help to confirm their contemporaneity with the use of the kiln.

Following a general truncation of deposits the surviving lower parts of these post-holes were sealed by the same yellow clayey make-up, *1092*, that also overlay the kiln structure. With the dating of *1092* and associated levels to the medieval period (a 12th–13th century date or younger – see Chapter 4 and Haggarty, Appendix D on CD) a considerable amount of time had clearly elapsed between the abandonment of the kiln in the 8th or 9th century and their deposition – some 300 years or more. Within this timeframe the *1210* garden soil, which partly overlay the kiln area, had evidently been created and subsequently abandoned, and the post-built structures then erected. The post-buildings must thus be substantially later than any occupation up to the 9th century. Given the absence of associated deposits their function remains obscure, and their more precise dating

uncertain. It is even possible that they represent an initial episode of later medieval activity and should be more properly included in the following chapter.

Anglian Kirk Ness? – An archaeological and historical contextualisation

The archaeological evidence for the early medieval occupation at Kirk Ness

While the dating of the early archaeological remains at Kirk Ness has prompted considerable academic interest, the extent and preservation of the surviving material has proven to be rather disappointing for the writing of a convincing narrative of this period for the site. The dates of the earliest deposits associated with the stone-footed structure have suggested a domestic occupation of the promontory of early 5th–6th century date, arguably Late Roman Iron Age into the early medieval period. It would, therefore, be tantalising to speculate about the character of activities at Kirk Ness in the context of large-scale political developments at this time, but any conclusion must remain speculative as the archaeological evidence on site has been undiagnostic in terms of arte-factual or structural evidence. Without the radiocarbon dates one would struggle to securely place the archaeological findings into any chronological context, since the remains could essentially be accommodated within any period, from later prehistoric until the late medieval period.

The evidence of several phases of use for the early structure, seemingly as a domestic building, possibly suggests a continuous, and judging from the original date and quantity of food residue as represented by the redeposited material to the west of this structure, at times quite thriving occupation of the site in the early period. These observations fit well with indications of cultivation of soils immediately to the west of this building, at a time when it seemingly stood empty or was possibly used as a byre. Phases of habitation seem to alternate with phases of agricultural use and the recovery of butchered seal bones could be linked with some form of craft work or even processing of skins and blubber.

The character of this occupation changed over time, especially if the interpretation of the intervening collapse for the early building is accepted, which would imply a hiatus of domestic occupation in the late 6th to early 7th centuries, with a clear shift towards agricultural use, at least in relation to the limited sample of the site as revealed within the excavated area. The main area of habitation may have moved at that time to another, as yet unidentified, part of the site. However, the early building seems to have seen reuse, most likely in the 7th century, and, given the quantity of stone, was rebuilt as a rubble structure. This might perhaps suggest a more prestigious use than the previous simple domestic function. With the date ranges obtained, is it possible to associate such evidence to wider events in the region and archaeological finds elsewhere?

The historical context for the archaeological evidence at Kirk Ness

The period of Northumbrian occupation of the Lothians has been traditionally defined by two historical events, the siege of *Dunedin* [Edinburgh] in AD 638, and the date AD 973, when Cinaeda mac Mael Coluim (971–95) gained control of the area from Edgar of Wessex (for a detailed discussion of the wider historical context see Smyth 1984; Rollason 2003; Lowe 2006, 191–8; Fraser 2009, Crone in prep.). Crone also hints at the evidence for early English place-names in East Lothian, supporting a mid-7th century date for the first settlement from Northumbria in this area (*cf.* Smyth 1984, 31). However, the term 'Northumbria' might have been a much later identifier, introduced in the early 8th century, at the time of Bede's writings, (*cf.* Rollason 2003, 34f).

The earliest expansion into the area by kings from Bamburgh has been historically associated with the reign of Ethelfrith in the late 6th–early 7th centuries (AD 593–617; *cf.* Smyth 1984, 21). Bernician influence on East Lothian was certainly growing by the beginning of the 6th century. In 1981 Simpson and Stevenson suggested there was sufficient archaeological evidence to support a date of the 6th century for settlement in the environs of North Berwick. This evidence consisted of a zoomorphic penannular brooch and a hand-pin recovered from a rock shelter (1981, 14). They also noted that a large mound which supposedly had contained Anglo-Saxon 'relics' had been destroyed during construction works in 1847 and that the location of those 'relics' was unknown (*ibid.*, 10). Writing 16 years later, Hall and Bowler referred to this evidence as 'scanty' but noted the proximity of the burgh to both the Castle Hill 'motte' site and to the possible Iron Age fort upon North Berwick Law which could suggest continuity of occupation, probably of more indigenous character (1997, 660). The place-name Berwick itself is commonly thought of as containing the Old English (OE) prefix *bere-* (barley) and the OE suffix *–wic*, meaning specialised farm (www.nottingham.ac.uk/english/ins/kepn/).

While the earliest occupation at Kirk Ness, starting in the late 5th–late 6th centuries (cal AD 410–590 at 95% probability and cal AD 485–565 at 68% probability) predates any historically recorded Northumbrian activity, the site has revealed no evidence for any continuity of settlement from later prehistoric times either.

Some kind of Northumbrian settlement or presence in this area is almost to be expected since North Berwick lies within the territories controlled by the kings of Northumbria and the excavations at Castle Park, Dunbar (Perry 2000) have demonstrated both continuity of settlement through the Northumbrian period and the richness of surviving Anglo-Saxon archaeological evidence. Dunbar has been identified as the important centre of secular power in the late 7th century, the Northumbrian king's Ecgfrith's *urbs sua Dynbaer*, the town of Dynbaer (Crone in prep., *cf.* Colgrave 1985). However, the distinct 'Anglo-Saxon' connotation of the mid-to-late 6th/early 7th century occupation at Dunbar (there phase 7) has recently been questioned by Blackwell, based on re-assessing a belt buckle fragment of early to mid-7th century date. In its archaeological context it seems to sit uneasily with the phasing as originally identified by the excavators – and given its evidence of wear and repair appears more likely to have been lost or abandoned in a fence ditch feature in the latter half of the 7th century (Blackwell 2009, 366). In the wider East Lothian context and with regards to high status objects of continental or wider pan-Anglian character, Blackwell has argued that a supra-regional English or Anglo-Saxon identity developed only during the 7th century (*ibid.*, 370, *cf.* Hines 1994). With the phasing at such a well-understood site as Dunbar in question, the understanding of the evidence at Kirk Ness is even more difficult, in particular since North Berwick, unlike Dunbar, is not explicitly named in surviving Anglo-Saxon sources.

Kirk Ness might have played a role similar to Eldbotle, some 5.5km further west along the coast from North Berwick. A medieval settlement had been known in the area for some time, confirmed in excavations in 1999 (Moloney and Baker 2001), but the presence of a much earlier settlement, originating at around the same time as the earliest structural phase at Kirk Ness, AD 400–670 (phase 1 at Eldbotle, *cf.* Morrison *et al.* 2008, 24), has only recently been confirmed. Without artefactual evidence from phase 1 at Eldbotle, the earliest occupation has been interpreted as "elements of a British settlement during the period of initial Northumbrian penetration into East Lothian" (*ibid.*, 40). A similar interpretation might hold true for the first settlement as recovered at Kirk Ness.

The dating of the deposits associated with the early occupation and the early building at Kirk Ness would correspond with this suggested early period of British settlement and 'Northumbrian' transition in East Lothian in the 5th–6th centuries. The small lead object, interpreted here as an early medieval fishing-weight or net sinker, as compared with parallels from York – there from Anglian and 11th–12th century contexts – might confirm an association of the site with the early Northumbrian influence in East Lothian. However, the simplicity of the object renders it chronologically and certainly culturally undiagnostic (A. Blackwell *pers. comm.* and McLaren/Hunter this vol.).

For Eldbotle it has been suggested that by the mid- to late 7th century the settlement can be seen in connection with the major monastery at Tyninghame as "a component in a pattern of secular and ecclesiastical estates running from Dunbar westwards to Edinburgh" (Morrison *et al.* 2008, 40). From all that we know from the excavated remains at Kirk Ness, the site may be similarly considered and could have played a very similar role, only in a much more prominent coastal position.

The early medieval ecclesiastical situation in East Lothian

The presence of a church building dating to the early medieval period, and thus considerably pre-dating the present structural remains of the church of St Andrew at Kirk Ness, has been suggested by several sources. Ferrier discussed a possible foundation of this early church by "St Baldred", as early as the 6th century (Ferrier 1869, 16; there is, however, no historical figure of St Baldred which is apparently a later corruption of St Balthere, *cf.* Fraser 2009, 370).

The spread of Northumbrian-influenced monasteries has been traced as a coastal development, geographically recorded from Spurn Head on the Humber Estuary via Whitby to Tyninghame and Auldhame, if the latter are accepted as Anglian foundations by St Balthere (see below; Petts 2009, 88).

The earliest known medieval parish church at North Berwick was dedicated to St Andrew. It is now called the 'old kirk' and has already been the subject of a number of excellent detailed investigations by both historians and archaeologists. All of these reports have focused to different extents on the hagiography relating to an even earlier and still rather obscure local saint called St Baldred who, we are informed, lived in the area in the mid-8th century (Arnold 1882–5, I, 48). Unfortunately, there is very little surviving information relating to St Baldred or St Balthere and his mission apart from a few references in English sources and later hagiography from the Aberdeen Breviary. Yet his figure overshadows the history of both the church of St Andrew and North Berwick to a considerable extent.

Any narrative about the early church at Kirk Ness will inevitably be based upon secondary sources since there are essentially no surviving Scottish documentary records from the pre-1100 period. This situation does not improve much for the period 1100–*c*.1550 because the North Berwick burgh records for that period have not survived. This leaves the cartulary of the medieval Cistercian nunnery of North Berwick as virtually the sole source for material relating to the 'old kirk' because its revenues belonged to the convent.

The evidence from medieval documents

Although the historical events as generally narrated in secondary sources seem to imply documentary accuracy for the wider area, the only reference to an 'Anglo-Saxon' presence in the North Berwick area comes from a medieval text written by the community of St Cuthbert, *Historia De Sancto Cuthberto*. The most recent editor of

this text has argued that it was written to record and legitimise the property claims made by the Cuthbertine community that had originated at Lindisfarne. The dating of this text depends on whether some 11th century charters within it are interpolations, i.e. later additions to an originally earlier text. If they are, the original text is 10th century in date. However, the editor of the medieval text on the whole favoured the idea that they were not later textual additions, which would date *Historia De Sancto Cuthberto* to the period between 1031 and 1050 (Johnson South 2002, 11, 35f).

Whatever the date, the list of territories claimed by the Cuthbertine community states:

> Et hic est Lindisfarnensis terrae terminus: a fluuio Tweoda usque ad Warnedmuthe, et inde superius ad illum locum ubi haec aqua quae uocatur Warned oritur iuxta montem Hybberndune, et ab illo monte usque ad fluuium qui uocatur Bromic, ct inde usque ad fluuium qui uocatur Till, et tota terra quae iacet ex utraque parte ipsius fluminis Bromic usque ad illum locum ubi oritur. Et illa terra ultra Tweoda ab illo loco ubi oritur fluuius Edre ab aquilone usque ad illum locum ubi cadet in Tweoda, et tota terra quae iacet inter istum fluuium Edre et alterum fluuium qui oucatur Leder uersus occidentem, et tota terra quae iacet ab orientali parte istius aquae quae uocatur Leder usque ad illum locum ubi cadet in fluuium Tweoda uersus austrum, et tota terra quae pertinet ad monasterium sancti Balthere, quod uocatur Tinningaham, a Lombormore usque ad Esce muthe.

> [And this is the boundary of the territory of Lindisfarne: from the River Tweed as far as the mouth of Warren Beck, and from there upwards as far as the place where Warren Beck rises next to Hepburn Hill, and from that hill as far as the river that is called Beamish, and from there as far as the river that is called the Till, and all the land that lies on both sides of the same River Beamish up to the place where it rises. And that land beyond the Tweed from the place where the River Blackadder rises in the north as far as the place where it flows into the Tweed, and all the land that lies between that River Blackadder and another that is called the Leader towards the west, and all the land that lies on the east side of that water that is called the Leader as far as the place where it flows into the Tweed toward the south, and all the land that pertains to the monastery of St Balthere, which is called Tynningham, from the Lammermuir Hills as far as the mouth of the Esk. (Johnson South 2002, 46–47). It should be noted that the editor has twice translated the word 'Edre' as 'Blackadder' when such a translation is not justified by the text. There is also a river in the area called the Whiteadder.]

Leaving the geographic details to one side for the moment, the important figure amid these claims is St Balthere (now known as St Baldred). Yet another medieval text, this time written by Symeon of Durham in the late 11th or early 12th century, adds the detail that St Balthere of Tyninghame was an Anglo-Saxon who died in AD 756 (Anderson 1908, 56). Symeon of Durham, who joined the monastic community there *c.*1090, would have witnessed first-hand the translation of St Cuthbert's coffin to Durham in 1104 (Piper 1989, 437–46). Since Durham would have had an interest at that time in controlling the lands and revenues that traditionally would have belonged to the cult of Cuthbert while it was successively resident at Lindisfarne, Norham, and Chester-le-Street, Symeon's attention to Balthere is understandable. Since the Cuthbertine community had earlier claimed possession of St Balthere's monastic lands in *Historia De Sancto Cuthberto*, so the final resting place of Cuthbert's body, Durham, could also legitimately lay a later claim to those same lands and revenues.

Problems of dating the take-over of East Lothian by the Northumbrians

It may be impossible to establish precisely when and how the cult of Cuthbert at Lindisfarne came to assume superiority over the lands of the Balthere community at Tynningham. Part of the problem here is that we have no detailed chronology for the conquest of the Lothian plain by the Northumbrians, and the nature of this "conquest". Perry, for example, has recently asserted that the *obsesio Etin*, recorded in the Annals of Ulster in AD 638, completed the Northumbrian conquest of Lothian and presumably *Y Gododdin* (Perry 2000, 7; Koch 1997). Yet, this is not what the annal states. In fact, the reduction of *Etin* in AD 638 could have been undertaken by any number of different war-bands from north Britain, and with no identity given of the besiegers or the besieged (Rollason 2003, 34, 89; *cf.* Fraser 2009, 171–2).

Goldberg recently remarked that the medieval Welsh poetic references are the only occasion that the Gododdin, identified as the *Votadini* in Roman histories, have been associated with territory north of the Tweed. No contemporary reference – such as the *Annals of Ulster obsesio Etin* – mention them. Earlier references by Roman sources such as Ptolemy indicate the location of the Votadini as much further south, in the Tyne valley area (M. Goldberg, *pers. comm.*). This dislocation and the gap in historical references between 2nd century Roman and 10th century Welsh sources would further question the accuracy of the claim of a Northumbrian victory over the dominating tribe of the area at Edinburgh. It is similarly likely that conflicts in the 6th–7th centuries were not fought on ethnic, but on social links (G. Stratton, *pers. comm.*).

The later 7th century Northumbrian occupation

Matters are a little clearer for the latter half of the 7th century. According to Eddius Stephanus, a roughly contemporary 8th century hagiographer, the Northumbrian Bishop Wilfred was imprisoned at Dunbar in AD 680 (Colgrave 1985, 72). Smyth identifies Wilfred, educated at Lindisfarne and subsequently in Rome, as having evolved as one of the politically most prominent episcopal figures after the Synod of Whitby in 664. Wilfred became the bishop of Northumbria in 669 (1984, 24, 121), but his influence seemed to have waned under king Ecgfrith (670–685), resulting in Wilfred's imprisonment and exile. Shortly after the battle of Nechtanesmere in 685, Bede states that the Northumbrian Bishop Trumwine abandoned the episcopal seat at Abercorn on the Forth, apparently founded only four years earlier (Farmer 1990, 255). Taken together, these pieces of evidence seem to imply a complete Northumbrian takeover of Lothian before the end of the 7th century to a point at which new episcopal sees were being formed – this before the intervention of Nechtansmere. In all likelihood, the coastal location of Kirk Ness in the Firth of Forth might have given a strategic advantage for Northumbrian influence, intended to radiate out towards the Fife coast and its fertile hinterland.

The Northumbrian advance had been subsequently reversed to some extent by the Pictish king of Fortriu, Brude mac Bili at Nechtansmere with no record of either Bishop Trumwine or any subsequent Northumbrian bishop ever returning to Abercorn. However, it cannot be assumed that after Nechtansmere the Picts were able to establish effective overlordship in East Lothian since there are later 8th century records of Pictish–Northumbrian armed clashes somewhere in the Plain of Manau around the Firth of Forth (Mac Airt and Mac Niocaill 1983, 710.3). Unfortunately, it is unknown whether these were either Pictish warbands attacking other areas under Northumbrian overlordship or Picts defending territory they had previously conquered post-AD 685 from subsequent Northumbrian reconquest. The debate about control over the Forth is complicated as earlier sources assumed the battle of Nechtansmere to have taken place much further south than is assumed now (Fraser 2009, 215–16). The location of the battle is important for understanding which lands were controlled by Picts or Northumbrians in the aftermath of the battle. With the location of the battle of Nechtansmere now placed in Strathspey at Dunachton (Woolf 2006, 187), it is possible to argue that Northumbria still had some influence on the Forth region, and certainly within the Lothians (*cf* Fraser 2009, 216).

The mission of St Balthere in the 8th century

It is against this political backdrop that the 8th century mission of St Balthere into Lothian must be viewed. Clearly, he cannot have been a part of the initial Anglo-

Saxon advance northwards into Lothian since 70 years separated the abandonment of Abercorn by Bishop Trumwine in 685 and Balthere's death as recorded by Symeon of Durham for 756. It would undoubtedly be easier to interpret this evidence if the geographic extent of the original Northumbrian diocese of Abercorn was known but it now appears impossible to resurrect these boundaries exactly. Matters are further complicated by the fact that parts of the Lothian plain, consisting of the detached parishes of Abercorn, Cramond, Preston and Bunkle, belonged to the medieval diocese of Dunkeld, whereas the remainder of Lothian belonged to the diocese of St Andrews. Accordingly, it seems unlikely that the boundaries of these medieval Scottish dioceses were based upon earlier Northumbrian ecclesiastic patterns (McNeill and MacQueen 1996, 353).

A strong Northumbrian influence on East Lothian – in the 7th or 8th century?

The situation as discussed above leaves the 11th century perambulation, i.e. the description of geographical boundaries as "walked along", of the lands of Lindisfarne between the Rivers Tweed and Esk in *Historia De Sancto Cuthberto* as the sole piece of evidence for the extent of the influence of Lindisfarne, and ultimately Northumbria, over East Lothian, even though almost 400 years separate this description from the original creation of the see of Abercorn, probably in AD 681 (Smyth 1984, 32). In the light of the sparse historical evidence, it is worth questioning whether these Lothian lands as claimed by the see of Lindisfarne in the 11th century either represented what had always been an entirely separate see or whether they had once formed part of a larger and earlier Northumbrian see based at Abercorn, before its abandonment in the late 7th century. Kirk Ness' central position – not quite halfway between Abercorn and Lindisfarne – must have presented a prominent landmark between these two eminent ecclesiastical places at that period.

One clue to answering the question of Lindisfarne's relations to East Lothian lies in the *Historia Regum Anglorum*, an early 12th century text attributed to Symeon of Durham, which incorporates earlier Northumbrian material compiled by Byrhtferth of Ramsey *c.*1000 and a possible lost Pictish source:

Anno .DCCCLIV., natiuitatis Regis Elfredi .vi., Wlfere, regnante rege Osberto super Northimbros, suscepto pallio confirmatus est in archiepiscopatum Eboracensem, et Eardulf suscepit episcopatum Lindisfarnensem. Quo pertinebant Lugubalia, id est Luel, nunc dicitur Carliel, et Northam, quae antiquitus Vbbanford dicebatur. Omnes quoque ecclesiae ab aqua quae uocatur Tweda usque Tinam australem, et ultra desertum ad occidentem, pertinebant illo tempore ad praefatam ecclesiam, et hae mansiones, Carnam et Culterham, et duae Geddewrd

ad australem plagam Teinetae quas Ecgredus episcopus conditit: et Mailros, et Tigbrethingham, et Eoriercorn ad occidentalem partem, Edwinesburch, et Pefferham, et Aldham, et Tinnigaham, et Coldingham, et Tillmuthe, et Northam supradictam.

[In the year 854 in the sixth year after the birth of King Alfred, in the reign of King Osbert over the Northumbrians, Wulfhere received the pallium, and was confirmed in the archbishopric of York, and Eardwulf received the bishopric of Lindisfarne; to which pertained: Lugobalia, that is Luel, now called Carlisle, and Norham, that was anciently called Ubbanford. And also all of those churches between the river called Tweed and the southern Tyne, and beyond the desert to the west, pertained at this time to the aforesaid church, and these estates, Carnam and Culterham and the two Jedworths and the south side of Teviot which Bishop Ecgred donated: and Melrose, and Tighbrethingham, and Abercorn to the western extent, Edinburgh, and Pefferham, and Aldham, and Tyninghame, and Coldingham, and Tillmouth, and Norham, as said above. (Johnson South 2002, 119; Forsyth 2000, 19–34). It seems likely that Pefferburn could refer to the village now called Aberlady since Anglo-Saxon material has been excavated from there too.]

This text clearly indicates that at one point in time the see of Lindisfarne claimed to possess jurisdiction over the whole Lothians to Abercorn. Its possessions are listed in a circuit going down the Tweed to Melrose, then up through the unlocated *Tighbrethingham* to Abercorn, then down the Lothian coast to Coldingham and Tillmouth. The differences between this list of Lindisfarne possessions preserved in the early 12th century *Historia Regum Anglorum* and the list contained in the 11th century *Historia De Sancto Cuthberto* can perhaps be rationalised by the conquest of much of the Lothian plain by kings of Alba during the intervening period. Unfortunately, however, there is still a period of over 150 years between the abandonment of the see of Abercorn in 685 and the list preserved in *Historia Regum Anglorum* (assuming that it is accurately dated – see Johnson South 2002, 84*f.* It has been noted that the list begins and ends at Norham, where the Cuthbertine community was based *c.*850, so this text may well be contemporary). All this means that in theory the possessions of the see of Abercorn could have been absorbed by the see of Lindisfarne after the retreat of Bishop Trumwine southwards to Whitby in 685.

Accordingly, the activities of St Balthere must be placed within this second phase of Northumbrian ecclesiastic activity in Lothian, after the abandonment of Abercorn and the likely claiming of its properties by the bishops of Lindisfarne. Given the strength and power of the Cuthbertine community, the *Haliwerfolc* (people of the holy man, devotees of Cuthbert), and the fact that Cuthbert was being promoted as the *Reichsheiliger* of the Northumberland kingdom in imitation of the cult of St Martin in Gaul, it seems likely that Johnson South was correct to suggest that the Balthere mission in Lothian could have been a daughter house administered from Lindisfarne (Liddy 2008, 186; Thacker 1989, 115; Johnson South 2002, 80).

Notice has also been drawn by art-historians to a contemporaneous Northumbrian school of sculpture within the boundaries of the see of Lindisfarne. Rosemary Cramp in particular has argued that vine scroll from Abercorn, Jedburgh and Hexam; a strange bird from Tyninghame; animal interlace from Bamburgh and Coldingham; together with geometric interlace from Lindisfarne, add up to a distinctive regional style (Cramp 1989, 226–7).

The local cult of St Balthere must have received a setback in 941 when Tyninghame was sacked by Amlaíb son of Gothfrith, king of the Gaill, who also sacked Clonmacnoise in Ireland, fought at *Brunanburh*, and had a recognised claim to the kingship of Northumbria. The sacking of Tyninghame was, however, the final act in Amlaíb's career. He died a few days afterwards and the northern annals claimed that he had been struck down by the power of St Balthere (Woolf 2007, 174). Whatever damage that had been done to the community of St Balthere by Amlaíb must have been shortly rectified since two of the three churches associated with his cult, Auldhame and Tyninghame, and the triplication of the saint's body (Constable 1892, 84–5), were obviously still of value to the Cuthbertine cult based at Durham at a later date.

Unfortunately, the vague but seemingly straightforward story of St Balthere is further complicated by hagiography in the Aberdeen Breviary, of 16th century date, which tells a very different story. In this text it is stated that St Baldred [*sic*] was a disciple of St Kentigern. This claim poses something of a problem since it has been argued that St Kentigern died *c*.614, some 140 years before the recorded death of St Balthere in 756, and these dates are obviously irreconcilable (Macquarrie 1997, 234). This has led to speculation that there were two St 'Baldreds', St Baldred of Lothian and St Baldred of Strathclyde. The Aberdeen Breviary also seems to be the first surviving source to directly associate St Baldred with the Bass Rock.

The major problem with the claims made by the Aberdeen Breviary is that it is a relatively late text printed for a particular purpose in 1509–10, long-divorced from the times of the saints whose lives it purports to describe (http://www.lib.ed.ac.uk/resources/collections/specdivision/ch200803.shtml). Accordingly, there must be a suspicion that the association it makes between St 'Baldred' and the Bass Rock could be a late invention, particularly in light of the fact that a new chapel dedicated to St Baldred had recently been built upon the Bass Rock by Robert Lauder just before 1492 (NAS, GD103/2/44); this is discussed more fully in the following chapter.

A similar problem might occur with the association of the dedication of the early church at Kirk Ness to St Andrew. Reference to a medieval hospital or pilgrimage hostel at Kirk Ness attests North Berwick's importance as the ferrying point for pilgrims to St Andrews in the high medieval period:

> *duo hospitalia unum iuxta portum maris australem, alterum iuxta portum eiusdem transitus aquilonalem que pater meus statuit in susceptionem pauperum et perigrinorum*

> [two hospitals, one beside the southern sea-harbour (North Berwick), the other beside the northern harbour of the same crossing (Earlsferry), which [hospitals] my father established for the reception of the poor and pilgrims (North Berwick charters, no. 3).]

However, how early this pilgrimage was established remains unclear. The foundation of St Andrews has hagiographically been assigned to Acca of Hexam (Phillimore 1929, 11). Skene comments that the:

> "king who placed the kingdom under the patronage of St Andrew, and founded St Andrews, was Angus, son of Fergus [Onuist son of Wrguist, king of the Picts] who reigned AD 731 to 761, and that the year of the foundation was AD 736, when the expedition to Dalriada, afterwards called Argathelia, took place". (Skene 1860, 309)

Skene suggests that Acca's flight from Hexam to St Andrews is traceable by the number of early St Andrew dedications; this Skene thought notable because historical evidence suggests that St Peter was the patron saint of the Picts prior to Acca's introduction of St Andrew. The St Andrew dedication at Kirk Ness has therefore traditionally been viewed in this historical context. However, similarly to the association of St Baldred with the Bass Rock, the early association of Kirk Ness with the St Andrew pilgrimage might be a medieval invention. Independent from whether we accept that the 12th century pilgrim's route was a new creation by the nunnery or whether this represented the formal establishment of a pre-existing tradition utilising the shortest crossing to Fife, any pilgrimage to St Andrews cannot have started before the middle of the 8th century, and therefore generally post-dates the main activities as archaeologically evident on site.

Early medieval Kirk Ness in context

The geographical situation of Kirk Ness, on a headland on the southern coast of the Firth of Forth and presenting the closest sea travel to the Fife coast, might have suggested itself as a strategic position. It must have been particularly attractive in the 6th and 7th centuries, from Ethelfrith to Ecgfrith, at a time when Northumbrian (Bernician) ambition was to strengthen its control over East Lothian and to expand onto the north side of the Firth of Forth and beyond. The advantage of a short sea journey to the fertile Fife peninsula – always a strategic point in manifesting control over southeast Scotland and beyond (Smyth 1984, 39f) – might have encouraged controlling Kirk Ness. Fraser has argued that at least by the middle of the 7th century the Northumbrian expansion into Lothian was arguably motivated to control the passage between Iona and Lindisfarne, not simply for ecclesiastical but also for economic purposes (Fraser 2009, 171–2). A Northumbrian base at Kirk Ness around this time could be regarded as a possible conclusion in the wider territorial ambitions of both king and church.

Purely based on the date range for the early occupation at Kirk Ness, as obtained by the recent excavations, it could be suggested that the stone-footed building was erected as early as the 5th century, but certainly by the 6th century, seemingly pre-dating any Northumbrian influence on the area. The recovery of the lead object, although it has parallels with Anglian occupation in York, cannot in the present context be diagnostic of ethnic identity (A. Blackwell, F. Hunter, *pers. comms*).

The quantity of stone found within the final collapse horizon of the early building suggests that the repair, or even rebuilding, of the early structure – after a period of abandonment or agricultural use – had produced a seemingly more substantial structure than the earlier assumed turf construction. It may be that at this later stage the building had been rebuilt with stone walls, indicative of a more prestigious use; however, what function this served must remain a matter of speculation. Given the approximate date for this rebuilding in the 6th–early 7th centuries, the stone construction might fall into the period when the Northumbrians strengthened their foothold in East Lothian.

Given the date range for the corn-drying kiln, centring on a mid-7th to 8th century date (less likely early 9th century), its construction and use also falls within the period of Northumbrian influence on the area. Activities on the Kirk Ness site might have increased or even thrived under the influence of the new bishop's seat at Abercorn – and may have been similarly short-lived. However, the evidence for the protracted use of the kiln, re-occupying the site of the earlier building, suggests a permanent occupation of the site for the 7th–8th, possibly even 9th centuries.

The evidence and dating as indicated by the excavations at Kirk Ness are, unfortunately insufficiently defined, both by the archaeological evidence as preserved, as well as from the finds assemblage and radiocarbon sequence. Without any direct association with the historical context reflected in the archaeological evidence, we have to view the early activities at Kirk Ness in the light of these seemingly unsettled times in the 6th (or even earlier) and 7th centuries AD, with the conflicts of emerging kingdoms and different strands of Christianity attempting to gain influence in East Lothian and with the political situation in an even frailer position after Nechtansmere. However, it is impossible to assign any direct social, political or cultural identity to the occupation. Any occupation of Kirk Ness at this period need not necessarily be Northumbrian. Changing political fortunes might explain the changes in use and frequency of activity on the site from the 5th to the 8th, possibly into the 9th century AD, before the formal establishment of the pilgrim's route to St Andrews. Whether a more substantial and permanent ecclesiastical foothold was established at Kirk Ness by a pre-existing local community or as a new 12th century foundation through the Cistercian nunnery, as discussed in more detail in the following chapter, remains uncertain. It is very frustrating that the wider interpretation of the dated deposits and features from the excavations is hindered by the fragmented and sporadic nature of the archaeological evidence, and by the restrictions of the investigated area. The direct association of Kirk Ness with an Anglian kingdom may thus have been much looser than the historic evidence or Kirks Ness' geographical position may suggest.

Cross incised grave-marker discovered at the site of North Berwick Abbey, *c.*1896

with Rosemary Cramp and John Borland

While assessing finds from Dr J. S. Richardson's earlier excavations at Kirk Ness in the Haddington store of East Lothian Council Museum Service, an early cross-incised stone from North Berwick was recognised. This matches a description and illustrations published by Richardson in 1906–7 (Richardson 1906–7b, 432–3; Figure 3.24),

... a sandstone slab, 2 feet high, 1 foot broad, by 3½ inches thick. Sculptured on the one side is an incised cross, formed by parallel lines about 1 inch apart, with plain square angles and shaft, and on the other side a cross of equal arms, formed of similar incised lines. The horizontal arms of both crosses project slightly on the sides of the stone, and on both sides, in the upper corners formed by the arms, there is bordering the edge of the stone an incised line joining the arms of the cross.

Richardson's quoted dimensions for the stone were confirmed, at 0.62m, by 0.34m at its widest extent, by 0.09m. Of a fine-grained, pale grey–cream crystalline sandstone, the surface of the stone on both sides is relatively roughly

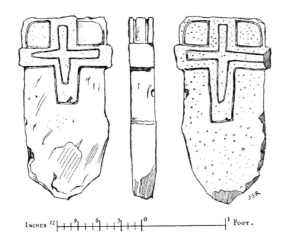

INCHES 12 | | | | 9 | | | | 6 | | | | 3 | | | | 0 | | | | | | | | | | 1 FOOT.

Fig. 3.24: J. S. Richardson's record of the cross-slab as published in 1907 (We are grateful to the Society of Antiquaries of Scotland for permission to reproduce)

Fig. 3.25: RCAHMS photo of cross slab. (© Crown Copyright: RCAHMS. Licensor www.rcahms.gov.uk)

dressed, with side A (more regular cross) having received a slightly smoother finish and certainly the more balanced cross carving (Figures 3.25 and 3.26). The cross on side B is smaller in height and seemingly also in width, with the right arm stopping short of the edge of the stone, and also not accurately aligned with the projecting left arm of the cross on side A. Overall the lower 0.15–0.20m of the stone is less well finished, this zone likely indicating the depth of insertion of the stone into the ground (?or socket).

The stone has seen some weathering and accidental damage, the latter possibly through later usage or alteration. There are small chips at the edges of the lower part of the stone and on the edge to the left of side A, towards the bottom end of the side A cross shaft. Weathering occurred primarily on the projecting cross-arms and at the top where the upper edges appear to have been particularly exposed to the elements. There are also a number of seatings or small notches that may have been intentionally formed. On the left edge of side A there is one placed at about the horizontal axis of the stone; a second, less deep and more worn, at the centre of the projecting left cross-arm – these two are about 0.15m apart. A further example appears at the horizontal axis towards the left edge of side B; and another possibly at the apex. The significance of these remains unclear – possible fixings?

There has been some suggestion, though evidently mistaken, that the stone was a find from Kirk Ness (site inspection in 1996, entry in CANMORE). However the actual circumstance of its discovery, in *c*.1896, was noted by Richardson,

… found about eleven years ago, while digging out a duck pond situated in the vicinity of the Abbey, and has since been preserved in the Lodge grounds.

At J. S. Richardson's instigation the stone was subsequently removed from the Lodge, in *c*.1954–5, and relocated to the old church site where it was erected upon a buried cement base within a purpose-built iron-railed enclosure. It was subsequently removed, between 1975 and 1980, to North Berwick Museum.

The particular interest of the stone is that it may be of comparatively early date – possibly pre-dating both the existing church ruin at Kirk Ness and the foundation of North Berwick Abbey, both of the 12th century. If this were the case then a predecessor site of origin would need to be proposed – one possibility might be an earlier ecclesiastical foundation at Kirk Ness, as has been long-suggested.

The stone has been variously reported, by J. T. Richardson (1911), by the RCAHMS (1924), by Graham (1960–1), and by Ferrier (1980). Among these a broad range of possible dates has been suggested. Ferrier notes the stone 'is thought to be of about 9th or 10th century date', this likely reiterating Richardson's opinion. Indeed in an earlier statement by Richardson the stone is described as a 'ninth century cross-slab' (Town Council minutes, 7 September 1954). By contrast Graham, who compared it to a disk-headed cross at Gullane Church, East Lothian, suggested it to be 'probably of the thirteenth century or possibly earlier'. However Graham's dating of the cross slabs, both at North Berwick and Gullane, seems to have been by association with the construction dates for the respective ecclesiastical buildings. In the case of the former, he associates it with its find spot as described by Richardson, the 12th century nunnery (Graham 1960–1, 236). The Gullane stone resembles parallels that have been assigned a 10th or 11th century date.

The widespread appearance of cross-bearing stones is linked to the adoption of the cross as a universal Christian symbol in the 5th century and could have fulfilled various functions, such as grave markers or memorials, boundary stones, landmarks or praying stones. References to "crosses (?crossed stones)" are a common feature mentioned in the *vitae sancti* of various early saints (Nash-Williams 1950, 18). The simple versions of double-incised outline crosses generally appear from the 7th to the 9th centuries, but also continued into the high medieval period.

Comment from Rosemary Cramp

It is extremely difficult to date these cross incised grave-markers which seem to have a long life which spans the Conquest. However, if one considers the English examples, one might assign the North Berwick example to the mid-10th to mid-11th centuries. The closest parallels I can find are those from Lindsey and Lincoln city (Everson and Stocker 1999). These include Gayton le Wold, Hackthorne and Glentworth; Glentworth being particularly important because it was built into a tower of the mid- to late 11th century. These examples are all upright (rectangular) markers with crosses on both broad faces and all the crosses are of the simple rectangular (type A1) shape and double-incised. But their outlines are less crude than the pecked outline of the North Berwick stone, and the cross is framed all round by a cable moulding so that it does not overlap the edge. Those grave markers which are clearly 11th–12th century tend to have crosses with splayed arms.

The distinct attributes of the North Berwick stone are the rounded top and the way in which the moulding only frames the upper arms of the cross (although it is so battered that perhaps it did once extend even though no traces are immediately obvious). The rounded head of the marker does seem to be typically Northumbrian or perhaps 'North British'. From the early name stones of Holy Island to the Ovingham, Tynemouth or Warkworth grave-markers (see Cramp 1984), a rounded head is the norm, but, even though Ovingham 2 is quite like the North Berwick stone in form and layout none have the double cross like the Lincolnshire group. The North Berwick grave-marker is so far unique in some details, but like enough to the others for it to be plausibly pre-Norman.

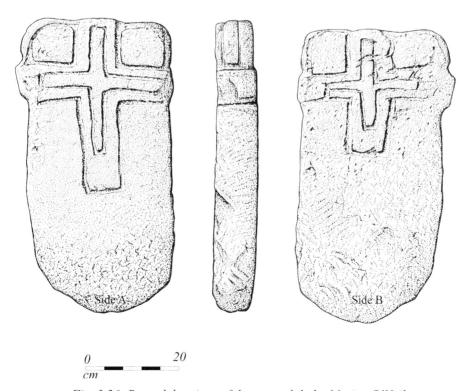

Fig. 3.26: Record drawings of the cross slab, by Marion O'Neil

4. Kirk Ness in the Medieval and Early Post-Reformation Period

Thomas Addyman and Alasdair Ross

Introduction

The only tangible remains of archaeological significance to be seen today at Kirk Ness are the much-restored footings and surviving south porch of the medieval church of St Andrew at Auld Kirk Green, now known as Anchor Green (Figure 4.1). This church is known from at least the 12th century and functioned as the principal church for the parish and burgh of North Berwick and focus for pilgrimage traffic seeking passage across the Firth of Forth en route to St Andrews in Fife. Over the succeeding five centuries the structure evolved and expanded to become a substantial burgh church. However, its exposed position was vulnerable to the ravages of the sea and, ultimately, storms caused the collapse of the eastern parts of the structure in the middle part of the 17th century. At this point the site was abandoned for a new location inland, at St Andrew Kirk Ports, erected in 1659–64. The ruins were progressively robbed for building material and by the later 18th century consisted solely of the upstanding south porch and the lower part of the west tower. From this time there are a number of important antiquarian sources that record aspects of the structure's earlier appearance. In time the west tower also disappeared, its site partly built over by a later structure. Following its initial collapse the eastern parts of the church and the associated burial ground continued to erode into the sea though the cemetery did see some continuing use.

The site was finally stabilised by the construction of the existing sea wall by the Hamilton-Dalrymple family, proprietors, in the mid-19th century. For over a century, up to the mid-20th century, the only visible remnant of the church had been the upstanding vaulted south porch, itself a structure much altered and adapted for alternative use (see Chapter 5).

An extensive excavation of the church site was conducted in 1951–2 by Dr James S. Richardson, retired H. M. Inspector of Ancient Monuments for Scotland and resident of North Berwick, and was subsequently consolidated and laid out for public display.

The various archaeological interventions associated with the construction of the Scottish Seabird Centre revealed much new information about the archaeology of the medieval kirk, and parts of the associated cemetery were also exposed. Proposed repairs to the Scheduled church ruin were preceded by a systematic new record and reassessment of its analysis; the repairs themselves involved further localised exposure of archaeological remains within the church interior. With the excavation of the tunnel link further north additional evidence for medieval occupation was revealed that was more domestic in nature and was perhaps associated with the operation of a hospice for pilgrims adjacent to the harbour.

The necessary reporting of these works presented the opportunity to review the known history of the medieval and early-post-medieval site, to revisit antiquarian accounts of the ruins, and to gather together knowledge both of individual antiquarian finds made at the site over two centuries and, from various sources, attempt a detailed appraisal of Richardson's unpublished excavation.

Historical context

Medieval records

The medieval history of North Berwick has already been discussed by a large number of authors and it is well-established that these lands were under the control of the earls of Fife by the 12th century. A now destroyed royal charter issued between 1150 and 1153 by King David I confirmed an earlier charter issued sometime between *c.*1136 and 1153 by Earl Duncan I of Fife, which had granted the lands of *Gille-cameston* to the nunnery of North Berwick (Barrow 1999, 260). This initial grant was confirmed (and possibly enhanced) by Earl Duncan II of Fife (1154–1204) between 1160 and 1172 when the two hospitals for pilgrims at either end of the ferry between North Berwick and Earlsferry in Fife were also listed as belonging to the Cistercian nuns of North Berwick (Innes 1847, no. 3).

A subsequent pre-1199 charter issued by Malcolm (later Earl Malcolm I of Fife between 1204 and 1230),

Fig. 4.1: Artist's impression of the 14th century church site and associated domestic occupation at Kirk Ness by David Simon

son of Earl Duncan II of Fife, also confirmed his grand-father's earlier grant and the other lands belonging to the nunnery, and this document (Scottish History Society 1926, 308) includes the first mention of the 'old kirk',

> that he has granted to God, St Mary, and the nuns of North Berwick in free, pure, and perpetual alms, the church of North Berwick with the land thereof, tiends, offerings, and all other rights justly pertaining thereto, and the land on which their house is built, usually named Gillecolmestun; the hospital lands of North Berwick and Ardros [by Earlsferry, Fife].

This latter charter provides unequivocal proof that the nuns had built their nunnery upon the lands of Gille-colmestun and so indicates that the earlier grant of *Gillecameston* to the nuns by Earl Duncan I of Fife must surely have been the foundation charter of the nunnery. These charters are important for another reason: the place-name Gillecolmestun is clearly composed of two elements, the Gaelic personal name Gillecolm (servant of St Columba) and the Anglo-Saxon *-tun* suffix, meaning village/settlement. If W. J. Watson is correct, such a place-name must date to the post-1000 period when *gille-* began to replace the older word *maol-* (servant) and so this place-name might conceivably have been first coined during the period when Lothian was gradually absorbed into the Gaelic kingdom of Alba (Watson 1926, 134). Whatever the case, it also demonstrates that the burgh of

North Berwick has absorbed at least one outlying village during its history.

The earls of Fife were not the only important patrons of this nunnery. As early as *c.*1210, Earl Duncan of Carrick granted the nuns three merks annually from his lands of *Berrebeth* and the lands, chapels, and tiends pertaining to his churches of Maybole and West Kilbride (Curran 2005). Unfortunately, nothing is known about the names of either the nuns or prioresses of North Berwick before 1295 but Carrick's links with North Berwick lasted for almost 200 years as an Elena of Carrick was prioress of the nunnery between 1379 and 1410 (*ibid.*). Given the strength of these links it is legitimate to speculate that a daughter of an early earl of Carrick could either have been a nun or prioress of North Berwick in the late 12th or early 13th centuries. There is another possibility which might explain the links between Carrick and North Berwick: there is some circumstantial evidence to suggest that Earl Duncan of Carrick's mother could have been a sister of Earl Duncan II of Fife (Oram 2001, 89).

Of course, the 'old kirk' only formed a small part of the property portfolio gradually assembled by the nuns of North Berwick and this ranged from lands and rights in Fife, a church and lands in Stirlingshire, a toft in Leith, lands near Livingston in West Lothian, and their holdings received from the earls of Carrick in the south-west of Scotland (Barrow 1971, no. 516). Unfortunately, there appears to be no surviving detail relating to the lands attached to the 'old kirk' of North Berwick until the 16th century when it was stated that the major lands and rights

Name	Date
Richard	1177
Hugh	1219–26
J.	1242
David	1279
Waldeve	1292
Alexander	1302
William	1312
John Fabri	1365 × 80
William de North Berwick	1380 × 88
James	1418
William Sinclair	1543 × 47
Patrick Sinclair	1547
James Brown	1548
Archibald Barre	Nd
Alexander Wood	1550, last Catholic vicar
John Young	1567, first Protestant minister
Patrick Creich	1568

Fig. 4.2: List of incumbents of the vicarage of North Berwick transcribed from Ferrier (1980)

belonging to the nunnery consisted of 23½ husbandlands of the *Hewch*, the north meadow, three mills, North Berwick Law, various grazings, and a teind of fish landed at the harbour. These properties were obviously extensive but they cannot all have been directly attached to the 'old kirk' since both the hospital and the nunnery itself must also have had North Berwick lands attached to them for their respective upkeep (Innes 1847, xxv, 59 and 62; Harvey and Macleod 1930, nos 793, 794 and 1028). It is also entirely possible that each of the altars within the 'old kirk' would have been provided with lands for their upkeep. Regrettably, early references to such lands are missing and it is not until the post-Reformation period that a 'Virgine Marie's croft' appears in the burgh records so it cannot be definitely proven that the profits from this croft paid for the maintenance of the altar to the Blessed Virgin Mary in the original parish church (NAS, B56/7/1).

More importantly, perhaps, because of this lack of detail it is impossible to be sure if the nuns had possessed all of these rights and properties in North Berwick since the foundation of their house. The major problem in relation to this lack of detail is the simple fact that the formal cartulary that once must have been kept by the Cistercian nuns of North Berwick in accordance with 13th century papal decree has been either destroyed or lost. The so-called cartulary compiled, arranged, and edited by Cosmo Innes and published by the Bannatyne Club in 1847 is an entirely false creation compiled from stray documents extracted from different collections, which perhaps helps to explain the chronological gap within it relating to the nunnery between 1293 and 1373 (Ross 2006).

What is clear is that, by the 16th century, the nuns had extensively developed their lands and rights in North Berwick since there are references to a system of aqueducts and dams that serviced their mills. This points towards cereal production and processing and their possession of property in Leith, which became the major export port in Scotland after the loss of Berwick upon Tweed, may indicate an interest in processed grain export. It has already been pointed out that there are 13th century Italian references to wool from the sheep of North Berwick's Cistercian nunnery and the nuns certainly possessed grazing on both North Berwick Law and Bass Rock (see Innes 1847, 59; Hall and Bowler 1997, 669). There are also strong hints that the nuns had either constructed or been donated rabbit warrens on North Berwick Links for the production of meat and fur and this too would have been a very valuable economic asset (Harvey and Macleod 1930, no. 798; Bailey 1988). It is likely that the nuns also had business interests in the processing of young gannets caught on Bass Rock for their fat from an early date since they complained to the Pope at the end of the 15th century (NAS, GD103/2/44) that those rights were being eroded by the Laird of Bass, Robert Lauder:

Innocentius episcopus servus servorum Dei dilectis filiis Priori et Archidiacono ecclesie Sanctiandree Salutem et apostolicam benedictionem Conqueste sunt nobis Priorissa et Conventus Monasterii de Noarchberuyk per Priorissam soliti gubernari Cistertiensis ordinis Sanctiandree diocesis quod nobilis vir Robertus Laudir dominus Insule de Bas et modernus Rector parrochialis ecclesie dicte Insule noviter erecte dicte diocesis super quibisdam Barilibus pinguedinis avium silvestrium ad Monasterium predictum spectantibus injuriantur eisdem Ideoque discretioni vestre per apostolica scripta mandamus quatinus vocatis qui fuerint evocandi et auditis hincinde propositis quod justum fuerit appellatione remota decernatis facientes quod decreveritis per censuram ecclesiasticam firmiter observari Proviso ne in Insulam predictam ac alias terras dicti Nobilis auctoritate presencium interdicti sententiam proferatis nisi super hoc a nobis mandatum receperitis speciale Testes autem qui fuerint nominati si se gratia odio vel timore subtraxerint censura simili appellatione cessante compellatis veritati testimonium perhibere Quod si non ambo hiis exequendis potueritis interesse alter vestrum ea nichilominus exequatur Datum Rome apud Sanctumpetrum anno Incarnationis Dominice millesimoquadringentesimo nonagesimosecundo Quarto Idus Julii Pontificatus nostri anno octavo

[Innocent the Bishop, servant of the servants of God, to our beloved sons the Prior and Archdeacon of the church of St Andrews, Greeting and apostolic blessing. The Prioress and Convent of the Monastery of North Berwick (used to be governed by a Prioress of the Cistercian order and of St Andrews diocese) have complained to us that a noble man Robert Lauder, lord of the Isle of Bass, and the present parson of the newly erected church of the said Isle in the diocese aforesaid, are doing them injury in the matter of certain barrels of the fat of wild birds belonging to the foresaid Monastery. Therefore we commit it to your discretion by these apostolic writings that calling in the parties who should be called and hearing the arguments on both sides you decide according to the justice, forbidding appeal, and by church censure causing your decision to be firmly observed. Provided that you are not to pronounce sentence of Interdict against the foresaid Isle and the said Nobleman's other lands by authority of these presents, unless you have received from us special commission to that effect. And if those who are called as witnesses shall withdraw themselves for favour disfavour or fear you shall compel them by the like censure without appeal the bear testimony to the truth. But if both of you cannot take part in the execution of this mandate, one of you is to execute it nevertheless. Given at St Peters Rome, 12 July 1492, the eighth year of my pontificate.]

George Ferrier, writing in 1869, noted that 12 solan geese with their feathers on were paid to the post-Reformation ministers of North Berwick (Ferrier 1869, 44). This may have been the continuation of a much older custom but it is impossible to prove this from the surviving documentary record.

As Simpson and Stevenson remarked (1981, 1, 14) it is now impossible to tell whether North Berwick owes its origin to the nunnery, the ferry, or the sea. However, they did also note that pilgrimages to St Andrews were popular from at least the 8th century and so seemed to be suggesting that they favoured the presence of the ferry route as the most likely rationale for the existence and initial growth of North Berwick. Such a suggestion is entirely possible but cannot currently be proven since no source actually records the existence of the ferry before the 12th century. Nor do we know the numbers of pilgrims that used the ferry on an annual basis: in 1988 Weir stated that it was common for 10,000 pilgrims to pass through North Berwick each year but such an estimate is entirely fanciful (Weir 1988, 50).

It is also not entirely clear where the belief came from that King Robert III granted North Berwick the status of a royal burgh *c.*1391 when he visited the burgh. Such a claim is not present in the Old Statistical Account, produced in the 1790s, but is present in the New Statistical Account that was produced between 1834 and 1845 (NSA 1834–45, 323). Assuming the author of the first account had undertaken his research properly, it would seem that this belief first surfaced between 1790 and 1845 and the claim has been regularly repeated as late as 1980 (see Ferrier 1980, 14). However, Simpson and Stevenson refuted this supposition (1981, 1). There is no record of King Robert III granting North Berwick royal burgh status when he visited the town in the early 1390s (Exchequer Rolls iii, 255).

At that time the burgh barony of North Berwick still belonged to the earls of Fife, represented at that time by the second eldest son of King Robert II, Robert Stewart, Guardian of Scotland and later duke of Albany. It is clear from a document issued on 2 August 1388 that Robert Stewart had previously granted the barony of North Berwick to James, second earl of Douglas, who had been killed at the battle of Otterburn in 1388 (Brown 2007). However, in 1388 there was an ongoing dispute over the Douglas inheritance as Robert Stewart attempted (successfully) to manipulate the succession to that earldom to ensure that the illegitimate contender, Archibald the Grim, inherited the title. Possession of Tantallon Castle, one part of the barony of North Berwick, was involved in the resolution of this dispute (Boardman 1996, 159).

Even though there is next to no surviving information about the 'old kirk' of North Berwick during the period before 1560, apart from the fact that the vicarage had been annexed to the nunnery by 1360 (Cowan 1967, 157), slightly more information has been assembled about the priests by the Rev. Walter Ferrier (1980, 20–37). His listing of incumbents of the vicarage, some of whom only appeared in sources that have been recently lost (Figure 4.2). Undoubtedly the most famous of these vicars was William de North Berwick who fought alongside the earl of Douglas at the battle of Otterburn in 1388. His exploits were such that he drew the attention of the French chronicler Froissart (Brereton 1968, 344),

They found beside him [the dying earl of Douglas] one of his knights who had kept with him throughout, and a chaplain of his who was not there as a priest but as a worthy man-at-arms, for he had followed him all night through the thick of the battle with an axe in his hand. This doughty warrior was laying about him near the earl, keeping the English back with the great blows he dealt them with his axe, for which service the Scots were truly grateful. It earned him great renown and in the same year he became archdeacon and canon of Aberdeen. The name of this priest was William of North Berwick. It is a fact he was a tall, finely built man – and brave, too, to do what he did. Nevertheless, he was severely wounded.

William's exploits during the battle were later recounted by another occasional inhabitant of the burgh in the 16th century, the historian John Major, who had been born in nearby Gleghornie (Constable 1892, 321).

It was also around the time of Otterburn that the Lauder family seem to have been first granted lands in the burgh of North Berwick by the earl of Douglas (NAS, GD1/1386/1). The Lauders quickly became customers of the port and the Exchequer Rolls regularly report on the export of wool, woolfells and hides from North Berwick. Interestingly, there are also infrequent references to the export of rabbit skins, thus lending weight to the suggestion that the nuns possessed rabbit warrens. In 1425, 620 rabbit skins at 6s 2d each were exported. In 1426, 300 skins at 3s each were listed and, in 1434, another 300 skins priced at 3s 6d each were listed as exports (Exchequer Rolls vi, 386, 402, 559).

By 14 December 1425, and after the forfeiture and execution of the duke of Albany, Sir Robert Lauder, by then a royal councillor for King James I, had been granted lordship over half of the Bass Rock, as well as further interests in and around North Berwick (RMS ii, no. 29). The Lauder family were on record as still only possessing half of the Rock, the northern side, in 1507–8 (RMS ii, no. 3185). In fact, despite calling themselves lords of Bass, the Lauders do not seem to have gained formal possession of the other, southern half of the Bass Rock until just before 1609, when King James VI confirmed a charter of this from the archbishop of St Andrews to them (RMS vii, no. 152, see RMS x, no. 428).

All this evidence indicates that during the 15th century the Bass Rock was wholly controlled by two parties: the Lauders and the archbishops of St Andrews. Before 1492, the Lauders built a new chapel dedicated to St Baldred upon the rock and shortly afterwards hagiography that for the first time associated the historical saint with the rock was printed in the Aberdeen Breviary (NAS, GD103/2/44). Given the ownership of the rock, together with the long-established ferry that operated between North Berwick and Fife, it is surely legitimate to question whether the Lauders and the archbishops of St Andrews were attempting to raise extra revenue for themselves by building the new chapel to St Baldred upon the rock, thus giving a local saint a new lease of life. The fact that the new chapel sat beside a recognised

pilgrimage sea-route and within easy sailing distance of the ferries between North Berwick and Fife may have made it very attractive to pilgrims.

Evidence for the church from later records

Later records for the site, discussed in more detail in Chapter 5, are valuable in that, from 1649, they record the presence of two altars within the 'old kirk', dedicated to the 'Lady' and to 'St Seybastion' (NAS, GD110/59). It seems highly likely that these dedications were to the Blessed Virgin Mary and St Sebastian. The Reverend Ferrier noted these latter two dedications during his research and mooted that the dedication to St Sebastian could have been made post-1348 to ward off the plague. This suggestion is eminently sensible. He also suggested that the high altar would have been dedicated to St Andrew and noted the presence of a fourth altar in the north transept dedicated to St Ninian and a Pietà (Ferrier 1980, 19). The presence of an aisle to St Ninian is also noted in the Royal Commission report on the 'old kirk' and Richardson, in his preliminary report of 19–20 February 1951 to the town council, had clearly seen some further information about its construction; he noted:

> The north transept, otherwise St Ninian's Aisle, was built about 1496 by the Earl of Angus, but William of Carrick, indweller in the Mains of Tantallon, contributed to the cost, and in 1497 he was given permission by the Baillies and Community of North Berwick to erect an altar in this part of the church.

> Unfortunately, neither Ferrier nor Richardson noted the source(s) of their information about St Ninian and the Pietà aisle and no trace of any record relating to such an altar or sculpture was found during the current investigation. There are, however, a number of post-1539 references to a previously unknown altar of the Holy Rude (Holy Cross) within the 'old kirk' (see Innes 1847, xxv, 55, and Brown 2007).

Newes from Scotland – the witch trials of 1590–1

Notoriously, the old kirk featured in the earliest publication on Scottish witchcraft, *Newes from Scotland* (1591), recording the trial, in the presence of King James VI, of a number of East Lothian witches. Its subtitle is as follows,

> Declaring the damnable life of Doctor Fian a notable Sorcerer, who was burned at Edenbrough in Ianuarie last. 1591. Which Doctor was register to the deuill, that sundrie times preached at North Baricke Kirke, to a number of notorious Witches

Whilst under torture one of the accused witches, Agnes Tompson, had described events at North Berwick,

Fig. 4.3: St Andrew's church as depicted in Newes from Scotland, 1591 (by permission, University of Glasgow Library, Special Collections)

Item, the saide Agnis Tompson was after brought againe before the Kings Maiestie and his Counsell, and being examined of the meetings and detestable dealings of those witches, she confessed that vpon the night of Allhollon Euen last, she was accompanied aswell with the persons aforesaide, as also with a great many other witches, to the number of two hundreth: and that all they together went by Sea each one in a Riddle or Ciue, and went in the same very substantially with Flaggons of wine making merrie and drinking by the waye in the same Riddles or Ciues, to the Kerke of North Barrick in Lowthian, and that after they had landed, tooke handes on the land and daunced this reill or short daunce, singing all with one voice.

Commer goe ye before, commer goe ye, Gif ye will not goe before, commer let me.

At which time she confessed, that this *Geilles Duncane* did goe before them playing this reill or daunce vpon a small Trump, called a Iewes Trump, vntill they entred into the Kerk of north Barrick.

These confessions made the King in a woderful admiration and sent for ye said *Geillis Duncane*, who vpon the like Trump did playe the said daunce before the Kings Maiestie, who in respect of the strangenes of these matters, tooke great delight to bee present at their examinations.

Item, the said *Agnis Tompson* confessed that the Diuell being then at North Barrick Kerke attending their comming in the habit or likenes of a man, and seeing that they tarried ouer long, he at their comming enioyned them all to a pennance, which was, that they should kisse his Buttockes, in signe of

duetye to him: which being put ouer the Pulpit barre, euerye one did as he had enioyned them; and hauing made his vngodly exhortations, wherein he did greatlye enveighe against the King of Scotland, he receiued their oathes for their good and true seruice towards him, and departed: which doone, they returned to Sea, and so home againe.

Other than this colourful and fanciful episode purportedly relating to the old church, the published tract is only directly significant to the present study in that it presents a woodcut illustration of the church itself, to which Dr Fian and companion approach on horseback (Figure 4.3). While the representation seems to bear little topographic accuracy it does give an overall impression of a substantial and developed structure. The account of the North Berwick witches was further popularised by Sir Walter Scott in his *Letters on Demonology and Witchcraft* (1830).

Earlier cartographic sources for the church

Early cartographic sources shed little light upon the actual church site but considerably more on its immediate setting. The earliest of these that shows Kirk Ness in any detail is the manuscript map of East Lothian by John Adair of 1682 (Figure 4.4). While only in sketched detail the long-established components of the settlement are nonetheless clearly expressed – *northberwick abbey* to the west, the east–west aligned High Street and, to the north of this and connected to the mainland by a narrow spit, Kirk Ness, with church, harbour wall and anchorage clearly represented. These topographic details remain constant in a printed version of the same survey, engraved in 1736 by Richard Cooper of Edinburgh.

General William Roy's Great Map of 1747–55 provides a clear impression of the topographical situation of Kirk Ness, here unequivocally expressed as an island with an intervening band of beach sand (Figure 4.5). This is the earliest representation to feature the successor church of St Andrew Kirk Ports, itself now ruinous, to the south of Main Street. The access to Kirk Ness, the line of the modern day Victoria Road, is now clearly expressed. The early church – presumably the west tower – is expressed as are the two walls to its north-west that enclosed the harbour.

On account of their scale, subsequent maps of the later 18th century and first half of the 19th, mostly county maps of Haddingtonshire, add little significant detail worthy of comment. These include maps by George Taylor and Andrew Skinner (1776), William Forrest (1799), John Ainslie (1821), John Thompson (1822), Sharp, Greenwood and Fowler (1824 and 1844), and the Great Reform Act burgh boundary plan (1832).

However, a manuscript plan of the North Berwick Estate, surveyed by William Forrest in 1804, provides exceptional detail of Kirk Ness, illustrating the sandy spit

Fig. 4.4: 'East Lothian', manuscript county map by John Adair, 1682 (reproduced by permission of the Trustees of the National Library of Scotland)

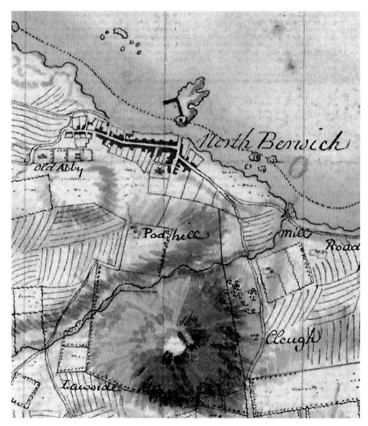

Fig. 4.5: Detail of North Berwick from General William Roy's Great Map 1747–55. (©British Library. Licensor www.scran.ac.uk)

and access road connecting it to the mainland, the church ruin (tower and porch), a newly built granary, and the extent of the harbour (Figure 4.6). This representation corresponds well with a series of early views of the site discussed in the following section. Of additional note is the presence of a further finger of dry land that extends beyond the eastern corner of the harbour; this was largely removed during harbour works in the early 1860s.

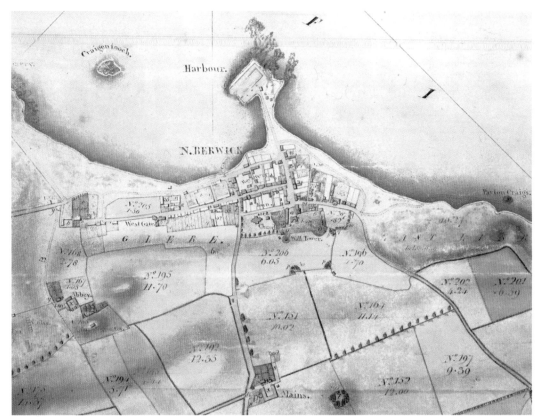

Fig. 4.6: Detail of the North Berwick Estate plan by William Forrest, 1804 (by kind permission of John Dalrymple-Hamilton; held by the National Records of Scotland: RHP1726/1)

Earlier antiquarian sources for the church

Early written sources, such as visitors' accounts, reveal comparatively little about the church site, and this often erroneously. For example Bishop Pococke (Kemp 1887, 319), visiting in 1760, notes,

> We descended to North Berwick, a small, ill-built town situated on a strand – a promontory stretches out from it which seems to have been an island, from the north end of which a pier is built that extends to the west … On this promontory is a small ruined chapel, arched over, and a tower a little to the north-west of it: They told me it was called St Elan and was a Monastery: I suppose it must have been the Cistercian nunnery built to the honour of the Virgin Mary in 1266 by Malcolm son of Duncan Earl of Fife.

In a similar vein the Rev. Henry Hill in the *Statistical Account* (1789, vol. 5, 443) described the remains,

> A small ruin, supposed to have been a chapel, belonging to the monastery, or to an hospital, stands a little to the east of the harbour. The adjacent ground was probably a burial place of the family of Douglas.

However, a series of important early views are more reliably revealing. The earliest, a dramatic ink and wash sketch by Paul Sandby of *c*.1750, shows the west tower of the church, this with vaulted lower stage and, on the basis of window openings, two further stories (that Ferrier suggests contained a priest's room and ringing chamber) whose west and north walls still remain (Figure 4.7). To the north the structure appears to survive to its wall head, where a crenellated parapet is still apparent. Richardson (report, February 1951) suggested that the surviving detail depicted at parapet level suggested the tower had had a pyramidal roof set within the parapet, 'covered with slates from Dundee'. The mass in the left foreground must be the porch and one in the right foreground may be a vestige of the south aisle at its south-east corner. Above the latter, more lightly sketched, is an upstanding section of walling displaying two arched openings at the upper level; what may be an engaged pier is visible at the lower level. It is possible that this is a depiction of a fragment of the documented hospice, its position as depicted would approximately coincide with that of the existing granary building, erected *c*.1800.

A view of 1782 by George Henry Hutton shows the remains of the west tower of St Andrew's church from the north-west (Figure 4.8). In the foreground appear the harbour walls, with the beach, town and North Berwick Law beyond to the south. Immediately in front and to the right of the tower appears a section of upstanding masonry, this possibly part of the same wall section as

Fig. 4.7: Part of an Old Chapel at North Berwick. *Ink and wash. Paul Sandby, c.1750 (National Galleries of Scotland, D165)*

shown by Sandby though further reduced, and a possible remnant of the hospice or *maison dieu*. The masonry fragment visible to the left may be the top of the porch or, perhaps more likely, the upstanding remains of the north-west angle of the north transept.

This is also suggested by an engraved view presented in Francis Grose's *Antiquities of Scotland* (1789, vol. 1, 77) which dramatically illustrates the misfortunes that had befallen the church site, as shown from the south-east, where the sharply sea-eroded scarping along the east side of the site is readily apparent (Figure 4.9). To the left is the west tower, with vaulted lower stage; to the centre is the south porch, as more or less extant, and the high fragment to the right may be part of the north wall of the north transept; below this there is what appears to be further masonry remains or a temporary revetting of part of the seaward side. The tightly constrained nature of the ecclesiastical site is clearly evident, as is the absence of an improved link to the mainland shore. Grose notes:

This picturesque little ruin stands on a small sandy mount on the shore of North Berwick, a little to the eastward of the harbour.

Various are the opinions and reports concerning it, some making it a chapel belonging to the adjacent nunnery, others the chapel of an hospital, or

hermitage; but no proofs in support of either of these opinions are adduced from history or records.

The adjacent ground appears to have been used as a burial place, from the number of human bones scattered about it. This view was drawn A.D. 1789.

Overall this view corresponds both to Roy's map and Hutton's view, albeit the latter is taken from the opposite direction. A further engraved view of the church, this time taken from the north-east in 1788 by Adam de Cardonnel, was published in *Picturesque Antiquities of Scotland* (1788). Confirming the details of Grose's view, it also includes representation in the immediate foreground of what must be parts of the north transept (Figure 4.10).

These views in turn correlate well to a notable ink and wash measured plan of the site by Andrew Morton, dated December 1816 (Figure 4.11). This demonstrates that little had been lost of the upstanding fabric at the site in the intervening quarter century, with the possible exception of the fragment of the north transept which is illustrated. His outline of the perimeter of the site appears simply to have been sketched and of dubious accuracy, particularly to the north.

However the remains of the west tower must have eventually been wholly cleared away, or recycled for its

Fig. 4.8: Hutton's 1782 view looking S across the harbour, with the church ruin to left, part of the west beach, to right, and the town beyond, all overlooked by North Berwick Law (© National Library of Scotland. Licensor www.scran.ac.uk)

materials, by the mid-19th century. Swan notes that 'the north side [of the church ruin] was removed when operations were proceeded with to erect a gaswork on the ground in 1845' (1910, 9). These works may have involved the dismantling of the west tower; though the detail is poor there is no suggestion of it by the time of the 1st Edition Ordnance Survey, surveyed in 1853 (6in: mile, Haddingtonshire, Sheet 2).

The sole remaining portion of the structure, the south porch, was utilised by the coast guard in the mid-19th century when certain alterations were made to the fabric. The structure was maintained and regularly limewashed until the middle of the 20th century; the surrounding ground of Anchor Green, which was laid to lawn, was crossed by a metalled path running from the church site to the stair at the northern end of the green (Figure 4.12, and Figure 4.14, below).

Later commentary and discovery

There are numerous guide-books and a selection of learned articles and histories of North Berwick, from the mid-19th century onwards. Most of these refer to the remains of the old church which, with the ruin of North Berwick Abbey, formed the principal monuments of antiquarian interest in the town. The more significant include G. Ferrier (1869, 1881) J. T. Richardson (1911), Williamson (1908), Swan (1910; 1926–7), RCAHMS (1924), W.

M. Ferrier (1980) and Jamieson (1985; 1992). Though much of the material is secondary in nature the accounts cumulatively contain many details and observations of the Kirk Ness site, and provide record of miscellaneous discoveries over the years – church artefacts, coins, grave goods, carved stones and the like. Some of the latter saw individual publication (a badge mould – Cooper 1906; Richardson 1906–7a, etc; a brass seal matrix – OSA 1789; MacDonald 1904, etc; coins – Robertson 1960–1; monuments – RCAHMS 1924; Graham 1960–1). Finds from the church site and records of their discovery are assessed in more detail in relevant sections later in this chapter, and in the appendices.

More recent studies of the archaeology of the medieval burgh provide some assessment of the Kirk Ness site and also reference some of the individual discoveries (Simpson and Stevenson 1981; Hall and Bowler 1997; Dingwall 2009). However, none had Kirk Ness as its primary focus.

James Richardson and the excavation of the old kirk site in 1951–2

A biographical note

James S. Richardson (1883–1970) excavated the site of the old church at Kirk Ness in the early 1950s (Figure 4.13). He was a native of North Berwick and son of Dr

Fig. 4.9: Ruin on the Shore of North Berwick, *Francis Grose, engraving, taken from the SSE, 1789 (Reproduced by permission of the Trustees of the National Library of Scotland)*

Fig. 4.10: Adam de Cardonnel, engraving from the NE, 1788 (© courtesy of RCAHMS. Licensor www.rcahms.gov.uk)

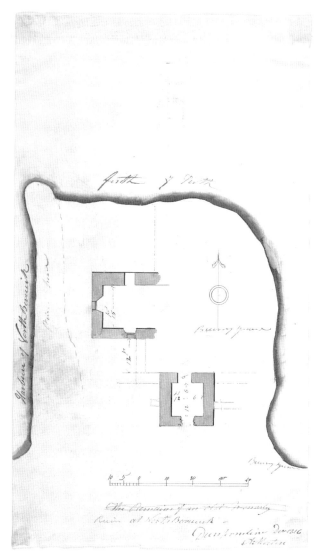

Fig. 4.11: Survey plan by Andrew Morton, 1816 (©
National Library of Scotland. Licensor www.scran.ac.uk)

James T. Richardson, a local antiquarian and author of
the 1911 *Guide to North Berwick*, who had settled in
North Berwick in 1889. The career of James Richardson
(younger) spanned the transition of antiquarianism to the
modern discipline of archaeology. According to the obituary in the *Proceedings of the Society of Antiquaries of
Scotland* (102, 1969–70), he inherited his father's 'di-
verse interests and considerable artistic talent'; he had
training as a draftsman and had worked as an architect.
However, his antiquarian interests were so well recognised that he was appointed the first HM Inspector of
Ancient Monuments for Scotland in 1914, and re-ap-
pointed after the First World War in 1920. He had a busy
career, and worked on many important buildings and ruins in Scotland, including major remains of cathedrals
and abbeys. He increasingly established a reputation as a
writer, historian and teacher.

From his youth Richardson had taken an active role in
his home town, eventually becoming one of its most respected inhabitants. He was instrumental in the formation
of the East Lothian Antiquarian and Field Naturalists Society, leading their first field excursion in 1924. After
retirement in 1948 he dedicated himself to voluntary and
local projects, including the excavation of the old kirk
site, and the establishment, in 1957, of the North Berwick
Museum, of which he was also Curator.

Circumstances and progress of the 1951–2 excavation

By the middle of the 20th century the site of the church
consisted of an irregular low grassy mound bounding the
west, north and north-east sides of the upstanding porch.
In 1951–2 this area was excavated by Richardson. It
seems that, after a very full career, retirement may have
afforded him the long-awaited opportunity to examine a
site with which he was closely familiar. Richardson never
formally reported on his excavation at Kirk Ness and the

*Fig. 4.12: Vignette of the south porch, showing Auld Kirk Green and some exposed masonry remains beyond, from
Phillimore's* Guide to North Berwick, *1913*

obituary notice is one of the only published sources to refer to it, albeit only briefly.

A sequence of early photographs that have recently come to light, and a further three photographs in the East Lothian Museum Service archive, are the only images identified of the archaeological works in progress (Figures 4.14–17, and Figures 4.18, 4.21 and 4.76 respectively). The former were taken in the early stages of work, probably in February 1951, and the latter when works had further progressed, these evidently taken in April or May of the same year. While no primary field documentation appears to survive, the minutes of the Town Council and associated correspondence in the National Archives of Scotland record the progress of works and from these can be gleaned some information on what was discovered (NAS B56/17/23). Progress of the excavations was also reported in a series of articles in the *Haddingtonshire Courier* between February and July 1951.

Richardson seems to have persuaded the burgh council to provide financial support for the project. The excavation was carried out in part by the Burgh Surveyor's staff, under Mr Richard Hume and a Mr Brash, with Richardson, in constant attendance, providing overall direction. It is recorded that a Mr G. Forsyth and a Mr F. Shiels formed part of the excavation team; local volunteers were also involved, one mentioned is Miss Betty Jardine. The Council minutes record that excavations were under way in early February 1951, as Sir Hew Hamilton-Dalrymple expressed annoyance that he had not been consulted about them, the land being under his proprietorship.

The initial intention of the excavation seems to have been exploratory, to establish whether buried remains of the church still survived. In his *Preliminary Report* to the Town Council, read on 20 February, Richardson noted: 'The inspection trenches have confirmed that the outline of the western parts of this ancient and historic building exist and could be exposed'.

The first group of surviving photographs clearly show the excavation of these inspection trenches. One extends out from the porch, running northwards into the area of the nave, and the other lies further west, evidently following the west wall of the south aisle and then angling into the area of the west tower (see Figure 6.1). Exposures of the footings of the west end of the south aisle and parts of the west tower can be made out.

The three later photographs reveal the work of the more general excavation of the site to have been rudimentary rather than a very formally conducted process, extending to much of the area of the nave and west tower of the church (for the estimated extent of the excavation area see Figure 6.1). It clearly involved very extensive removal of overburden, evidently principally sand with some rubble content, to an estimated depth in some areas of as much as 1.0m (Figure 4.18). The rubble must have been the demolition debris generated during the dismantling of the structure from the mid 17th century onwards; the general absence of larger stones in the three photographs suggests the process had been systematic.

Fig. 4.13: Dr James S. Richardson (© East Lothian Museum Services. Licensor www.scran.ac.uk)

Richardson specifically noted in May 1952 that 'excavations were only carried down to the floor levels of the kirk'. A *Courier* article of 8 June 1951 reported Richardson's discovery of a clay floor surface (quoted below). Re-excavation in localised areas in 2003–4 failed to identify the clay surface. In the areas examined it seems that Richardson's excavation was taken to just below what must have been the abandonment period floor levels; the latter, whether of clay or other material such as flags, were wholly absent.

Most parts of the church were evidently exposed in this first campaign, with the exception of the north transept. Enough was revealed by late February 1951 for Richardson to suggest the sequence of evolution of the structure (see following section). On the basis of his findings to date Richardson's *Preliminary Report* concluded with the recommendation that the Council:

> should promote a scheme to show off the remains of the building – lowering the ground outside to a considerable level – and setting in turf the floor of the church as determined by expert examination. ... Any work of consolidating the walls could be done later.

While Richardson's proposal for further excavations was well received by the Council, they forbade any further excavations in spring 1951 (letter from Town Clerk to

Fig. 4.14: The early stages of J. S Richardson's excavation, in February 1951: test trenching commencing against the N and W sides of the south porch; general view looking NE showing the pre-existing stage of Anchor Green with the rear of the Harbour Pavilion beyond (courtesy of Mrs Lorna Burton)

Richardson, 6 March 1951). There is no explanation for this decision, but it is suspected that the council did not want an unkempt archaeological site next to the Harbour Pavilion or the swimming pool, two of the principal attractions of the upcoming tourist season. However, articles on 30 March, 6 April and 8 June in the *Haddingtonshire Courier* demonstrate that work continued on site for some time thereafter. The latter notes:

> Further evidence concerning the structure of the old church is daily being brought to light in the form of wall foundations, and the uncovering of a low-lying surface of hard clay, thought to be the flooring of the building. To the north, a new aisle has been located, and Dr Richardson states that this may be the one associated with the altars of St Ninian and Our Lady of Pity. These were presented to the church by John Carrick, who lived at the Mains of Tantallon at the end of the 15th century.
>
> When the excavators extended the digging in the north eastern part of the nave they discovered a fallen gable, but were not able to decide which part of the building it came from

The excavated remains of the gable seem likely to be rep-

resented today by three carved stones still preserved at the site, these of greenish sandstone, each comprising a sloping skew stone that tied back into the wall head and detailed with a raggle (see Figure 4.35, below). The article also records the discovery of 'The remains of the octagonal 13th century font … discovered directly opposite the south porch, together with pieces of the platform on which it stood'. The platform still remains (it was consolidated in 2004) but the evidence that the font was octagonal is no longer evident – perhaps this had been an impression upon the platform surface. Excavation in 1951 also seems to have involved the grading down of the ground beyond the western side of the church; on 30 March the *Courier* reported:

> Work is at present concentrated on the west side of the porch, where the turf is being skilfully replaced after the removal of quantities of earth and sand. The old walls of the church now rise to a height of two feet above the new ground level …

The same *Courier* article reported that spoil was also used for improvement of the appearance of the ground around the base of the Kate Watson Memorial at the south end of Anchor Green.

A visitor to the excavations in 2001 reminisced that

Fig. 4.15: Detail of the trenches close to the south porch, looking SE (courtesy of Mrs Lorna Burton)

Fig. 4.16: The test trenching operation nearing completion, looking SW (courtesy of Mrs Lorna Burton)

Fig. 4.17: View looking south, showing some of the building debris and monument fragments generated by the excavation (courtesy of Mrs Lorna Burton)

Fig. 4.18: General view of the 1951 excavation in progress, with Dr J. S. Richardson crouched, centre following the discovery of the red sandstone table tomb close to the junction of the west tower and nave, looking ENE (Courtesy of East Lothian Council Archives & Local History Service)

the spoil from the 1951–2 excavation was deposited on the beach and that, when washed by the sea, finds, particularly shroud pins, were recovered by hand. That this was the case is confirmed by a similar report in the *Courier* of 8 June recording the find from the sea-washed spoil of 'several silver shroud pins'. Small-finds in 1951 included a billon penny of James IV and a silver coin 'probably of late 13th century origin'. The 8 June article also records the recent discovery of 'six old Scottish coins' and goes on to note:

All coins discovered on the site have been sent to the National Museum of Antiquities for identification and special treatment. Dr Richardson states that they belong to the reigns of James IV, and James V, and Francis and Mary (Mary Queen of Scots).

Additionally described is the find of 'a gravestone of a well-known North Berwick merchant of the 17th century'. The latter must certainly be the upper parts of a red sand-

stone table tomb found in a number of fragments within the nave of the church that appears in two of the early photographs and remains at the site today (see Figures 4.18 and 4.76–7).

The 8 June article concluded 'The site of the church is at present being tidied up for the benefit of summer visitors, but excavation work will be resumed at a later date.' Excavation only resumed later the following spring by which time it seems that Richardson's scheme for 'laying bare of the foundations of the Pre-Reformation Kirk of Saint Andrew' had been fully accepted by the Council (minutes, 8 April 1952). There was again concern that work should be completed before the visitor season began, and work actually started on the site on the 14 April 1952.

On the 21 April at a site visit attended by the Provost, the Burgh Engineer and G. P. H. Watson from the Royal

Fig. 4.19: The newly excavated church site as temporarily laid out in summer 1952, following Richardson's excavations (© East Lothian Museums Service; Gordon Collection. Licensor www.scran.ac.uk)

Commission for the Ancient and Historical Monuments of Scotland (RCAHMS), work was proceeding well. One of the concerns voiced was the disturbance of human remains (minutes of 21 April 1952). It was resolved that 'All human bones to be collected in bags and buried immediately in a pit appointed for that purpose'.

In mid May 1952, there must have been continuing concern over the disturbance of human remains for Richardson submitted to the Council a 'Statement concerning the human bones unearthed during operations' (14 May 1952), explaining how such remains were to be handled, and defending his actions. The statement contains much information about the occurrence of human remains at the site, discussed below. Minutes of a meeting of 21 May records:

> The Town Council met at the Auld Kirk Green with Dr James S Richardson, who pointed out to them the final work to be carried out in connection with the excavations as contained in a report of this date. The Council approved of the work being completed as suggested by Dr Richardson and expressed their satisfaction with the whole work.

In his report, dated 21 May but recorded in minutes of 3 June, Richardson makes several suggestions for the presentation of the site, particularly stating that he would have to advise on the setting out of stones to indicate the position of the lost walls, and the location of a path. It is clear from the report and a contemporary photograph that, though the excavations were complete, the work of presenting the site permanently was not yet begun (Figure 4.19). A *Courier* article of 13 July noted the site 'has now been tidied up and the exposed part of the church clearly identified by sign boards'. The same article, which records a visit to the site by the East Lothian Antiquarian and Field Naturalists' Society, concludes 'The Society appreciates greatly what the Town Council of North Berwick are doing in the way of arousing new interest in the burgh by exposing the remains of the Church of St Andrew.'

In the same year, Richardson had been in correspondence with the Church of Scotland General Trustees regarding one or several pre-Reformation stone grave markers, one referred to as the 'Lauder gravestone' (minutes, 8 April 1952). These stones had become part of the Manse rockery at some point, and Richardson proposed to bring them back to the old kirk site. The Church of Scotland replied in June, stating that they were happy for the stones to be taken by the council for their better preservation, but only if the gaps in the rockery were filled.

Following the 1951–2 excavation, and after some considerable delay, the site was eventually landscaped and the ruin laid out for interpretative display, a process that is described in Chapter 5.

The architecture and archaeology of St Andrew's Kirk a synthesis

Introduction

In 2000, after 50 years as a consolidated ruin with unrestricted public access, the surviving remains of the old church were suffering the effects of prolonged wear and tear. Proposed repair and re-interpretation of the monument involved, as a preliminary stage, the comprehensive record and reassessment of the masonry fabric (for survey drawing set see Appendix O on CD).

The existing ruin of St Andrew's Church, as revealed by Richardson and subsequently consolidated, consists of the outline of the majority of the nave, the western part of the north transept, the north aisle, the west tower and the western parts of the south aisle. As already described the south porch remained upstanding. The eastern parts of the church were destroyed by winter storms in the 1650s and, doubtless, erosion continued thereafter until an estimated half of the church plan had eventually been lost, this to the east of a diagonal line running north-eastwards from the eastern side of the porch across the nave to the mid-part of the north transept.

In his *Preliminary Report* of 19–20 February 1951 Richardson proposed a basic developmental sequence:

> The first, or Norman Church, was an aisles [aisleless] rectangular building. In the 13th century it was enlarged; north and south transepts were added in the 15th century, and then, apparently the nave necessitated reconstruction. This work provided a western tower and a south nave aisle with an attached porch.

He also noted 'the north transept, otherwise St Ninian's Aisle, was built about 1496 by the earl of Angus'

It is unfortunate that Richardson's final conclusions about the evolution of the church are not recorded in detail; clearly his thoughts developed during the course of his investigations. For instance he subsequently suggested that St Ninian's Aisle might be identified with the north aisle rather than the transept (*Haddingtonshire Courier*, 8 June 1951).

Detailed assessment and survey of the remaining wall bases was undertaken in 2000 in advance of proposed repairs; this permitted a general reappraisal of the surviving evidence. A number of unambiguous stratigraphic relationships were recorded though, with the general absence of surviving architectural detail, the suggested chronological framework must be treated with some caution. Assessment was also somewhat hampered by vegetation growth (turf) upon the wall tops and by the substantial areas where the ruin had been consolidated in the 1950s. Thus it was not always clear whether walling constituted undisturbed early fabric, original stones re-bedded in cement, or sections of

cement-bedded rubble masonry that had been newly formed. Further investigation of the surviving masonry and some interior areas of the church occurred during repair works in 2004. In many places only the very base of walling survived and the remaining footings were found to be very insubstantial, often directly built upon underlying deposits of sand.

The recordable evolutionary sequence appears typical of that of many a medieval parish church, characterised by successive piecemeal expansion and modification that doubtless reflects the increase, not to mention stasis or even decline, in both the population and the wealth of the burgh over a period of 500 years. The reinterpretation of the structural sequence differs in some details from Richardson's. For example it is not clear what his evidence was for expansion in the 13th century; no evidence remains for a south transept – this was evidently presumed. The west tower was also found to pre-date the aisles (Figure 4.20).

The surviving remains demonstrate the church was predominantly rubble-built at each stage of construction, with freestone (sandstone) principally employed for dressings – entrances, windows, gable heads, plinths and piers. The basic masonry fabric employs a trachybasalt of a type known as mugearite, this more generically referred to here as whin. Of this David McAdam (2004) notes:

> It is dark to pale purple or grey-purple in colour, depending on freshness and weathering. The rock is finely crystalline, not visible with the naked eye, and usually non-porphyritic, with no large crystals or phenocrysts. It has a platy texture, and in places has a concentric structure or iron-banding.

The angular nature suggests they were quarried, rather than rounded glacial or beach stones. Of the three basaltic lava flows that are present on the Kirk Ness peninsula the middle one, visible at Plattcock Rocks, is of mugearite, to which the stone of the church can be matched – this evidently the quarry source; Richardson (1961) describes the colour of the stone as of a 'warm madder tint'. McAdam further observes that the rubble stone most commonly used in North Berwick, the distinctive red igneous Law rock, a phonolitic trachyte from a quarry on the north side of the Law, is notably absent at the old church site.

The predominant freestones present include a pale-cream to greyish fine-grained sandstone, generally referred to as white sandstone, of a type that is commonly found throughout central Scotland though not in the vicinity of North Berwick. The most common freestone is a greenish sandstone (the greenish hue suggesting the presence of volcanic ash) for which there is no immediately local source, the closest possibly being Point Garry or, more likely, Gullane or Tantallon.

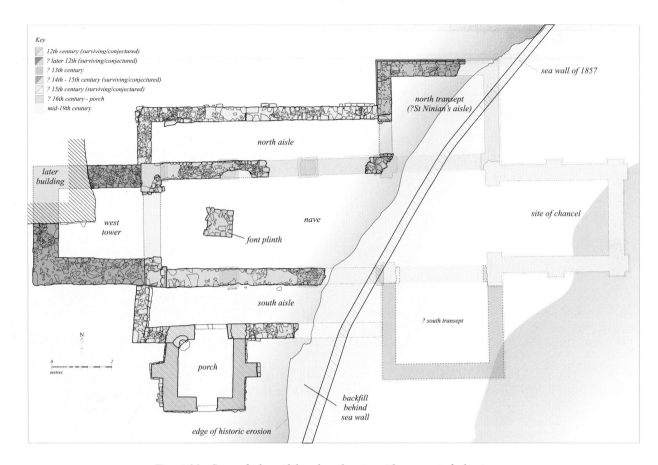

Fig. 4.20: Ground plan of the church ruin with suggested phasing

The early church – nave (12th century)

The earliest remaining parts of the church ruin appear to consist of the lower walling and/or footings of the north and south walls, and fragments of the west wall of what had evidently been a simple aisle-less nave. That this is early fabric was deduced almost solely on the evidence of the last substantial upstanding remnant of the structure at its south-west angle where a dressed external base course or plinth survives, and the fact that this is deeply embedded within later masonry. Richardson had recognised this; he had informed the *Courier*:

> The clearing of the exposed walls of the tower and the south-west end of the nave … [resulted in] the discovery of dressed freestone within the core of the walls. Has marked the south-west corner of the Norman Church. … it was evident from the size and nature of the stones, that the walls of this building were of a dressed ashlar, square-hewn stone, similar to that used for the Church of St Baldred at Tyninghame, and at Dalmeny Church, West Lothian.

The plinth dressings, which form the actual SW angle, are best seen in the foreground of one of the three photographs taken during Richardson's excavations in 1951 when newly revealed (Figure 4.21). These, and further cut blocks that form the internal re-entrant, are of a fine-grained pale sandstone (which Richardson, 1961, suggests may have been quarried at Gullane, or even in Fife), are the only *in situ* dressings from the earliest church building. The plinth stones retain the significant detail of a narrow upper chamfer (Figure 4.22). While less diagnostic than more developed moulded detailing, this is consistent with Romanesque or early gothic construction and, in the context of what is known of the history of the site, the dating of the earlier inhumation burials, and the structural sequence of the church itself, can likely be identified as of 12th century date. The presence of the plinth course suggests the original church was of some moderate architectural pretension; the course is of similar detail to that seen at Dalmeny (mid-12th century). It is also possible that, as is the case of the north transept, a further stage of the footing existed above, but is now missing. The remains of the transept itself are faced externally with cubical blocks of fine-grained sandstone that appear, perhaps, to be reused. If so these are likely to derive from the original building.

Though based on such minimal survival one may imagine that the early church was of a typical two-cell arrangement, comprising a nave and a smaller chancel, such as that surviving at Duddingston, Edinburgh. The precise form of the latter, whether or not more elaborate than a simple rectangle (perhaps also incorporating an apse, as at Dalmeny), cannot now be known.

Fig. 4.21: The SW angle of the nave, left foreground, as newly revealed by the 1951 excavation, looking NW. The chamfered base course, which can be clearly seen forming the angle, has been cut through and overlain by the moulded pier base of the inserted nave arcade (Courtesy of East Lothian Council Archives & Local History Service).

North transept (?later 12th century)

Of the north transept, only parts of the north and west walls now remain, these rising to a maximum height of about 1.2m. Though the direct stratigraphic relationship of the transept to the early nave no longer survives it is possible that this was an addition to the earlier church. As already noted its lower external facings, all of pale sandstone, may be recycled cubical blocks from the earlier building – in their present position their coursing is somewhat irregular. However, the quoining of the external angle is of neat ashlar and early character. The external wall foot rises from a plinth of two chamfered stages, the stones forming the lower stage are of similar character to the *in situ* plinth stone of the early nave (Figures 4.23 and 4.24). Though the surviving remains are fragmentary, the presence of ashlar blocks defining the *internal* re-entrant is a diagnostically early feature (as noted, it also appears at the south-west corner of the nave), a detail employed in Romanesque construction that saw continuing use into the earlier 13th century (Figure 4.25); the well-preserved late 12th century church of Auchindoir, Aberdeenshire, for example, provides exact parallel for this detail. Some internal wall plaster still adheres at the re-entrant angle.

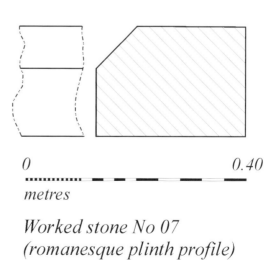

0   0.40

metres

Worked stone No 07 (romanesque plinth profile)

Fig. 4.22: Profile of the external plinth at the SW corner of the nave

Fig. 4.23: The upstanding NW corner of the north transept, looking SE

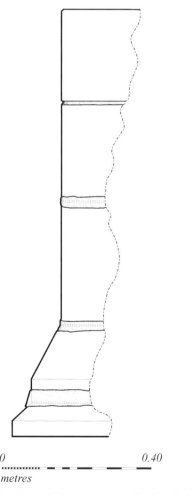

0   0.40

metres

Fig. 4.24: Profile of the external plinth of the north transept

Fig. 4.25: North transept: dressed freestone blocks defining the internal re-entrant of its north and west walls – a diagnostically early feature, looking NW

Fig. 4.26: Font base photographed from the SW, recorded during repair works in 2004

In summary if the transept did not form part of the original build of St Andrew's Church then it seems to have been a very early expansion of it. Although the evidence has been lost to the sea it seems probable that the transept had had a southern partner (the existence of a secondary south aisle probably implies this). The church at this early stage (if not originally) had thus likely been cruciform in plan, a considerable rarity in the Scottish context for a lesser church of early date. A lateral extension may relate to a deliberate concentrated investment in the harbour area and Kirk Ness generally by North Berwick nunnery in the 12th century. Possibly it was a direct response to an increase in pilgrimage traffic, that also necessitated the provision of the documented hospice that was likely located close by, towards the harbour. A transept or transepts would have significantly increased the capacity of the building and permitted the provision of additional altars.

Font plinth (13th century)

In the centre-west part of the nave survives the square base for the font. Having deteriorated since its exposure and initial consolidation under Richardson in the 1950s, the feature was examined in detail in 2004 (Figure 4.26). The plinth was stepped, edged with squared dressings of pale sandstone; one of these was a reused architectural fragment – a window jamb stone still displaying a glazing groove but whose moulded detail had been clawed back. The edging stones enclosed a loose rubble core and the feature overall was found to directly overlie deposits of sand. No evidence to suggest the base of the font had been octagonal, as observed by Richardson, can now be seen,

and neither is it clear why he should have specifically assigned a 13th century date to the feature.

West tower

A clearly recognisable addition to the early church structure are the remains of the west tower whose very substantial foundations unambiguously abut the east end of the nave and are now themselves partly overlain to the north-west by an existing 19th century building, Church Cottage. While a break in the west wall of the nave is apparent, no remains survive to demonstrate the details of the entrance into the tower. The details recorded by the various early views of tower suggest it to be of later medieval date – the vaulted lower stage, the parapet detailing, etc (this assuming it to have been a structure of one period).

Aisles and nave arcade

Stratigraphically the next demonstrable phase consisted of the addition of the north and south aisles. These resemble each other closely in overall form and surviving detail, where this can be compared, and appear to be coeval. The construction of each is generally in dark whin-stone (mugearite) but employing sandstone dressings of a distinctive greenish hue. The west wall of the south aisle clearly abuts the south-west corner of the nave and the west tower. Although much of the existing masonry of the north aisle is original work its western parts appear to have been reconstructed in the 1950s on their

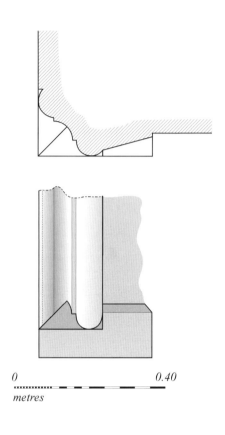

0   0.40

metres

Fig. 4.27: The western jamb of the south entrance to the church preserved within the upstanding porch (note the fireplace and chimney breast above, inserted in the 19th century)

Fig. 4.28: Profile and basal stop of the west jamb of the church entrance as exposed above present ground level

presumed line. While the junction of the west wall with the north-west corner of the nave is thereby obscured it may be reasonably presumed to have abutted in a similar manner.

The western jamb of the principal, south entrance into the south aisle survives within the porch; enough of this remains to demonstrate the entrance to have been round-headed. It is adorned with a moulded surround consisting of two quirked rolls on either side of a hollowed chamfer, a detail diagnostic, as noted by the RCAHMS in 1919/24, of a 16th century date (Figures 4.27 and 4.28). The north aisle also preserves the remains of an entrance, its west interior splay only, mid-way along its north wall.

The addition of the north aisle necessitated a new opening at its east end, through the pre-existing western wall of the north transept. The projecting ashlar base of the respond (half-pier) of the arch inserted at this stage survives on the north side, this detailed with a chamfer. A continuation of the lower stage of the plinth of the west wall of the transept was found to underlie this base when exposed during works in 2004 (Figure 4.29).

The addition of the aisles clearly implies the insertion

of the nave arcades of which the lower part of one respond, at the west end of the south wall of the nave, is the only survivor (see Figure 4.21). The base displays a roll above a broad chamfer; the lower course of the pier shaft survives *in situ* upon the base, this detailed with simple 3in (7.5cm) chamfer at the angles (Figure 4.30). These details are also preserved in a large number of *ex situ* stones from the Kirk Ness site, incorporated *c*.1659–64 into the successor church at Kirk Ports. Between the west end of the nave and the crossing (the line of the west wall of the north transept) there is comfortable space for an arcade of three arches.

South porch (?16th century, 17th century, and later)

The surviving south porch, which is a construction of a number of periods in its own right, was described in some detail by the RCAHMS (1924), (Figures 4.31 and 4.32). Earlier still, in 1911, J. T. Richardson had supposed the structure to be of great antiquity:

Fig. 4.29: Continuation of the plinth of the west wall of the north transept, overlain by the later addition of the north aisle, looking E

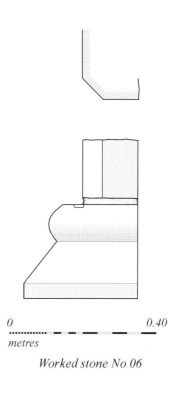

0   0.40

metres

Worked stone No 06

Fig. 4.30: Profile of the surviving nave pier base

All that has been left of the church of St Andrew is the porch ... The porch ... or at least its foundations (for the upper portion of the walls and the roof is later), is a much earlier structure and must go back to the 8th or 9th century, at which time it probably served as the chapel or cell of one of the local anchorites, of whom St Baldred's is the only name preserved by tradition. The fact of its lying north and south lends support to this theory, as the oldest of our ecclesiastical remains almost all have their long axis in that direction – another example of which may be seen on the Mey Island. We are therefore justified in looking on this building as among the earlier ecclesiastical structures in the country.

However, no subsequent writer proposed such early origins.

The earliest, lower parts of the masonry of the porch clearly abut the south wall of the south aisle and must thus represent a subsequent construction episode. The lower parts of the east and west porch buttresses are partly of ashlar-work (recycled stone?); these appear in turn to abut the masonry of the porch proper and thus

seem to be a further sub-phase – perhaps these relate to the subsequent construction of the vault.

The upper parts of the porch, including the barrel vault, the upper walling and upper stages of the two buttresses (integral to the adjacent walling), and perhaps the south entrance, all appear to be a reconstruction, perhaps of the later 16th century. The entrance is detailed with a substantial quirked angle roll (Figure 4.33). Dressings are of mixed sandstone types. A curious feature of the structure is a crudely wrought sandstone basin set into the masonry of the east jamb of the porch entrance, this traditionally presumed to have been a holy water stoup (Figure 4.34).

The altered wall heads of the porch, including the crow steps on the south gable, as well as the slated roof can probably be associated with the mid-19th century works evident on the interior of the structure. The latter include an inserted fireplace and chimneybreast at the interior north-west angle (see Figure 4.27), and a substantial widening of the earlier entrance into the south aisle on its east side. This new opening necessitated the insertion of a low relieving arch formed of two courses of brick, above a substantial timber lintel. The opening was

Fig. 4.31: Photograph of the lime-washed south porch taken at the time of Richardson's excavation in February 1951, looking N (courtesy of Mrs Lorna Burton)

Fig. 4.32: View of the south porch from the SE taken in 2000, before commencement of repair works

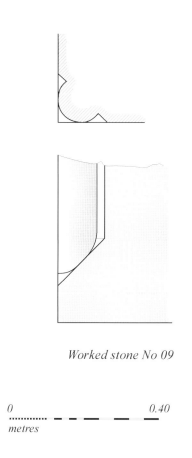

Worked stone No 09

0 .... – – – – 0.40

metres

Fig. 4.33: Profile and basal stop of the porch entrance

Fig. 4.34: Stone basin on the inner east side of the porch entrance

fitted with opposing doors. These works may relate to the activities of the Coast Guard and Rocket Brigade – perhaps the structure was converted as a shelter or lookout post (see Chapter 5). The chimney itself was reduced in the mid 20th century during repairs following Richardson's excavation, when the interior of the porch was also re-floored.

Architectural fragments and other building materials

Amongst the finds gathered from the site by Richardson was a small group of carved architectural stones, some of these generated by his own excavation, others repatriated from the Manse rockery and elsewhere, and put on display at the church in the early 1950s within a railed enclosure in the north transept. These comprise three skew stones of a somewhat argillaceous sandstone of greenish hue (as noted above these were likely parts of a fallen gable uncovered by Richardson – Figure 4.35), and a further stone of a pale fine-grained creamy grey sandstone, apparently part of the jamb of a window (a glazing groove is evident) though it is so mutilated that little else can be deduced of its former detail.

In full accord with documentary references to the dismantling of the old kirk for the building of the new in

*c.*1659–64, at Kirk Ports within the town, many reused architectural fragments are clearly to be seen in the second church, which is itself now ruinous (Figure 4.36). Richardson had also noted their presence; in his *Preliminary Report* of February 1951 he noted:

> 'In the building of the 17th century parish church I have found evidence that the builders used as corner stones, the dressed ashlars taken from the pillars that carried the arcading between the nave and the south aisle of the older building.'

He also reported to the *Courier* (6 April, 1951): 'some of these cubicle [sic] stones [of the Romanesque stonework of the church] are still to be seen built into the walls of the post-Reformation kirk'.

Of the numerous dressings deriving from the earlier church the majority that bear carved detail are certainly sections of the piers of the nave arcades and are of sandstone of a similar greenish hue; these dressings tended to have been reused for the lower and mid-level quoining of the original build of the later church (Figures 4.37 and 4.38). Of these, a minimum of 109 examples were recorded by visual inspection, of which at least 13 were certainly full-width stones, chamfered at each end. The

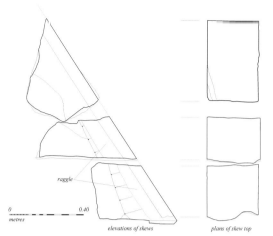

raggle

0   0.40
metres

elevations of skews   *plans of skew top*

Fig. 4.35: Three gable head skew stones recovered from Richardson's excavation

latter all measured 0.94–0.95m in length, this a precise enough match, at 0.95m, to the width of the solitary surviving pier section at the old kirk. It is perhaps notable that while at least one further moulded pier base was seen reused at Kirk Ports, there were no capitals or arch voussoirs in evidence. The Kirk Session Minutes of 30 March 1658 specifically refer to the use of the columns at the old church (NAS CH2/285/1):

> Considering that the pillars of the old church were now useless thair & that free stone is hard to be gotten did thairfor appoint the said Matthew Wilson mason to caste down the said pillars & to make use of the stones thairof for such hewan work of the new Kirke as they will be most suitable unto & agree with him that he shall have halfe the price both of hewan stone of such which he should cast down which they wold give for such stones respective if they were winn out of ane quarrell & that he should have halfe the price agreed upon keepe stanes.

It is also apparent that there are *ex situ* dressings of varying stone types. In addition to the greenish stone already noted there is further freestone of a fine-grained pale greyish cream variety (often cubical blocks – these evidently the ones being referred to by Richardson), and orangey-brown to medium brown fine to medium-grained sandstone, with more or less pronounced bedding visible (Figure 4.39).

Other stones bearing moulded detail include a series of pieces of the greenish stone bearing single quirked angle rolls, including two lintel sections; and two window or entrance jamb stones that were detailed with a broad angle roll, double-quirked (Figure 4.40).

Other structures in the harbour area contain stone that was recycled from the church site. Richardson noted that a section of a 13th century grave cover was recovered from the harbour/swimming pool wall. The earlier parts of the top of the north-west facing harbour breakwater

contain sections that display the same variety of stone types as seen at the church (Figure 4.41). The south and east walls of the existing building that overlies the footings of the west tower, Church Cottage, certainly contains material deriving from the church (Figure 4.42).

Numerous fragments of sandstone roofing tiles were recovered from dumps of redeposited material behind the sea wall in the vicinity of the church during the excavation of the services route (Figure 4.43). These are of a buff to purplish-brown medium grained sandstone of a type typically found in Angus and generically referred to as 'Carmyllie' (one of the Angus quarry sources). These must certainly derive from the church. Indeed, Richardson commented in February 1951 that the west tower of the church must have been covered with slates from Dundee, a comment he would not have made if he had not recovered such material from his excavation.

The recovered fragments are typical of the type, being 1.5–2.5cm in thickness and displaying chipped edges and large punched holes for wooden pegs. Some also retain mortar residues suggesting either remains of fillets or their reuse in construction (broken tiles were often employed as pinnings and levellers). Occasional fragments of slate from the same deposits, some of blue-grey Highland Line type, seem more likely not to relate to the church.

A solitary section of lead window *came* was one of the historic finds from the site. Its cross-section indicates a medieval date and the twisted nature of the came section clearly suggests its window was the victim of materials recycling following the demise of the church (Figure 4.47, below, and Appendix F).

Architectural visualisations

An undated sketch reconstruction by Richardson of St Andrew's Church in perspective view and plan is held by the National Library of Scotland (NLS, 30. 5.23 (26E)) (Figure 4.44). Though the plan is too cursory to suggest his detailed conclusions on phasing, both images show the fully evolved church as a major structure with paired transepts; the view presents overlaid alternative proposals for the roof form of the tower – both pyramidal and gabled.

A perspective cut-away reconstruction of the church building was commissioned in 2004 from the artist David Simon for the new interpretation at the site (Figure 4.45). This image combines information available from the surviving remains following its reassessment with the evidence of historic sources and other architectural precedents; Dr Richard Fawcett also advised on appropriate details, in particular the likely internal arrangements in the immediate pre-Reformation period. In contrast to Richardson's view this omits a south transept and assumes the retention, little-altered, of a Romanesque chancel. The cover illustration of this volume, also by David Simon, represents the church and the church site at a slightly earlier period, nominally in the 14th century,

Fig: 4.36: The church of St Andrew, Kirk Ports, erected c.*1658–64; view from the SE*

Fig. 4.37: Pier sections from the old church employed as quoins in the church of 1659–64

Fig. 4.38: Detail of reused pier sections showing tooling

Fig. 4.39: Much of the general lower walling of the 17th century church, contains reused stonework, this demonstrably from the Old Kirk

Fig. 4.40: Individual stones displaying moulded detail: lintels with quirked rolls (above), and jamb stones with twice-quirked angle rolls, and part of a pier base, inverted (lower right)

Fig. 4.41: Part of the northwest-facing harbour breakwater, interior face, showing an assortment of reused stones likely recovered from the medieval church site

Fig. 4.42: The south and east walls of Church Cottage contain reused stonework from the church

Fig. 4.43: A selection of sandstone roofing tile fragments recovered during monitoring in 1999

Fig. 4.44: Sketch reconstruction of St Andrew's Kirk by Richardson, based on the evidence of his excavations of 1951–2 (© National Library of Scotland. Licensor www.scran.ac.uk)

Fig. 4.45: An artist's impression of the appearance of St Andrew's Church at its most developed extent, on the eve of the Reformation, c.1550. By David Simon with input from Dr Richard Fawcett

before the erection of the west tower and the addition of the aisles (see also Figure 4.1).

Church artefacts

The church bell (1642)

An important survival from the Old Kirk is its bell, cast in 1642 (Figure 4.46). This former occupant of the west tower was noted by the Rev. James Burt in 1930–1:

'The bell was first erected in the church at the har-

bour. After that church was disused it was still left there. And on 21st October, 1666, it is "reported the bell to be in hazard of falling by reasone of frequent raines falling upon the trees, (or beams) whereupon shee hings, and on her stocke'

Four years after this, in 1670, it is recorded 'This dat thee Session finding thee timber whereon the bell was hinging to be failing, thought good that shee should be taken down and brought up and layd in the kirke'. The bell remained unused within the new kirk of St Andrew at Kirk Ports until the erection of a bell tower there in 1770. Mounted in the tower, it remained there even after the removal of the congregation to the third St Andrew's kirk, in the High Street, in 1882–3. It was hung within the bell tower there when the latter was finally completed in 1907. The bell itself was finally replaced in 1928. In 1924 the RCAHMS noted:

> In the bell chamber of new St. Andrew's Church is a bell measuring 2¼ feet from skirt to crown with a diameter of 1 foot 5 inches at crown and 2 feet 9 inches at skirt. Below an anthemion cresting is the inscription in Roman capitals: "JACOBUS MONTEITH ME FECIT EDINBUGH [sic] PRO TEMPLO NORTH BERIK ANNO DOMINI 1642 SPERO MELIORA." Below the inscription are two thistles alternating with two shields each surmounted by a crown, and bearing a hammer.

The inscription translates, 'James Monteith made me in Edinburgh for the church of North Berwick – AD 1642 – I hope for better things'

Other artefacts from the church site

A variety of miscellaneous finds have been made at the church site, many of which now reside in the collection of the East Lothian Council Museums Service (formerly at North Berwick Museum), or at the National Museum of Scotland. The former group (Figure 4.47), mostly likely deriving from Richardson's excavation, is assessed overall in Appendix F. Objects of particular note from the site include the following:

Candle-snuffer

A church-related relic of individual note is the cope of a bronze candle-snuffer, this an historic find from the site and now in the care of East Lothian Council Museums Service (see Figures 4.47 and F.2). Though the exact provenance is not recorded, perhaps coming from Richardson's excavations in the 1950s or earlier, such a find would clearly directly relate to the functioning of the church itself.

Pilgrim's badge mould

This, the most celebrated find from the site of the medieval kirk, was discovered in *c*.1893, and has been variously reported (eg. Cooper 1906; J. T. Richardson 1906–7a; RCAHMS 1924; Yeoman 1999). Williamson (1908) states:

> About fifteen years ago an interesting discovery was made on the Kirk Green of MATRICES for badges of St Andrew and of the Saviour on the Cross. The find was made the subject of a communication by Professor Cooper to the Scottish Ecclesiological Society. As reported by the Scotsman :-

Fig. 4.46: The 17th century church bell, photographed c.1931 (© East Lothian Museum Services. Licensor www.scran.ac.uk)

> "... The matrices are formed of bed ironstone, with holes for fastening the badge to the clothing of the wearer."

J. T. Richardson (1911, 39) noted that the stone had been 'picked up on Anchor Green, having been scraped out of the ground by a dog'. J. S. Richardson (1906–7a, 431) provided the following descriptive notice and illustration (Figure 4.48):

> Notice of portion of a stone mould for casting pilgrims' signacula and ring brooches.
>
> This interesting relic, which was found a few years ago among some disturbed soil in the old churchyard of St Andrew's Church, situated near the harbour at North Berwick, was exhibited at a meeting of the Scottish Ecclesiological Society, and recorded in their transactions for the year 1905. It is the centre portion of a stone mould, formed of clay-bed ironstone, measuring about 4 inches square by ⅛ of an inch thick, having the lower end fractured. On the obverse are matrices for casting pewter or lead badges, such as were wont to be carried in medieval times by pilgrims, either as tokens or sewn to their garments. These badges are – a representation of Saint Andrew on his Cross, set in an oblong frame, with rings at either corner, an equal armed crucifix, and portion of a smaller one. At each corner of the arms are rings, serving as loops by which to fasten the

Fig. 4.47: Historic finds, pre- and post-Reformation, from the Old Kirk site in the collection of East Lothian Museums Service

badges to the dress. On the reverse are moulds for two unequally-sized ring brooches, with thistle-headed pins.

The find is further referenced in 'Donations to the Society' in *PSAS* (1922–23, 110),

By JAMES S. RICHARDSON, F.S.A.Scot. Stone Mould for casting Pilgrims' Badges, 215/16 inches by 25/8 inches by 11/16 inch, bearing on one face matrices for St Andrew on his cross, an equal-armed crucifix, and part of a smaller one, and on the other face matrices for two ring brooches of different sizes and two thistle-shaped pins: found in the old church-yard of St Andrew's Church, North Berwick.

The original is now in the National Museum of Scotland (Figures 4.49 and 4.50); Richardson had arranged for the creation of a facsimile for display in the former North Berwick Museum collection (East Lothian Council Museums Service).

Crucifix

This historic find from the church site is without detailed provenance, though possibly from Richardson's excavation; it is now in the East Lothian Council Museums Service collection (Figure 4.51). The crucifix is described by Simpson and Stevenson (1981, 11) as a '12th century pendant cross', however, it may be considerably later in date, see specialist report in Appendix F. A small crucifix cut from bronze sheet, somewhat crudely executed and detailed with simple incised decoration (saltire-like incisions on the centre of one side are probably of no specific significance). Notches towards the termini at each cross-arm suggest this was intended to be stitched onto cloth – whether as part of a burial rite or perhaps as a badge is unclear; it is possible, perhaps probable, that this is a grave good from a burial from the site.

Jug

This was a find recovered during Richardson's excavations in the area of the north transept in 1952 (see Figure 4.52 and Appendix F). In a letter to the Town Clerk of North Berwick of 6 May 1957 Stuart Maxwell, Assistant Keeper, Museum of Scotland, noted:

Dr J. S. Richardson has brought here a small glazed stoneware jar, some three inches in height, which was found by workmen digging at the south-

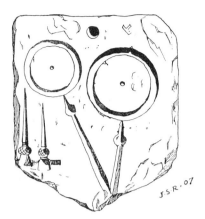

Fig. 4.48: Drawing of pilgrim badge mould by J. S. Richardson, in PSAS 1906–7 (We are grateful to the Society of Antiquaries of Scotland for permission to reproduce)

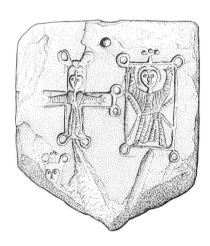

Fig. 4.49: The sandstone mould as drawn by Marion O'Neill for Historic Scotland (Yeoman 1999) (Historic Scotland)

Fig. 4.50: The rear of the badge mould (© National Museums Scotland. Licensor www.scran.ac.uk)

west [subsequent correction – 'north'] transept of the pre-Reformation kirk of St Andrew … It may be of 16th century origin, or a little later. ….

Of salt-glazed stoneware from Raeren (lower Rhine), 16th century, the jug is unusually small.

Coins

J. T. Richardson (1911, 39) noted:

> Before the retaining wall was built by the late Sir Hew Dalrymple quite a hoard of small copper coins, such as boodles and hardheads of James VI and Charles I, used to be picked up on the beach after a high sea. These were generally supposed to have been washed out of the graves, where they had been buried along with the dead – a propitiatory offering to the powers below of the smallest coin that the sorrowing survivors possessed

In addition to the coins recovered from Richardson's own excavations on the church site, Anne Robertson (1960–1, 141) recorded:

> In January 1953, Dr J. Richardson reported the discovery, a few weeks before, of a small bronze coin of Caligula, minted at Berytus in Phoenicia, when sand from the sea shore to the east of the Auld Kirk green, near the harbour at North Berwick, was being screened at the filters for the town's reservoirs. A small copper Scots coin was found at the same time.

Burials within the church and the surrounding cemetery

Human remains at Kirk Ness – background

The exposure of graveyard materials, particularly human remains, had long been recorded at the old church site, this particularly where erosion affected the eastern side of the promontory in the vicinity of the church ruin.

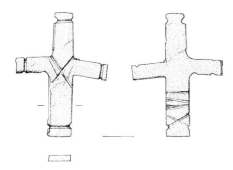

Fig. 4.51: Small bronze crucifix, possibly 12th century by Marion O'Neill

These remains were often strewn across the beach following major storms and, ultimately, this embarrassing circumstance led to the erection of the existing sea wall in 1857.

Evidence for burial activity both within the site of the ruined church and about it was recorded at the time of Richardson's excavations in 1951–2. In his *Statement concerning the human bones unearthed during operations* (14 May 1952) he makes a number of key observations about human remains found at the site, both disturbed in the past and encountered during his own excavations:

During the Pre-reformation period interments were made within the Kirk, under the floor [..] and more often outside the building in the east, south and west sides. In the 17th century the Kirk Session prohibited further burials on those parts of the Kirkyard, and ordered all future burials to be on the north side of the building. Excavations were only carried down to the floor levels of the kirk therefore no burials under that level have

been interfered with – Only one post-reformation burial was located in the nave, it had been made after the church had been demolished. It was left undisturbed.

1) From time to time, before the seawall was constructed, human remains were washed out by the sea; these were collected and buried in dumps under the turf.

2) When the Gas Work project was started [*c.*1845] it was stopped owing to encroachment on the graves – All disturbed bones were buried in dumps.

3) When the sea wall was constructed a large number of similar remains were disturbed and reburied in dumps.

4) When the Coast Guard house and enclosure were built a similar disturbance of graves took place & the bones collected buried.

Human remains uncovered under No. 2, 3 or 4 found a resting place in the Parish Kirk land in 1856.

Instructions

When work was started in 1951 instructions were given that no skeleton, in a burial position, was to be disturbed but that all dumped or stray bones were to be collected and reburied at once on the site. This [...] was strictly adhered to.

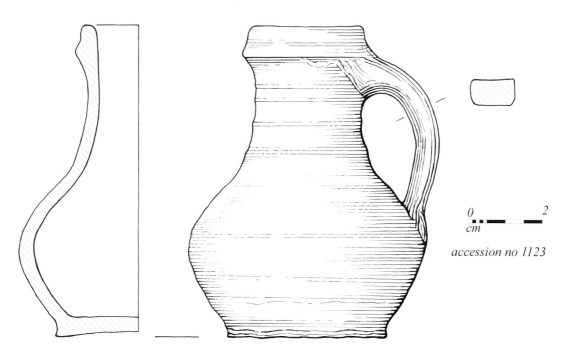

accession no 1123

Fig. 4.52: Small jug, from Richardson's excavation by Marion O'Neill

What was done

During this years work – numerous dumps were found just under the turf – These were reburied in pits on the north side near the building on the west side of the Kirk Green. A carnal house was found within the N Transept at the N.W. Corner – on locating this dump the bones were immediately reinterred.

To the W. of this transept – skeletons were located – these were not disturbed – hence the steep incline of the ground at that part.

With reference to burial to the north of the church Richardson was evidently aware of the entry in the Kirk Session Minutes, of Sunday 3 of April 1608 (NAS CH2/285/1):

The quhilk day the haill session all with ane consent statute and ordaint that herefter ther be no more graves maid bot on the North syd of the kirk, because the ground is more solid on that side and ordains Alexr Gibsoun to break no [e]rd efter the dait therof but upon the said North syd under the paine of depryving him frome his office.

In relation to the reference to the gas-works his father had written (Richardson 1911, 37):

Sixty years ago [thus *c.*1850] the ground here was in course of being dug for the foundations of a proposed gas-works, which operation was happily interdicted by Dr Graham, the parish minister at the time.

Human remains encountered during the project works – introduction

An important aspect of the recent archaeological involvements at Anchor Green has been the exposure and assessment of parts of the cemetery associated with St Andrew's Church, particularly beyond its north side where human remains were encountered in a number of areas (Figure 4.53). These included a discrete group of inhumation burials exposed at low level behind the sea wall a little to the north-east of the north transept (Trench 6), and further inhumation burials within Trench 2 close to the north wall of the transept. In the large open area excavation to the north of the transept, Trench 8, a broad zone containing inhumation burials was encountered at higher level. Parts of isolated individual burials were recorded elsewhere, both within the church and further to the north. Deep exposures of cemetery-related deposits were made in section along the eastern side of the site, these on a south-west to north-east alignment that effectively bisected

the medieval church (its eastern parts having fallen into the sea) and extended from it further to the north-east.

In addition to this body of cemetery data for which a secure context survived, there were occurrences of loose charnel in most excavated areas. There were also a number of instances where charnel had been deliberately gathered and reburied, this generally consistent with Richardson's observations already noted.

It proved necessary to up-lift the remains encountered in a number of areas, particularly those encountered in Trenches 6 and 8; these were subject to osteological analysis, reported by David Henderson in Appendix I of this volume. It is the intention is to rebury these at a suitable location at Anchor Green. The approximately 60 individuals that may be represented by the excavated remains is self-evidently only a small fraction of the overall cemetery population, and a very small sample upon which to offer generalisations as to the organisation of burial within the cemetery and the demographics of the population. Perhaps more than half of the area formerly occupied by the cemetery, including burials within the church itself, has been lost to the sea, and within the remaining area no boundary features were defined.

Other evidence for burial practice at the site exists in the form of a handful of individual stone monuments, these mostly gathered following Richardson's excavations. One or two individual monuments, less certainly from the site, are also included in this section.

It should also be noted that further human remains, specifically deposits of charnel, were encountered in a recent watching brief carried out within the alley surrounding the former Coastguard station to the south-west of the church site, on its west side (see Figure 6.1). It was judged that these related to burials disturbed during the construction of the building in the mid-19th century (McCaig 2012).

Cemetery deposition

From the archaeological evidence it seems clear both that the natural topography at Anchor Green rose gently to the north of the church and that, in addition to this, there seems to have been considerable build-up of deposits following the erection of the medieval church whose remains can now be seen. This deposition must, in part, be accounted for by the density of burial activity within the cemetery – the build-up of ground within an intensely used cemetery is a commonly recorded phenomenon – and in part by a substantial accumulation of wind-blown sand, the latter an occurrence recorded in many past archaeological investigations in North Berwick generally.

It is also known from historical sources, discussed in the next section, that interment in the cemetery continued well after the demise of the church in the mid-17th century, and apparently as recently as the early 19th.

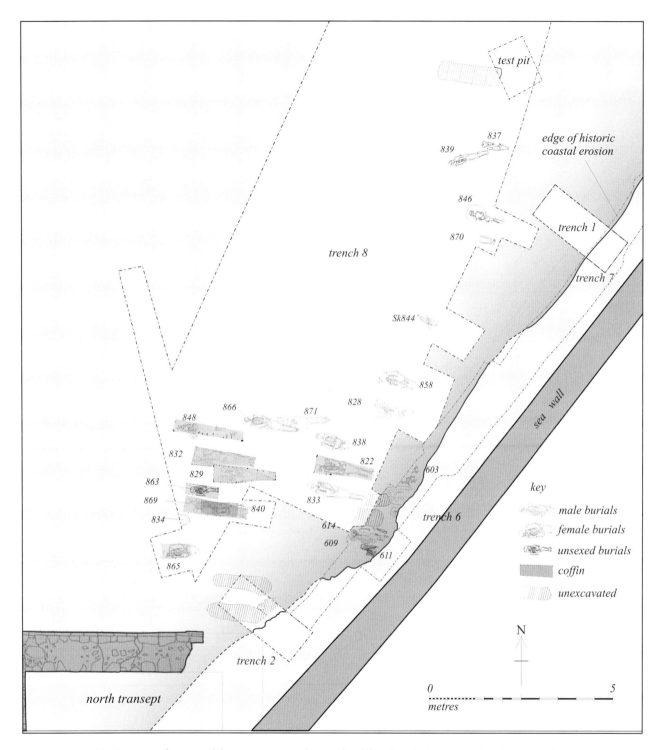

Fig. 4.53: Excavated areas of the cemetery to the north of the church, location plan for individual burials

Earlier burials

No evidence for inhumation burials was encountered at the site that might be associated with certainty to the earlier phases of occupation as described in the preceding chaper (i.e. before the 11th/12th centuries). However, exposure of stratigraphy that pre-dated the later medieval period, especially in the vicinity of the existing church ruin – which might possibly occupy the site of a predecessor – was extremely limited.

A group of seven inhumation burials were revealed during the excavation of the services trench behind the existing sea wall a little to the north of the north transept of the medieval church – trench 6 (Figures 4.54 and 4.55). The graves had been cut down through levels of clean sand into a deposit of more humic soil that may represent an earlier ground surface, *625*, the latter perhaps the same as deposit *231* revealed at somewhat higher level in trench 2. Grave fills tended to be of sand intermixed with this material.

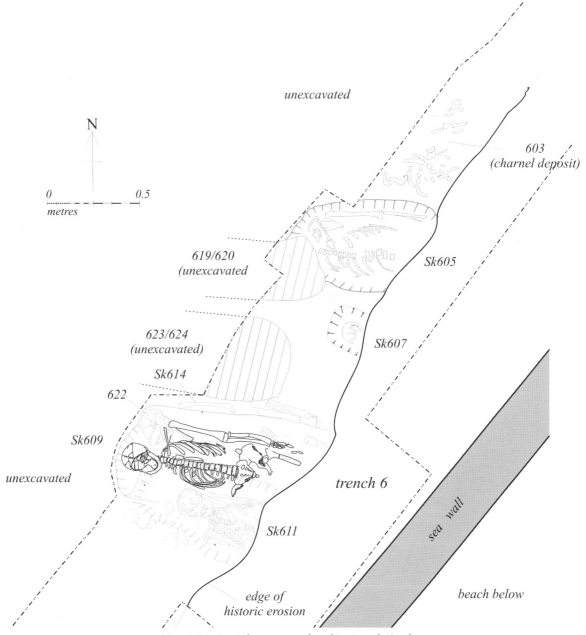

N

0 0.5
metres

unexcavated

603
(charnel deposit)

619/620
(unexcavated

Sk605

623/624
(unexcavated)

Sk614

Sk607

622

Sk609

unexcavated

trench 6

sea wall

Sk611

edge of
historic erosion

beach below

Fig. 4.54: Burials excavated within trench 6: plan

The remains of five individuals were fully excavated (*605*, *607*, *609*, *611* and *622*); two burials were only defined as grave cuts and not excavated (*619* and *623*). Relative to other burials at the site these were found at some considerable depth (between 0.6m and 0.8m below surface) and, on this basis, were assumed to represent some of the earliest individuals in the sequence of burial within the cemetery as sampled, a judgement subsequently confirmed by radiocarbon dating.

An intact section of the edge of the cemetery deposits was revealed within the constricted trench area as they had been exposed by coastal erosion in the years preceding the construction of the existing sea wall in *c*.1857. The lower extremities of each burial had eroded; in most cases only the torsos, arms and head remained while for

one, a neonate (*607*), only the head and uppermost parts of the torso survived. Deliberately placed localised deposits of loose charnel were also recorded in this area, *603* and *604*. This material, perhaps associated with the excavated graves, was evidently deposited at the time of the construction of the sea wall.

Amongst this group there was considerable evidence of intercutting, with grave *609* in particular disturbing two earlier burials (*611* and *614*) and containing charnel including a complete cranium and long bones (from *615–622*) (Figure 4.56); and grave *620*, disturbing the upper body of skeleton *605*. Burial *614* was represented by a single *in situ* humerus, the remainder having been destroyed by the cutting of grave *609* (and perhaps accounting for much of the charnel found with the latter).

The three earliest inhumation burials within this small

group, all inter-cut by later graves, were sampled for radiocarbon dating – the *622* cranium relating to skeleton *614*, and samples from skeletons *611* and *605*. These respectively dated to AD 1210–1300, AD 1020–1220, and AD 1150–1280 at 95.4% probability. There was no obvious archaeological evidence of earlier graveyard-related activity within this particular area.

Amongst these burials there was no evidence for coffined inhumations and no grave goods were recovered. The demographics and pathology of this group is examined in detail in Appendix I. Inhumation *605* was of outstanding individual interest as the victim of a repeated attack by pointed weapon, the detailed evidence for which is examined by Henderson and Franklin, in Appendices I and E respectively; and below.

Later burials to the north of the church

A larger sample of the cemetery population that on archaeological evidence appeared to be of later date than the group just described was encountered within the open area excavation of Trench 8, immediately to the north of the church (Figure 4.53, above). This comprised a group of 19 individuals, most of which were revealed at very shallow depth just below the existing Anchor Green lawn, towards the south end of the trench. This was an area that had clearly been considerably reduced by landscaping works in the early 1950s, lying along the east side of Anchor Green where the lawn begins to incline towards the sea wall. The lower extremities of many of the individuals in the latter area had evidently eroded away, further casualties of coastal erosion. Burials *822* and *833*, which had been thus affected, lay very close to the burials revealed in Trench 6. However, and in common with the other Trench 8 burials, these were encountered at a considerably higher level – generally between 0.6m and 0.8m above those in Trench 6.

In almost no case was a grave cut evident in the Trench 8 area, the burials having been made in a deep deposit of clean wind-blown sand, and back-filled with the same. In a few instances burials were found to intercut and a grave cut thereby traced or deduced (*832* was cut by *829*; *840* overlay *869* which was also partly cut by *863*; and *871* was heavily disturbed by burial *866*). However, for the most part the positioning of the burials respected one another, this suggesting they were broadly coeval and, in the absence of evidence for subsequent disturbance, were some of the latest in the burial sequence within this part of the cemetery. This seems to be consistent with the above-mentioned stipulation recorded in the Kirk Session minutes of April 1608 that new burials were only to be carried out on the north side of the church – many of the Trench 8 inhumations may thus be of such date and later.

There was also some suggestion of plot ordering within the cemetery, with two possible rows apparent within the greater concentration of excavated burials closer to the church. While clearly, in part, an accident of the ex-

Fig. 4.55: Trench 6 looking SW, showing the eroded edge of graveyard deposits and inhumation burials

tent of the excavated area, where the limit of excavation lay at a deeper level to the south, there was a discernable decrease in density of burials as one continued further north. Indeed no burials were encountered in section within the services trench extending northwards from Trench 6 (i.e. Trench 7), or in Trench 1. The most northerly burial was revealed in section, but not excavated, within a large sondage some 17m to the north-north-east of the north transept of the church ruin (cut *857*). However, such a decrease in burial density away from the church is not particularly surprising.

Where sex could be determined there was little unusual in the relative distributions of male and female inhumations, and the sample, though small, had representation of all age groups.

Coffined burials

In contrast to those in Trench 6, this burial group was notable for the number of coffined burials present – eight in total (Figures 4.53 and 4.61). While grave cuts were largely untraced, the wood of the coffin walls had left bands of mid-brown staining within the surrounding sand matrix. So well defined was this staining that, in most cases, it was possible to excavate the coffin interior and even, occasionally, to identify slight remains of base

An early murder victim?

Fig. 4.56: Trench 6: detail of inhumation burial 609 overlying skeletons 611 and 615

Fig.4.57: Trench 6, the remains of skeleton 605 as excavated

Inhumation *605* was the body of a young man, dating to the 12th or 13th centuries, who was fatally stabbed four times in the back, twice in the left shoulder and twice between the ribs on the left side of the torso (Figure 4.60). There may have been other injuries as the legs and some of the right side of the body were cut away by later burials. The man was over 20 years of age, slightly better built than average with wear to the shoulder, suggesting possible archery practice.

From the size, shape and relative positions of the injuries to the bones of *605* it was possible to infer some facts about the weapon that killed him. There was no indication that more than one weapon was used. The blade employed had a symmetrical lozenge-shaped section with very sharp edges and was probably at least 70mm long (but likely considerably longer). The locations of the wounds suggest they had been made by a stabbing point, a dagger being the most likely culprit (Figure 4.58).

The most likely course of events would seem to be as follows: the two shoulder injuries were inflicted first, over-arm and in quick succession, and were enough to bring the victim down (Figures 4.59 and 4.60). He was then stabbed twice through the ribs at close range, possibly while lying prone, with some accuracy and a knowledge of exactly the right angle

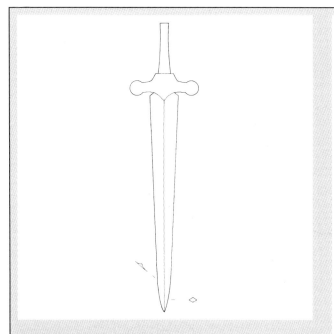

Fig. 4.58: A dagger of the type that may have inflicted the wounds, by Marion O'Neill

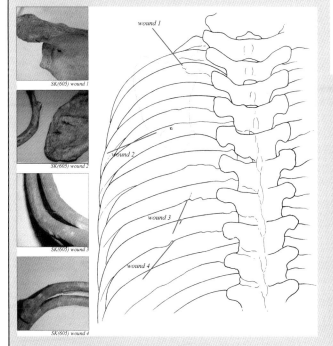

Fig. 4.60: Inhumation 605: blade injuries to left part of torso, by Marion O'Neill

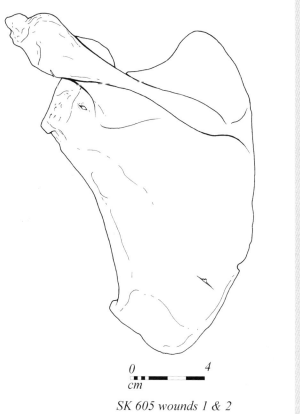

Fig. 4.59: Inhumation 605: scapula (shoulder blade) showing blade punctures, by Marion O'Neill

needed to reach the heart (Figure 4.60). It seems certain that either of the last two blows would have been fatal.

Daggers with a lozenge-sectioned blade are a specialist military weapon and carried mainly by military men. This, combined with the accuracy of the stab wounds, implies a degree of professionalism in the killing and arguably a degree of calculation. It would seem likely, then, that this man was murdered, rather than slain in battle, whether for the purposes of robbery or more complex political or personal reasons, it was perpetrated by someone who was well armed and who knew how to kill. However, the particular historical context for this brutal event may only be guessed at.

boards. In one case, inhumation *863*, a child burial, some possible evidence for the coffin lid remained; here staining above the skeletal remains suggested the coffin lid may have been keeled. In all instances where evidence for a coffin stain was identified, coffin nails were also present, generally as concreted iron lumps. Where observable the nails were wrought with flat, rounded heads. The arrangement of regularly spaced nails was well preserved in most cases, this principally representing the construction of the coffin base; however, some nails were located at higher

level (the coffin walls at the angles) or were clearly *ex situ* (slumped from higher up). Larger nails were present at the heads of the coffins of three skeletons – *822*, *829* and *848*, perpendicular to the long axis of the coffin; these indicated the coffin side-boards had been *affixed to* the base boards and/or the end pieces. In the case of the surviving south side of coffin *848* quite substantial nails had been hammered into the base board at regular intervals.

From this group of burials a single sample, from burial *865*, was taken for dating; this particular burial was

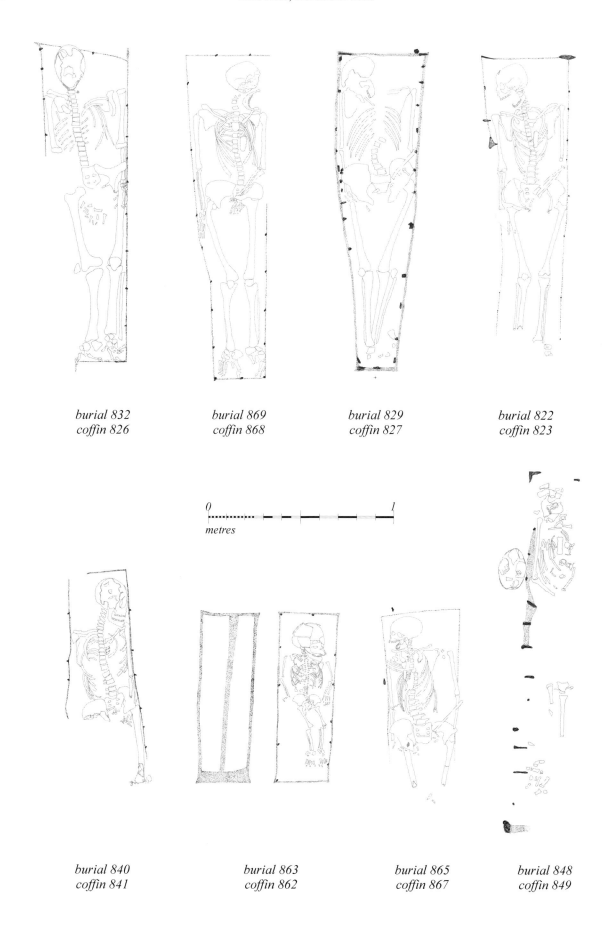

burial 832
coffin 826

burial 869
coffin 868

burial 829
coffin 827

burial 822
coffin 823

burial 840
coffin 841

burial 863
coffin 862

burial 865
coffin 867

burial 848
coffin 849

Fig. 4.61: Coffined burials recorded in trench 8

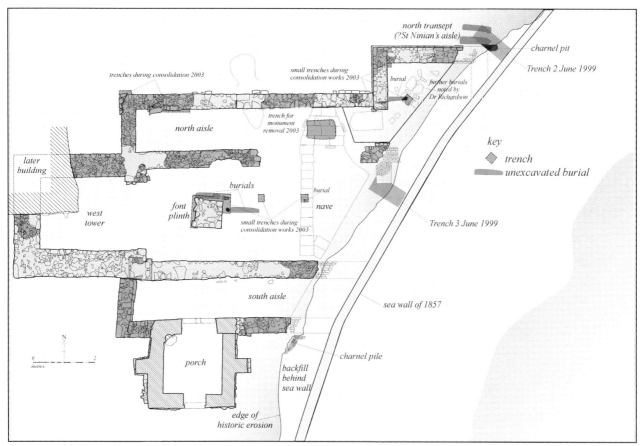

Fig. 4.62: Plan of the church showing sondages excavated during repair works, with burials exposed. Also shown are areas of cement repair to the ruined wall footings carried out under Richardson's direction in 1953–4, and slab paths and interpretation installed in 1977

chosen because of the presence of significant grave goods of varying date. A calibrated date of AD1450–1660 (SUERC-28302; 325±40 BP, at 95.4% probability) was obtained.

Other burials

Three further burials were identified as grave cuts in Trench 2, immediately to the north of the north transept of the church: cuts *222, 225* and *228* (Figure 4.53). While none of these were excavated, parts of the actual skeletons were visible at the surface (see Figure 4.66). The base of each burial had been cut into a pre-existing surface, *231*. In 1951 Richardson reported encountering burials during clearance works on the west side of the north transept, evidently in this area.

The church interior

Within the church interior a series of small sondages required during masonry repairs revealed a number of *in situ* inhumation burials, notably in the area of the apparent font plinth; however, it proved unnecessary to disturb these further (Figure 4.62). A particular significance of this group was the level at which the remains were encountered, these apparently only just below the

historic floor level – of which Richardson described a clay spread that he had revealed in 1951, though no trace of this was encountered in the works of 2003–4. A possibility may be that burial continued within the church interior even after its ruination by the sea and abandonment in the mid-17th century; this appears to be confirmed by the presence of the later 17th century table tomb discovered at the west end of the nave in 1951. It is possible that other burials may have been encountered at high level within the interior, perhaps in part represented by a mass of charnel apparently reburied by Richardson, revealed in Trench 2 and described in the following section.

Ex situ *skeletal material*

No evidence for *in situ* cemetery deposits was identified within the tunnel excavation at the northern extremity of Anchor Green; it appears that this area lay well beyond the cemetery perimeter. In spite of this a limited quantity of charnel was recovered from parts of the upper stratigraphy there, particularly from the substantial levels of sand, *1063, 1074* and *1088*. However, these appear to have been redeposited from further south (i.e. from the cemetery area) in the 19th century; they were also notable for the large quantity of copper alloy wire pins

Fig. 4.63: Trench 5, showing east section and charnel deposit 509

Fig. 4.64: Trench 8: two ex situ crania buried in a pit, 825

Fig. 4.65: Trench 2: general view looking WSW, showing unexcavated charnel pit 209 cut through undisturbed cemetery deposits and, in the foreground, the backfill behind the mid-19th century sea wall

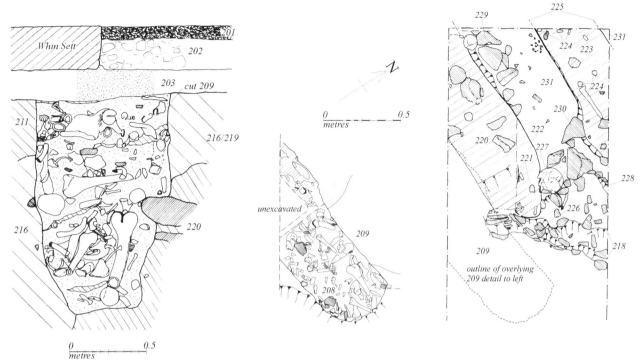

Fig. 4.66: Trench 2: section and plan of charnel 209 *pit and, right, undisturbed burials and, right, section of pit through* 209 *charnel pit*

Fig. 4.67: Trench 2: the part-excavated 209 *charnel pit, looking SW*

recovered, presumably shroud pins (52 pins of a total of 53 from the site as a whole came from this area).

Charnel was recovered generally from the cemetery excavation areas – Trenches 1–4, 5–6 and Trench 8. Individual deposits of *ex situ* remains included gathered material evidently placed during the construction of the present sea wall, in Trench 5, *509*, and trench 6 as already noted (Figure 4.63). Individual instances in the Trench 8 area included, most notably, two crania in a small pit (*825*) (Figure 4.64), and a further pit containing larger human bones (*830*). In only occasional instances could this material be directly related to *in situ* burials, being, for the most part, charnel placed within individual subsequent grave cuts.

Perhaps the most significant find of charnel was

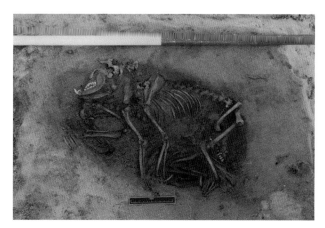

Fig. 4.68: Trench 8: burial of two small dogs in pit 860

Fig. 4.69: Engraving of seal of 'William, Lord of Douglas' in Sir William Fraser's, The Douglas Book (1885, 549)

within the substantial grave-like pit encountered and part-excavated in Trench 2, *209* (Figures 4.65–4.67). The sample excavated produced a minimum of 11 individuals based upon a count of femurs; perhaps the entire pit represented in excess of twice this number. It was deduced on stratigraphic grounds that this must have been a gathering of material from Richardson's 1951–2 excavation and therefore likely to contain much material from the interior of the church, possibly the north transept area (though ground reduction along the north side of the church will likely also have exposed burials).

Several femurs from this pit showed clear evidence of having been gnawed at the knee by dogs. It is most likely that these particular bones had been gathered from the eastern side of the site where coastal erosion had exposed them. Possibly they had been re-interred in the area subsequently excavated by Richardson.

Two dog skeletons were found in an oval pit (*860*), above burial *866*, encountered at the south end of Trench 8 (Figure 4.68). Both skeletons were aligned north–south and were placed on their sides with feet to the west. The head of the top dog dog, *859*, lay to the north; that of the under dog (*864*), directly below, lay to the south. The bones were well preserved, suggesting that this was not an ancient burial.

Grave goods

Of the excavated burials only one contained associated grave goods, inhumation *865*, the skeleton of a young woman from which was recovered a silk button, found lying to the left of the body between the ribs and the arm, and a bone pin – a possible hair pin – recovered from the neck area (see Figure 4.59 above). The latter appears to be of unexpectedly early date in relation to the inhumation itself, for which the radiocarbon dating range centred on the 16th century. These finds are discussed in detail in Appendices G and E respectively.

None of the considerable quantity of copper alloy wire shroud pins from the site was recovered from an *in situ* burial. However, they are nonetheless an important

assemblage (see Appendix E). As previously noted, many such pins were recovered from the wave-washed spoil from Richardson's 1951 excavations.

Other recorded finds from graves

Further discoveries of grave goods have been made at the site over the years and variously recorded. They include a brass seal matrix, of which the Rev. Henry Hill in the *Statistical Account* (*OSA* 1789, Vol. 5, 443), notes 'In 1788, a seal with the inscription 'Sigillum Willielmi Domini de Douglas,' was found in one of the vaults'. This find, recorded in 1850 as in the possession of Lady Jean Hamilton, was variously published, including engravings by Fraser (Laing 1850; Fraser 1885; MacDonald 1904) (Figure 4.69). Describing the object as of 'elegant 14th century design' Richardson (1911, 37) concluded the inscription referred to 'William Lord of Douglas, who lived from 1300 to 1333'.

Archaeologia Scotica (Vol. 5, 1890, appendix, 59) records the presentation by Daniel Wilson to the Society of Antiquaries of Scotland of:

> A Skull and Sword, with the words IN SOLINGEN and the initials J. G. L. on the blade, found in an ancient grave near .a ruin exhibiting Norman ecclesiastical features, on the west side of the harbour of North Berwick.

The sword seems to be no longer extant. Of German manufacture, it most probably dated to the 17th or 18th century (D. Caldwell *pers. comm.*).

Funerary monuments

Remains of only four sepulchral monuments are known to have certainly come from the old church site; three of these are medieval and one is of 17th century date. Of these, one not previously commented upon consists of a section of a foliated cross-slab built into the wall of an adjacent property, Church Cottage. J. S. Richardson had gathered the

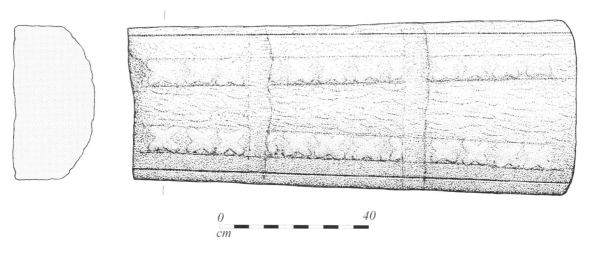

Fig. 4.70: 13th century coped grave cover, by Marion O'Neill

Fig. 4.71: Coped grave cover following reassembly from three fragments

other three and placed them, along with carved architectural fragments, in a small iron railed compound within the remains of the north transept. Two were inventoried by the RCAHMS in 1919; all three were subsequently described by Graham (1960–1, 244–5, North Berwick, St Andrew's Church, Nos 2, 5 and 6). In 2003–4 they were repositioned within the church ruin and the interior of the porch. Graham also suggested a further stone may have come from the site (North Berwick, St Andrew's Church, No. 4).

Coped grave cover (13th century)

This monument is first referred to by the RCAHMS in 1924 (visited in 1919) 'Two fragments of a grave slab *c*.13th century are preserved within the structure [the porch], while a third fragment has been built into the coping of the boundary wall of the swimming pool'. One source (Williamson 1908, 24) noted that 'within the porch … are … kept two moulded and carved stones which were removed from one of the harbour walls where at least three or four other similar stones may be detected'. Graham groups this stone with three at Oldhamstocks. He describes 'Parts of a coped grave-cover, of thirteenth century date, which was once decorated with rows of dog-tooth ornamentation. It may be compared with Nos. 1 to 3 at Oldhamstocks'.

The fragments are mentioned by Richardson who, in *c*.1952, gathered them together and had them placed within the site. In 2003–4 the three fragments, which were found to conjoin, were re-assembled by the conservator Nicholas Boyes, and the monument re-set in the vaulted porch (Figures 4.70 and 4.71). It is of fine-grained pale cream sandstone.

Now built into the south wall of the building overlying the footings of the west tower of the church ruin, a weathered fragment of greenish sandstone bears the remains of relief decoration that may represent part of the shaft of a foliated Calvary cross – part of its mid-section, enriched with two tiers of foliage springing from the cross shaft; perhaps of early 14th century date (Figure 4.72).

Fig. 4.72: Fragment of a foliated cross slab embedded in the south wall of Church Cottage

Recumbent slab – Lauder monument? (?15th century)

A substantial fossiliferous limestone slab of 1.18m (original width) by 2.06m (1 broken end) by 0.11m in thickness. A probable tomb slab its upper surface displays 17+ drilled holes of 14mm diameter, likely fixing points for decorative brass-work. Many of the holes retain lead in-fills (Figures 4.73 and 4.74). There is a shallow rectangular depression of 6 x 40cm in the central part of the slab. The stone is of non-local origin; while Graham refers to it as a *Tournai matrix stone* implying it to be of Tournai marble; it was perhaps more likely imported from the northeast of England. Probably of 15th century date.

In 1907 J. T. Richardson noted 'A flat stone which lay till comparatively recently near the centre of the Green was supposed to mark the burial place of the Lauders of the Bass.'It appears from minutes of a Town Council meeting dated 10 December 1953 that the slab had subsequently been taken to the Lodge; the minutes record the decision that the 'Tournai stone to be brought from the Lodge ground and laid beside the other stones' at Anchor Green. Graham (1960–1; North Berwick, St Andrew's Church, No. 6) records 'A Tournai matrix-stone measuring 6 ft. 10 in. by 3ft.10in. A few details are faintly visible'.

Recumbent slab

This monument, described by Graham (1960–1, 245 – North Berwick No. 4), was judged by him likely to have come from the old church site:

> Two articulating fragments of a large recumbent slab, the larger of which bears, in low relief, the head of a knight wearing a pointed helmet and ca-mail and resting on a pillow within a canopied niche. Of the inscription, which is in Gothic characters and runs round the margin, the words

ORATE PRO ANIMA [????] DE appear to have been legible in 1907. The larger fragment was formerly in the Manse garden, but the smaller one was found by Dr J. S. Richardson at the Abbey Farm, where also a stone very closely resembling the larger one was noted in 1847; these circumstances suggest that the slab originated at St Andrew's Church, and that it was removed to the farm as building-material when the structure was demolished. It is thus tempting to identify it with the stone recorded by Nisbet as 'in the aisle of the lairds of Bass' and as commemorating Robert Lauder of Congleton and the Bass, though the fragment of the inscription does not agree with Nisbet's record; Nisbet gives two dates for his monument, MCCCXI and MCCCCXI, and the second of these would suit the armour worn by the figure as it is of the late fourteenth or early fifteenth century. (cf. Nisbet, A., 1816)

> … in the aisle of the lairds of Bass, in the old church of North-Berwick, where they were interred, there is a tomb-stone, whereupon are cut, in Saxon letters, these words, Hic jacet Bus. (i.e. bonus) Robertus Lander mns. (i.e. magnus) Dus. (Dominus) de Congleton et le Bass, qui obiit mense Maii; some read, MCCCXI. and others read, MCCCCXI.

The stone was illustrated by J. S. Richardson (in J. T. Richardson 1911, opposite p. 25 – Figure 4.75). It is now in the collection of the East Lothian Council Museums Service.

Table tomb (later 17th century)

Recovered from within the nave of the church in 1951, as demonstrated by photographs of Richardson's excavation, this monument appears to have been a table tomb of 17th century character (Figure 4.76). Four fragments of a heavy slab of deep red sandstone were evidently recovered during the excavation, of which three pieces now remain. This stone is detailed with robust bolection-moulding to the edge. Also recovered and apparently associated are four 'legs', perhaps of an original six of moulded baluster form with flattened rear sides, these of the same red sandstone (Figure 4.77). Three further square slabs may also represent part of the monument, perhaps bases for the legs. It is not clear whether the monument was a fully free-standing table tomb or whether the 'legs' were applied to a supporting plinth beneath the slab. The monument is perhaps closely comparable to a table tomb at Innerwick Church, which Graham dates to the 17th century but whose date is illegible (Graham 1960–1, 240; Innerwick No. 3). There the slab is supported by baluster legs at the corners (though here integral parts of a single vertical slab at each end), and in the centre by vertically set plain slab-like piers. The elaborate Seton table tomb at Tranent, dated 1707 (Graham

Fig. 4.73: Recumbent grave slab

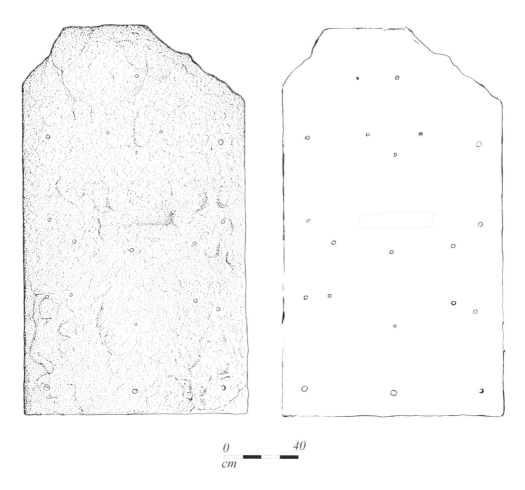

Fig. 4.74: Recumbent grave slab showing, right, distribution of lead-filled seatings for affixing brass-work, by Marion O'Neill

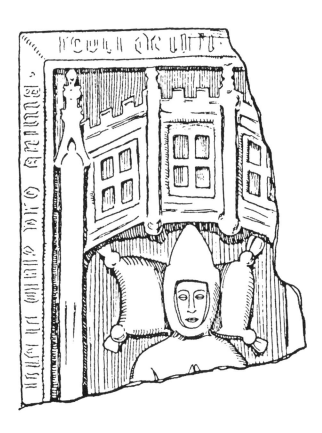

Fig. 4.75: Carved recumbent slab commemorating Robert Lauder, as illustrated by J. S. Richardson (1907)

Fig. 4.76: J. S. Richardson (with brush) following the recent discovery and piecing-together of parts of the top of the table tomb; the lower left-hand fragment is now missing (Courtesy of East Lothian Council Archives & Local History Service)

Fig. 4.77: The tomb fragments as laid out on site before their partial reconstruction in 2003–4

Fig. 4.78: Detail of the inscription on the tomb-slab

1960–1, Tranent No. 30), is supported at the corners by free-standing baluster legs as at North Berwick.

A report on the find was provided by Richardson to the *Haddingtonshire Courier* (8 June 1951):

> unearthed were the remains of a table tombstone cut from red rock resembling the Garvald variety. The fact that it is of late 17th century origins reveals that burials continued to take place within the church after it had become a ruin. The end of the stone has unfortunately been destroyed and so the interesting epitaph is cut short in the middle of the fourth line. On the upper half is a skull and crossbones, the initials R.W. and M.O., and the inscription Momento Mori. The verse commemorating the dead begins, "Heir lyes a sone of Mars, Ceres and Pan, in whom was al their virtues though a man, a Christian endoued with true … a soldier stout …" According to a list of ratepayers of North Berwick in 1660, Robert Walker was a prominent merchant of the times, and the only names beginning with the letter O were Oliver and Orrock. It is to two of these families the initials on the stone are presumed to refer. The mention of Mars indicates that Walker had seen active service in his young days, and that later he became a wood merchant and farmer, whose patrons were Pan and Ceres respectively.

Parts of this inscription are readily legible (Figure 4.78).

Evidence for the hospital and domestic occupation in the later medieval period

Evidence for a hospital for pilgrims

In contrast to the finds made in the vicinity of the church ruin, the tunnel excavation at the northern end of Anchor Green revealed some evidence for occupation of a more domestic character, this possibly associated with the maintenance of a hospice for travellers and pilgrims at Kirk Ness.

The importance of the southern pilgrimage route to Fife, by means of the ferry crossing between North Berwick and Earlsferry, is well established for the medieval period (if not earlier) and has been discussed by a number of authors such as Simpson and Stevenson (1981), Ferrier (1991, 13–15), and in a useful synopsis by Hall and Bowler (1997, 663). Wider studies on medieval pilgrimage also describe the route (Yeoman 1999; Hall 2007, 83) and each of these also draws attention to the find of the pilgrim's badge mould previously described.

As far as associated accommodation in North Berwick, in his survey of Scottish medieval hospitals Derek Hall (2006) noted:

The earliest hospital that can be classified as a Poor-house is the one at North Berwick in East Lothian which is first recorded in 1154 (Cowan and Easson 1976, 186). This must be qualified by the fact that it was also set up to aid pilgrims and given that it is located on the main pilgrimage route to St Andrews from the south this may have been its main function.

As has been suggested by a number of authors the existing granary building by the harbour, now East Lothian Yacht Club, a three storied structure of variegated rubble with arched doorways and external stair, may lie upon the site of the earlier hospital. Swan noted that no reference had been found in local records or writs indicating the position of the medieval hospital, although he also suggests there had been some confusion between this and the 'hospital of the poor brothers', under the patronage of the Lauders of the Bass, which lay on Quality Street on the site of the Dalrymple Arms Hotel (1926–7, 57–8). He alternatively proposed:

> The hospital would be erected close to the harbour, and the most probable site was that now occupied by the granaries on the east side of the roadway … [this position] would be the best for all purposes. It adjoins the church and is the place where the pilgrims would embark or land on their journey to and from St Andrews.

Given what is now known of the early topography of Kirk Ness this would seem to have been the most favourable site for such a structure. Until land reclamation began *c.*1860, the area immediately beyond the granary to the north-east constituted a rocky foreshore inlet bounded by whinstone ridges, and most, if not all of the land on the western side of Victoria Terrace was successively reclaimed in the 18th and 19th centuries. Thus the existing granary site was formerly far more constrained, and perhaps the only suitable plot for such a hospital building – at the head of the road from the town, close to the church and adjacent to a localised area of non-cemetery land, possibly even partly cultivable, at the northern part of what is now Anchor Green. As Swan notes the most obvious advantage of this site is the immediate proximity to the early harbour – the embarkation point for travellers and pilgrims to Fife (and, evidently, the Isle of May and the Bass Rock). The harbour itself is clearly of ancient origin; as noted by Angus Graham (1968–9, 257–8):

> 'Ports' at each end of the pilgrims' ferry to Fife are mentioned in a charter of 1177, travellers were crossing to Earlsferry in 1304, commercial use is referred to in 1373, North Berwick being by that time a free port, and a novodamus charter of 1658 implies that a 'haven' had existed in an indefinitely distant past.

Fig. 4.79: Tunnel excavation area: plan showing the 1069 cobbled path and associated bedding, 1093

That an earlier building had existed at this point is suggested most forcefully by the visual evidence of Sandby (*c*.1750) and Hutton (*c*.1782), both taken before the erection of the present granary in about 1800, already discussed (Figures 4.7 and 4.8 above). The former image is particularly intriguing if it does indeed show part of the upper storey of the hospital building; here the pair of rounded arched openings and, possibly, engaged shafts between, may indicate a building of Romanesque character. The variegated rubble of the granary building itself contains occasional reused blocks of pale sandstone that can be matched to freestone types seen in the church ruin or as reused at St Andrew's Kirk Ports. Whether this material is recycled from the church ruin or the hospital or was brought in anew cannot now be determined.

It is possible that the existing granary superstructure structure incorporates *in situ* sections of earlier walling – a particular possibility may be the buried lower parts of the rear (east) wall where it backs onto Anchor Green, though this is now wholly inaccessible without invasive investigation. The lower parts of the southern gable wall also appear to be of a different build but too little can be seen to suggest with certainty that this even represents part of a pre-existing structure. A recent archaeological evaluation associated with the structure failed to identify any archaeologically significant remains (Dingwall 2009, 7).

If the hospice did occupy this site the immediate topography may have been significant. A structure here would likely have had to back onto the whinstone ridge that runs beneath this part of the site; perhaps the upper level of the structure (assuming it to have been of more than one storey) was directly accessible from what is now Anchor Green, and the lower level from the harbour side.

Domestic occupation at Anchor Green – evidence from the tunnel excavation

Within the area of the tunnel excavation were recorded various remains of medieval date that were clearly not directly related to the use of St Andrew's church and its associated cemetery. By contrast these seemed to suggest occupation of a domestic nature. The levels formed a discrete group that was datable, primarily on the basis of ceramics present, to between the later 12th and the 14th centuries. It was possible to further sub-divide the group on stratigraphic grounds into three separate sub-phases. Again this was not inconsistent with the limited ceramics evidence. Where not impacted by later intrusions the deposits extended across almost all of the trench area and had been cleanly sealed by an overlying build-up, with little evidence to suggest a continuation of occupation in this area thereafter.

Fig. 4.80: The cobbled path, 1069, as revealed, looking east (2m scales)

Site preparation

It would seem that most of the tunnel excavation area (and most likely extending well beyond the sections) was carefully terraced, this process apparently involving the removal of turf or overburden and then levelling off of the upper parts of the underlying soil, level *1097*. Doubtless some stratigraphy was removed during this truncation; for this reason it was not wholly clear to which period a number of features cut into the *1097* soil make-up belong – particularly the post-hole groups (*1217, 1243, 1244, 1246, 1257, 1258*) to the south-west and (*1269, 1272, 1275*) in the central part of the trench, described in the preceding chapter (see Figure 3.22). Certainly some such features on the eastern edge of the site more probably related to the medieval period. These include an apparent infilling of an irregular shallow depression or cut, *1224*, with deposits *1225* and *1238*, perhaps representing a deliberate localised levelling-up operation. From *1225* was recovered a rim shard of a Scottish White Gritty Ware cooking pot of 12th–13th century date. Two well-formed circular post-holes had then been cut, *1231* and *1222*, the latter impacting the *1225* deposit. A solitary circular post-pit of similar character was revealed close to the south section considerably further to the west, *1215*. This had itself been cut through part of the fill of a shallow depression *1208*, the fill composed of degraded crushed mortar residues *1209*; the latter might more commonly suggest a medieval date.

However, as discussed in the preceding chapter, these may also have been associated with the south-western post-hole group – *1217, 1243*, etc. While the three post-holes just described are of similar character and possibly elements of the same structure too little remained to suggest anything of its nature. The levelling exercise seems to have corresponded to the laying of a cobbled path, *1069*, and associated surfacing levels.

Cobbled path (1069)

In the middle-western part of the trench area there survived the partial remains of a comparatively well laid cobbled path, *1069* (Figure 4.79). This was formed from grey whin cobbles and coarse, flat whin slabs with a few individual pieces of red friable sandstone (Figure 4.80). Where they survived the edges of the feature are defined by cobbles that were much more deeply set. The line of the western edge was relatively well preserved and a few edge cobbles indicated the former extent of the feature on its eastern side. The path line ran from north-east to south-west, curving increasingly to the west. The remains of a possible branch extended for a short distance from the centre of the south-east side. Overall the path measured 1.1–1.3m in width.

These *1069* cobbles were found to have been bedded upon a well defined deposit of clean, coarse shell sand 0.10–0.15m thick, *1093* (Figure 4.81). Where the cobbles had been robbed their impressions could still be seen in

Fig. 4.81: View looking ENE showing the 1093 sand bedding for the 1069 path following removal of cobbles (2m scales)

some areas. *1093* was devoid of diagnostic finds.

To the west of this path line was a spread of a rubbly deposit/rough metalling, *1207*, formed from small angular stones within a soil matrix. These extended to the west side of the site area where they were cut through by the *1040* construction cut for the 19th century walled compound. A continuation of the *1207* rough cobbling was encountered underlying parts of the *1069* cobbling/*1093* sand deposit – *1239/1240*. This was similar to *1207* further west, but bedded in shell sand rather than soil and thus apparently part of the bottoming for the *1069* surface. A whetstone (SF95) was recovered from *1239*.

Prepared surface (1091, 1092, 1080)

An apparently prepared surface was recorded across most of the trench area – *1091/1092(1178)/1080* (Figures 4.82 and 4.83). This directly overlay the *1069/1207* paving and the underlying *1097(1210)* deposits. Stonier clay bottoming deposits were noted to the east of the site, *1211* and *1212*, overlying the *1097* soil.

An upper lens upon the surface, recorded particularly to the west, consisted of a thin mortar spread, *1091*, that perhaps represented bedding for a subsequently robbed paving, possibly of flagstones. However, this was fairly patchy and no clearly defined edges were identified.

Mortar spread *1091* was in turn bedded onto a hard, compacted clay-rich deposit that ranged in thickness between 0.03m and 0.1m, *1092*; this level was recorded as *1080* towards the eastern side of the site. A north–south aligned 'boundary' between the two marked the point where there was a distinct change in surface character, the surface of *1092* being somewhat stonier. *1080* was slightly sunken – or had become sunken, apparently settling into the natural hollow beneath this area or slumping somewhat towards the edge of the rock scarp to the east. Indeed to the east the deposit terminated abruptly where evidently eroded (cut – *1183*).

The excavations failed to locate structural features, such as post-holes, that might have provided better definition. With its apparently well-prepared, level clay surface it was thought at the time of excavation possibly to have formed an interior floor. The abrupt change in surfacing character between *1080* and *1092*, was clearly not incidental although it was unclear whether one or both represented interior space or external. In comparison the *1092* deposit was stonier than *1080*, containing a high percentage of sandstone fragments; this in turn suggested perhaps an exterior metalled surface – a yard? However, along the junction no obvious dividing wall structure was noted. With a lack of defining edges or associated evidence for an upstanding structure it was hard to interpret these remains.

Again these levels were notably devoid of associated diagnostic artefactual material. The solitary exceptions were two body shards from a green-glazed white gritty jug (?York glazed ware) from *1092*, and a further unglazed white gritty body shard recovered from within the matrix of *1092(1178)*. Their relationship to the immediately underlying features perhaps suggests that these levels are of medieval date.

Hiatus – a windblown sand event

Part of the considerable interest of these structural remains within the tunnel excavation area is that there was no evidence of later pottery types, finds, etc., for any form of continuing occupation in the later medieval period. Indeed the medieval occupation layers and surfacing within the tunnel excavation area were directly overlain and sealed by a substantial build-up of largely clean deposits of fine-grained pale yellow, evidently windblown sand (*1091, 1079, 1078* and *1074*, the latter two of about 0.15m in depth). Evidence for all later cultural activity within the trench area either overlay this sand deposit or cut down into or through it.

Historical documents record several catastrophic wind-blow events literally deserting Kirk Ness in the 18th century, see Chapter 5. Such events certainly occurred earlier more generally in North Berwick, evidence for a number of sand blows having been revealed in varied archaeological investigations in the burgh. At Dalrymple Garage on Quality Street, for example, 'thin

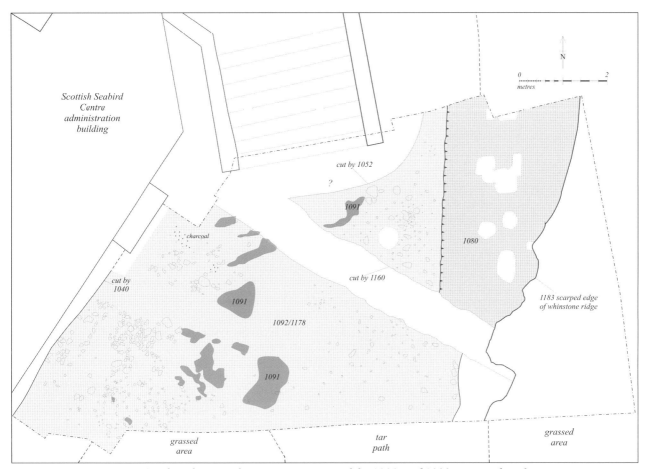

Fig. 4.82: Plan showing the surviving extent of the 1080 and 1092 prepared surfaces

Fig. 4.83: The 1080/1092 surface, fully excavated; parts of the underlying 1069 cobbled path can be seen towards the rear of the trench; looking W (2m scales)

bands of midden and windblown sand containing 12th–13th-century pottery' were recovered from excavations by SUAT (*cf* Dingwall 2009 for details of general stratigraphy throughout the burgh).

Pottery

Of the 11 shards of medieval pottery recovered from the tunnel excavation area most were residual and recovered from later deposits (see Appendix D on CD – contexts *1029*, *1063*, *1072*, *1092*, *1097/1210*, *1147*, *1161*, *1162*, *1178* and *1204*). Overall the majority were of white gritty fabric, and most of these from the Scottish White Gritty Ware tradition and generally datable to the 13th–14th centuries. One shard was comparable to wares recovered from Kelso Abbey (perhaps 12th century), and another was a rim shard from a cooking pot (12th–13th century). Imports included body shards possibly from a York glazed ware jug (late 12th–mid-13th century) and a fragment of high-fired white earthenware deep-dipped in a green lead glaze, this French, possibly from Beauvais.

Overview and interpretation

In stark contrast to areas of Anchor Green excavated further south, which relate to the church and cemetery, the medieval remains in the tunnel excavation area seem to be associated with domestic occupation. The limited bone assemblage from these deposits was notable for the total absence of human remains, even pieces of loose charnel (by contrast charnel was evident at higher level within deposits of much more recent date within material that was evidently brought in from the cemetery area). This absence of graveyard material strongly suggests that the northern part of Anchor Green lay within a zone outwith the cemetery perimeter, which had perhaps been defined by a formal boundary feature.

The excluded land area may have been of sufficient extent to support domestic occupation, the obvious context for which would be ancillary activities associated with the historically attested hospice that had likely existed immediately adjacent to the south-west – perhaps kitchens, sheds, yards, etc, and even cultivated plots, peripheral to the main structure(s). The purpose of the cobble path, where it led to and where from, was not determined, but its south-western extent may have formerly continued to the area presumed to be the site of the hospice.

In conclusion, historic references indicate the presence of a hospice, founded in 1154 by Duncan, 4th Earl of Fife for poor people and pilgrims, and thereafter granted by Duncan, 5th Earl, to the nuns of North Berwick, in 1177. Subsequently confirmed by Malcolm of Fife in 1199 and by William I in *c*.1213, there is no mention, thereafter (Cowan and Easson 1976, 186). It has been assumed that the hospice continued in use for some centuries as the pilgrim trade to Fife and St Andrews continued up to the time of the Scottish Reformation. A further possibility, in explanation of the domestic activity present at the north end of the site, might be a priest's house associated with the church. Although there is no historic reference to such specific to Kirk Ness, a vicarage existed in 1274. In *c*.1360 it was annexed to the nunnery, with whom all fruits continued, the parish being served by a vicar pensioner (Cowan 1967, 157: GRH. Papal Bull, no. 23. Assumptions, 154–5: thirds of Benefices, 89; RSS, iii. No. 2486).

The occupational activity at the north end of Anchor Green seems to have been curtailed, possibly as a direct result of a major windblown sand event. The limited pottery from this group of levels, four unabraded shards, and residual material from other levels, is all of the white gritty tradition (12th–14th centuries) and thus of appropriate period to the known documentation for the hospice.

5. Kirk Ness – Later History

Nicholas Uglow, Thomas Addyman and Alasdair Ross

Introduction

There is little archaeological evidence on the Kirk Ness site for major activity after the abandonment of the church in the mid-17th century. It is the documentary record that illuminates the history of the wider site between that time and the mid-20th century when J. S. Richardson undertook his excavation. In this period of about three centuries Anchor Green and the adjacent areas changed their use from ecclesiastical, and continuing burial activity, through minor industry, to tourism by the end of the 19th century. The erosion of the shoreline by the sea, which had caused the destruction of the old kirk in the mid-17th century, continued, and was exacerbated by open quarrying of bedrock on the foreshore. By the mid-19th century, the erosion was such that Sir Hew Dalrymple, affirming his ownership of the site, built a new sea wall, perhaps concerned that the promontory, with its valuable harbour and buildings associated with trade and fishing, might eventually be cut off from the mainland.

However, it was not the development of the harbour and the progress of industry that affected the area of the Kirk Green most in the 19th century, but rather the rise of the tourist industry. From the mid-19th century, North Berwick became increasingly popular as a seaside resort, initially as an exclusive and undiscovered aristocratic haven, then, with the rise of middle class holidaymaking, made possible by the advent of the railways, a populous seaside resort. At the beginning of the century though, North Berwick had neither butcher nor post office. The situation was little improved when the Prince of Wales visited in 1859. However, when he visited again in 1902, as King Edward VII, the town was utterly transformed into a well-developed seaside resort, visited by both the wealthy and the middle classes. This rapid change in fortune is typical of the rise of many British and continental seaside towns in the period. Responding to this burgeoning tourist industry, various improvements were made to the Kirk Green and Kirk Ness areas by the burgh council, including the virtual banishing of industry and the build-ing of the public swimming pool. By 1900, the town's economy was almost entirely based on seasonal tourism and, unsurprisingly, was seriously affected by the advent of the First World War. Subsequently, efforts were made by the burgh council in the 1920s and 1930s to recapture the town's pre-war popularity, including improvements to the swimming pool and a permanent entertainment building, the Harbour Pavilion.

Many of the surviving North Berwick records, both burgh and family, have been successively investigated by local antiquarians and historians. Yet, reading the secondary literature it is clear that, in fact, many of these authors have been dependent upon each other as sources. The notable exception to this is *The North Berwick story* written by the Rev. Walter Ferrier (1980 and 1991), the local parish minister. It is obvious from his writing that he undertook extensive original research although it is unfortunate that he chose not to reference his sources. This makes tracing his research difficult and it is impossible to be sure precisely where he found his material.

The demise of the old kirk

It is clear from the material assembled by Ferrier and other works, that a chronology for the 'old kirk' structure can be established. It seems clear that the site of the old kirk was originally an islet that was connected to the mainland by a causeway consisting of an arched bridge (Ferrier 1881). The Kirk Sessions Records within which this information was originally found during the 19th century were thought to have since been either destroyed or lost; Ferrier, for example, was unable to trace them for his 1980 publication. This means that the original readings of these books in the 19th century have been greatly relied upon in the various subsequent accounts, but confidence in them may not be entirely justified (Ross 2006). However, a number of the early church records were identified in the National Archives of Scotland (CH2/285/1-/2), including manuscript entries copied from early minutes, now lost. Other minutes are to be found in the Old Parish Registers from 1604–1615

(OPR 727/1). Excerpts from these records have recently been transcribed by Joy Dodd.

The Kirk Session Minutes contain a number of entries relating to the later days and ultimate demise of the church. An entry of 10 February 1612 demonstrates the structure needed repair: 'The session thought good that Mr Thomas [the Minister, Thomas Bannatyne] sould speak the noble and gentleman of the parochin for a contribution to repair the kirk. Too mend the glass windows, to floor the kirk …'. The Haddington Presbytery Records (NAS CH2/185/6/51-3) record a visitation to North Berwick in July 1648, evidently in response to local concerns, during which it was reported that 'The fabric of the kirk is nothing found defective. The motione concerning changing the burial place is remitted till it please God to sett a minister ther'. However, the Kirk Session records demonstrate that an alternative site was already being sought. An entry of 10 October 1652 states: 'The Session seeing the paroch should be disappointed of ane convenient house for preaching and hearing of the word ordained some of ther number to see and take notice what timber will make Sir William Dick's house useful to that effect & report ther diligence the nixt day'. And for 15 May 1653: 'The sd day the session with the heritors present ordained ane hundredth merks to be caston upon the whole heritors for repairing the house where sermon is herd'.

Subsequent entries suggest some vacillation between the need to repair the old building and the desire to find a new site:

Julii 10 1655

[The heritors present with the session] did resolve that the old Kirke should be repaired & a convenience should be thought upon of going out & coming in to the same.

Oct 20 1656

This day the Minister & elders considering that the heritors have submitted the designation of a plan of where a new Kirke may be built & a burial place thairto in regaird that the old Kirke is altogether ruinous & that the place where it was formerly situate is altogether very incommodious / unto Mr Robert Kerr Minister of Hading: John Macghie Minister of Dirlton & Andw Macghie Minister of Aberlady or any tuo of them providing the quantitie of ground to be designed exceed not the full measure of ane aiker & halfe of land doe heartily approve therof & declare that they are most willing & desirous that the said ministers or nay tuo of them proceed in the said matter & that they will not only stand & abide at but likewise in whatsoever shall be competent to them further & promote their decreat & determine action in that business.

April 12 1657

This day a warrant was read from the Council of State for the receat of ane 100 lib sterling for the helping to build ane new Kirke whereupon the Session appointed a meeting of the heritors.

Mai 19 1657

Ane estimation of rebuilding the old church 160 lib ster: wood & slating

For keiping the church & making a way into it from the land through the high water 200 lib.

For building ane new church the stone carriage excepted as likewise lime & sand churchyard dikes & place 460 lib.

July 5 1657

Given for ane tree holding up the loft 28 sh & to George Henderson for his workmanship 12sh.

In any event this information implies that a large part of the site upon which the 'old kirk' was situated was lost through coastal erosion before 23 October 1656 when both the causeway linking the islet to the mainland and a large part of the cemetery to the east of the 'old kirk' were washed away during a storm. Thereafter, the local heritors decided to build a new parish church in the burgh well away from the coastline, after deciding that the cost of refurbishing both the islet and the causeway would be too expensive. The final decision regarding the fate of the old kirk is recorded in an entry for 8 July 1657:

This day the heritors after they had seriously considered & reviewed the place where the old Kirke was situate & how small difference ther would be in the mater of expense betwixt the fortifying of the samen against the violence of the sea & building of passages thairto together with the putting on of a new roofe upon the said old Kirke & the building of a new one in a more convenient place besides the great danger of that the said fortifications & passages if they are built might again be demolished by a new storme & so the Old Kirke made useless if they should rebuild the same & having considered several places in & about the bound which were spoken of as for building of a new kirke in did adhere to the designation made by the Ministers to whom the business was formally submitted & conclude that a ther was a necessitie of a new Kirke & burial place thairto, so the ground designed by them was most convenient for that use.

And on 30 March 1658 it is recorded that:

The heritors with the elders think fitt that the new Kirk should be built in the form of ane capital & which is the form quhairin the new Kirk of Glads-muir in now beginning to be built the body therof lying east to west to be of 70 or 80 feet within the walls & 22 foot in breed with four doors & compet-ent windows.

As noted in the previous chapter, the mason Matthew Wilson was employed to extract building materials from the old church site for the building of the new. The new building was ready for use by 1664 when, on 5 June of that year the Session Book briefly records: 'This day the paroch mett for worship in ye new kirke'.

Continuing coastal erosion

Because the earlier burgh council records have been des-troyed it is impossible to contextualise the autumnal 1656 storm and decide whether the 'old kirk' had previ-ously been subjected to similar extreme weather events. All that really can be said is that the fabric of the old kirk and the surrounding land were damaged by other violent storm events post-1656 so such occurrences do not seem to have been unusual at this site.

The Reverend Ferrier discovered that, even after the abandonment of the medieval kirk and cemetery, local families continued to bury bodies there, even as late as the 1830s, presumably because they had either purchased or reserved lairs at the site, even though it was recog-nised that such burials might easily be quickly uncovered again by erosion. On 7 January 1672 (Ferrier 1881, 51) the Kirk Session had resolved: 'that who should after the dait of this presents burie in the old kirke yeard should pay 20s Scots for sand and faill [turf] least the coffin should againe be discovered by winde and weather'.

Further evidence of continuing active erosion at the site is found in a reference to a particularly violent storm in 1727, which was notable because it forced the burgh council to go and visit the site of the old kirk to view the damage. Unfortunately, the council records do not go in-to detail but they do record that a total of £9 was paid to labourers to 'gather all the stones between the church and the town wall together' (NAS, B56/9/1; Gibson and Smout 1995). It is difficult to decide what is meant by this reference but it could refer to grave slabs and other such markers. This interpretation is also useful because it might explain why a mid-19th century report from 1857, claims that there were no grave markers of any kind to be found at the 'old kirk', the last having re-cently either been shifted or lost (NAS, B56/7/7/256). If this scenario is correct, it is to be regretted that the burgh council records do not state what happened to the 'stones' that were gathered together in 1727. A further storm must have occurred in 1737 when it was noted that the harbour required extensive repairs (NAS, B56/7/1/61).

It is also interesting to note that the 1857 report also refers to an unspecified number of storms that regularly resulted in erosion of the old kirk site, even if it is not specific about the dates of those storms. This lack of dat-ing evidence might cast doubt on the veracity of this claim and it should be noted that this report was prepared by an advocate, Mr Penny, working for the burgh council who were trying to establish their ownership of the site over the claims of the baron of North Berwick, Sir Hugh Dalrymple (NAS, B56/7/7/256). Therefore, despite the recorded references to storms in 1656, 1727 and 1737, the advocate could have been exaggerating the severity and regularity of the storms that affected the site to make the case for taking it into council ownership more imme-diately compelling. The final record relating to violent storms and erosion in this period before 1870 dates to 1852 when it was recorded that the harbour area had been damaged by a 'great storm'(NAS, B56/7/7).

The impact of quarrying on the foreshore

In general environmental history terms, such extreme weather events and associated erosion are not unknown along the East Lothian coast. However, it must be ques-tioned whether there could be a causal link between the development of North Berwick harbour and the erosion of the site of the old kirk. It is known, for example, that stone from North Berwick was regularly quarried during the later medieval period. In 1531–2 a baker called Walter Scot received a payment for 19 North Berwick stones that were to be used in flooring a new oven at Holyrood, cost-ing 32s each. Thirteen of the same kind of oven floor stones, this time at a total cost of £13, were required again for an oven at Holyrood in 1622–3, five in 1639–40 at a total cost of £9, and 18 were required to repair an oven in Edinburgh Castle in 1649 at a total cost of £46 (Paton 1957, lii and 71; Imrie and Dunbar 1982, 147, 390–1, 447). The stone in question was a deep pink-red volcanic tufa known *leck-stone*, or 'red leck,' derived from The Lecks, an outcropping upon the foreshore of Milsey Bay, immediately to the east of Kirk Ness. The value of the stone was that it was porous and thus absorbed the mois-ture from the bread; it also split readily into slabs. The North Berwick burgh court books contain considerable information about the rental of The Lecks, where the right to quarry the stone was let out to the highest bidder, a valuable source of income for the burgh (Joy Dodd *pers. comm.*; NAS B56). The stone was still favoured for the provision of hearth stones into the 19th century.

Perhaps more problematically, within 12 years of the damage to the harbour in 1656, the Privy Council gave permission for a voluntary contribution to be made from all parish churches south of the Forth so that North Ber-wick harbour might be repaired and made secure from the elements (NAS, B56/16/23). By 1700 the interior of the harbour had been dynamited at least once and was regularly quarried to remove both stone and mud over the next 160 years (NAS, B56/7/1/49; B56/9/1). The cumulative effects of these activities, particularly dynamiting, close to the old kirk ruin may well have had a lasting impact on its stability.

Perhaps something of these effects can be seen on the early sketch of the old kirk, by Grose (see Chapter 4). This sketch also matches a brief description of the church made in 1760 by Kemp (1887, 319). In Grose's view, the proximity of the harbour to the church can be seen in the background and there seems to be clear evidence that a bulwark had already been constructed on the right-hand side of the islet, probably as a defence against tidal activity. This drawing shows a building that is already in an advanced state of decay with only the porch and the base of a barrel-vaulted west nave tower surviving. The layout seems fairly accurate when compared against later 19th and 20th century plans and reconstructions of the same building.

It is perhaps unlikely that these ruins had reached such an advanced state of decay in only 120 years without human interference. Ferrier (1980, 59–60) suggests that the natives of North Berwick may have removed stone from the site for re-use elsewhere in the burgh. Some support for this theory can be found in the burgh records which regularly refer to carts of 'old stone' being taken away from that general area for re-use in new buildings in the burgh (NAS, B56/9/1). It has also been recorded that fragments of masonry from the graveyard were built into the swimming pool wall, not begun until 1900 (Macfadyen 2004b, 45).

It is also important to realise that just because this site contained a ruined medieval church does not mean that it was completely abandoned after 1658. In fact, the site seems to have been rented out for various industrial uses from the 1690s. Legal documents from a case in 1857, concerning the ownership of the Kirk Green area, discussed forthwith, list the buildings and the activities around the ruins of the old kirk since the 1690s, when the Dalrymple family had become barons of North Berwick. The first point to note is that previous holders of the barony of North Berwick, the Dicks of Lauder, had mortgaged the barony, specifically including the old kirk, to an Edinburgh merchant burgess, Robert Lockhart, on 12 November 1646 for 46,000 merks Scots (NAS, GD110/59). Within five years Lockhart had received infeftment of the barony but was then unable to persuade his tenants in North Berwick to pay their rents and dues to him and he obtained a summons against them. This does not seem to have improved the situation to any extent because, shortly after, Lockhart sold both the mortgage and title of baron of North Berwick to Sir Thomas Stewart of Kirkfield, on 5 March 1656. This family then held the title and the accompanying mortgage until 24 November 1696 when they were purchased by Sir Hew Dalrymple, President of the Court of Session (NAS, GD110/59). Dalrymple must then have proceeded to pay off the 46,000 merk mortgage, and presumably compensate the

Stewart family, as he was granted the free barony of North Berwick on 12 April 1707 (NAS, B56/13/4/38).

Later archaeological remains at the north end of Anchor Green

It was principally within the tunnel excavation area that archaeological evidence for episodes of later activity was revealed, although these seem to have been comparatively minor in nature.

Retaining wall (1086) and associated deposits

Within the excavated area the ground surface has been artificially made up from a pre-existing base level at a depth of 0.7m below the modern surface (below which existed the deposits of wind-blown sand, described in the previous chapter). This make-up consisted of substantial successive dumps of sands and rubble stone generally devoid of datable artefacts (*1066, 1067, 1068, 1087, 1090* and *1098*), overall lying to a depth of some 0.5–0.6m. These deposits were retained along the western part of the north side of the trench area by a revetment or low retaining wall of unworked, unbonded blocks of friable red sandstone, *1086* (Figures 5.1 and 5.2). The surviving parts of this revetment formed an 'L-shaped' construction surviving to a maximum height of 0.3m (two courses). The principal east–west aligned section extended from the west section for a distance of 4.8m before returning to the north on the line of the east side of the existing concrete stair (*1047*) that leads down to the lower level esplanade to the north. The revetment continued north under the stair wall beyond the limit of excavation. The north face of the main east–west section of walling lay 1.4m south of the northern trench edge (the top of the steps); parts of this stretch of the retaining wall had been impacted by later cuts (*1052*, a pipe trench, and *1160*, relating to construction activity, discussed below). Where better preserved the feature survived to a height of two courses, a maximum of 0.3m. The base of the feature directly overlay the much earlier prepared surface of medieval date described previously, *1091/1092*.

Though of probable post-medieval date, the more precise dating and function of this combined feature remained unclear: whether it was just a short revetment required when levelling up the ground behind (with a path to the north?), or perhaps a building platform, or even representing the lower remains of a more substantial structure above. However, the rear side of these facing stones was very roughly formed and, given the narrowness of the feature, at 0.30m, and the unbonded construction, it is unlikely to have formed little more than a low revetment defining a levelled upper area. Areas of associated collapsed rubble at the foot of the wall, *1173*, suggest that the upper parts of the structure had been reduced and the stone reused.

Fig. 5.1: Plan of post-medieval features of undetermined date within the tunnel excavation area

Fig. 5.2: General site photograph showing the retaining feature, 1086, lower right (this is cut by the later barrow-run, 1160, seen between the poles); looking S

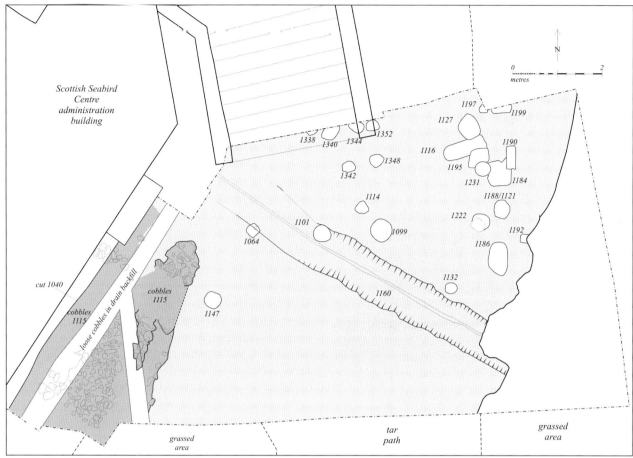

Fig. 5.3: Plan of major 19th century features within the tunnel excavation area

The surviving facing stones showed evidence of burning (blackening on their exposed side), and the *1092* surface extending to the north in front of the feature had similarly been heat-affected, with obvious burning and reddening that was most pronounced further to the east, *1179*.

Later constructional activity

The west side of the bedrock ridge running through the site area had been cut to a vertical face (cut *1040*) at the beginning of the early 19th century in order to allow the construction of a part-roofed walled enclosure at the lower level to the west (see following section). This enclosure first appears on the Great Reform Act town plan of 1832, and is shown in detail on the Ordnance Survey plan of 1893 (Figure 1.2, above) and later revisions, and in contemporary photographs (Figure 5.6, below, and Ferrier 1980, opp. p. 73). It consisted of a series of small yards and sheds intended for the storage of coal delivered by boat to the adjacent harbour, and perhaps also for fishing gear and other materials. Its walls, constructed of lime-bonded whinstone rubble, were in part incorporated into the structure of the existing Scottish Seabird Centre administration building – at cellar level the east wall and much of the westwards return at its north end still remain for much of their original height.

Following construction of the compound the *1040* construction cut was backfilled and the area of land on its east side at the north end of Anchor Green further infilled and made-up. In the north-west sector of the tunnel excavation area the lower-lying ground on the north side of the *1086* retaining wall was filled with a substantial series of dumps of sand and other material, including building debris, the latter likely relating to the construction of the compound (*1176*, *1156* and *1149*). Following the construction of the compound wall a cobble-sett surface was formed long its east side, extending out from it for about 2.5m, *1115* (Figure 5.3).

A major linear cut feature was also revealed running across the tunnel excavation area from close to its north-west corner to the east-south-east, towards the edge of the eastern edge of the bedrock ridge, *1160*. Measuring about 1.0m in width its upper extent had been truncated, its stratigraphic relationships lost, and the lower parts of this feature only remained to a depth of 0.3m. The cut had a flat, compacted base and steep, slightly inwards-sloping sides. It had apparently been formed as a barrow-run as a clearly defined wheel rut ran along the centre of its base; this rut displayed multiple passes of the barrow, the impression of the wheel indicating a flattened rim of about 0.06m in width (Figures 5.3 and 5.4). It was unclear from the excavated evidence in which direction the dumping occurred, or to which other activity on site

Fig. 5.4: The part-excavated barrow-run, 1160, looking NW

it might relate. Some spoil (*1162*) was dumped at the east end of the run (? the last few barrow loads before the cut was backfilled). This spoil was a mixed deposit of dark brown black soils within which was recovered a large unabraded fragment of a white gritty pottery. This find had evidently originated within excavations elsewhere on site.

The *1160* cut had been rapidly backfilled with spoil (*1161*) perhaps the same as removed during its original excavation and thus redeposited roughly from where it had originated – had the spoil from the cut been piled at the side of the trench? There was no obvious build-up of soil or rubbish in the base of the cut suggesting that the whole had been a rapidly undertaken operation.

Other truncated features cut down from above (mid–late 19th century)

A number of features, principally post-pits, were recorded that were truncated during ground preparations relating to the formation of the existing paths and staircase in the mid-20th century (cut/construction surface *1055*). They include a sequence of post-holes along the northern edge of the site area (*1340, 1342, 1344, 1348* and *1352*), a further series of post-holes along the eastern side of the ridge of bedrock (*1127, 1186, 1184, 1188, 1190, 1192, 1195, 1197* and *1199*), and three post-holes seemingly in alignment running east-west across the site

(*1099, 1101,* and *1064*). Each group represents successive boundary fence lines, alignments that appear on the Ordnance Survey maps of 1893 and 1906, and in early photographs of the site (such as Figure 5.6, and Ferrier 1980, opp. p. 73).

A small and decayed burgh?

By the 18th century, North Berwick was a small fishing port with a small export and import trade from its harbour. Graham (1968–9, 259) notes the early importance of the harbour, and comments on the extensive structural work done following several hard storms in the late 18th and early 19th centuries. However, by the early 19th century, the principal attraction for visitors was golf. Initially, local aristocracy and gentry gathered parties who drove from their estates to play for the day. A golf club was formally established in 1832, one member having served with distinction at the battle of Waterloo (Adamson 1980, 7). The environs of the town were also naturally attractive, with North Berwick Law and the Bass Rock, and various sites of antiquarian interest. It seems, however, that the popularity of the golf club was the key factor in changing the fortunes of the town.

In 1832, the Great Reform Act report describes North Berwick in the same year as the golf club was founded as a 'small and decayed Burgh, with little of or no Trade' (House of Commons 1832, 105). The burgh boundary plan that accompanied the report does not provide much enlightenment for the Kirk Ness area. It does not show the old kirk remains or the shoreline with any accuracy, and shows only a few buildings adjacent to the harbour. However, *The New Statistical Account of Scotland* describes a different situation altogether, North Berwick's chapter being completed in 1839. In the section dedicated to climate, it comments that 'the geniality of the summer and autumn is amply attested in the crowded influx of strangers for the enjoyment of sea-bathing and perambulation among the beautiful scenery around', and that there was a constant stream of boats touring the Bass Rock (*NSA* 1845, 318). It also mentions the prospect of the western links being feued for development of villas, 'a scheme which promises to be an essential improvement' (*NSA* 1845, 318). The change in the way the town is described, from the terse dismissal of the Great Reform Act, to the optimistic tone of the *NSA* suggests that in the 1830s, North Berwick was expanding and improving. It is in this context that the ownership of the old kirk site became an important issue for the burgh council.

A question of ownership and proprietorial improvements

In the 1850s, there was an important lawsuit concerning the old kirk site, whose ownership was disputed between the burgh council and Sir Hew Dalrymple Bt. It appears

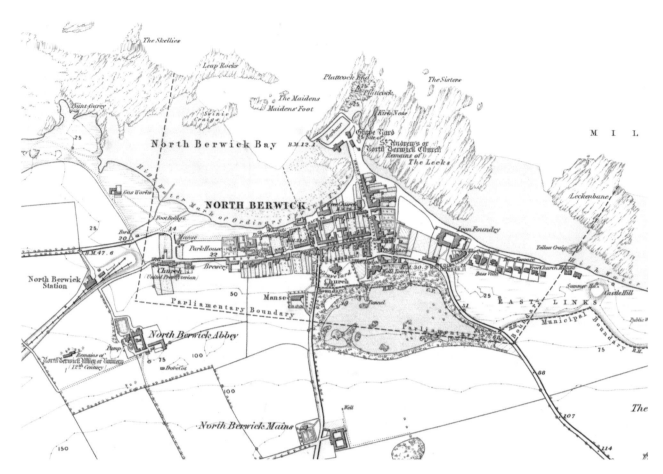

Fig. 5.5: First Edition Ordnance Survey map, surveyed in 1853, and published in 1854. Detail from Haddingtonshire sheet II (reproduced by permission of the Trustees of the National Library of Scotland)

that it was *c*.1840 when the burgh council first inquired who possessed the title to the site: the burgh or the Dalrymple family. On this occasion they were informed by the Dalrymples that the site formed part of the barony of North Berwick and had belonged to their family for more than 100 years. More importantly, the Dalrymple family had exercised rights of ownership over the property by granting feus and the burgh council had never objected to these grants in the past (NAS, B56/15/4/58). The papers note that for 'some time' local fishermen had been using the ruins of the old kirk to dry their nets, bait hooks, and repair boats, and these fishermen may have held a rental of the property from Sir Hew to that effect. If they did, it has not survived. In fact, the first recorded feu of the old kirk granted by the Dalrymples is just before 1800, to Mr Robert Burn, a slater in the burgh. Either the same feu or another section of the old kirk site was subsequently granted to a Mr Lorimer who erected two buildings on the site, a malt granary and a coal store. At some point after 1802 permission was given to a Mr James Somerville to erect a second coal store on the same site. On this occasion the council backed down, to the advantage of Sir Hew. It is evidently the granary that is represented on Forrest's estate plan of 1804 (see Figure 4.6); the structure now functions as the premises of the East Lothian Yacht Club.

In 1845 Sir Hew proposed to erect a gas works on the site, to produce and store coal-gas to North Berwick for domestic lighting. Ferrier hints that the initial selection of the Kirk Green site for the gas works may have been connected to an early proposal for the route of the railway in the late 1840s. This was for the line to run through the town and terminate at the harbour, presumably to enable the delivery and collection of goods from boats (Ferrier 1980, 66). As the line would have run over the Kirk Green, this would also have enabled the easy delivery of coal to the gas works.

There are conflicting accounts as to whether the works began or not. Richardson records that works never began and plans were stopped by an intervention, possibly by the parish minister, Dr Graham (1907, 37). However, the archaeologist Dr James Richardson, in the Minutes of the burgh council in 1952, stated that the works did begin but were stopped because of 'encroachment on the graves' (Burgh Minutes, 14 May 1952). A new site was found, between what is now West Bay Road and Point Garry Road and it was not until 1860 that the gas works moved adjacent to the station (NAS, B56/7/7/256). On this occasion then as the gas works plan was defeated, Sir Hew's exercise of his control of the site failed. These two incidents were merely the opening salvos in the main legal dispute that was to last until at least the late 1860s.

At this juncture it is worth briefly examining the carto-graphic evidence of the first edition of the Ordnance Survey of 1853 (Figure 5.5). As this area was only sur-veyed at 6in to the mile, it is difficult to rely on the accuracy of some of the detail compared to the later revi-sion of the survey. The granary appears, as does an elongated range on its south side though in slightly differ-ing alignment – this was evidently a predecessor structure on the site of the existing Fishermen's Hall of 1883. A small polygonal enclosure marked in dotted outline on Anchor Green remains unexplained and does not appear on other maps; it may have been temporary in nature.

There is a measured *Plan of herring stances* from July 1862 in the National Archives of Scotland (RHP24766/1). This shows all the buildings on the east of the road in line, and includes the southerly buildings. However, it does not show more than the part of these buildings that bounded the road, as the whole area apparently belonging to Sir Hew is shaded grey with no structures marked at all. This plan will be examined forthwith in connection with the appearance of the boatyard.

The next incident in the legal dispute over the owner-ship of the land occurred in 1857. The burgh council asked an advocate to give a legal opinion about the own-ership of the old kirk site, clearly looking for suitable locations to build more seafront villas. This was prompt-ed by Sir Hew's actions in late 1856 to assert his ownership, by employing masons on a number of related old kirk projects, the most significant being the construc-tion of a new retaining wall, around 'a considerable part' of the old kirk site, and erecting a locked gate on a road-way that led through the kirk yard to the beach that local businesses had used to harvest and cart seaweed (NAS, B56/7/7/256). How this 1857 wall round the site related to the earlier 1727 wall is unknown. The council hoped that these developments would not cut the site off from the public, and render it unsuitable for people taking walks (NAS, B56/7/8/4), but by May 1868 this was cer-tainly resolved as the town treasurer approved the expenditure of 2s 6d for painting the public seats on the kirk green (NAS, B56/9/5).

It is clear from written accounts that building the re-taining wall against the eastern edge of the burial ground to the foreshore had become a necessity. Ross mentions that the old burial ground had been damaged several times by storms, and various sources mention that its contents was regularly scattered over the beach, no doubt the cause of increasing civic embarrassment. One of the most poetic accounts is in *The New Statistical Account* which comments:

> Year after year, in the violent north-east storms which are not unfrequent in winter and spring, the sea makes melancholy ravages on this scene of an-cient sepulture, and continues to disturb and discover many forms which for centuries have re-posed there (NSA 1845, 328).

It may have been the necessity of building this wall that enabled Sir Hew to enclose the rest of the site and assert his ownership. On this occasion in 1857, the advocate, Mr Penny, was of the view that the old kirk site belonged to the heritors of the parish and that Sir Hew Dalrymple's charter of barony did not actually include the site, but no agreement can have been reached between the two parties, because the situation arose again ten years later (NAS, B56/7/7/256).

In 1867 the council asserted its claims for ownership and took the provocative step of enclosing a parcel of ground at the back of the harbour near the old kirk. Sir Hew's agents immediately contested this development but volunteered to forego compensation if the council would agree to three conditions. First, if the town agreed not to erect any buildings of more than one storey or with chimneys on the site; second, that the sea was to be un-derstood as the northern boundary of the Melbourne Park housing development and the council conveyed all their rights or interests there to Sir Hew; and, finally, that the Mill Burn would be straightened in a mutually agreeable line (NAS, B56/7/8/263).

The burgh council quickly replied that it had no inten-tion of building houses with chimneys on the old kirk green, that the straightening of the Mill Burn was desir-able, but that the boundary of the Melbourne Park development was not negotiable (NAS, B56/7/8/264). However, it seems that this was just a negotiating posi-tion because by 5 November 1867 the burgh council and Sir Hew had reached agreement over the Mill Burn and Melbourne Park, but the Council now assumed that the piece of land they had illegally enclosed next to the old kirk now belonged to them (NAS, B56/7/8/280).

This dispute between Sir Hew and the Council contin-ued, and there is an archival trail that could be further explored. For the present purpose, it is only important to note that the Kirk Green area remained the property of Sir Hew and his descendants. The record of the enclosures and annexations of the Kirk Green site narrated above, provides valuable dating evidence for some of the features of the site. Changes to other parts of Kirk Ness continue the narrative of the site in the 19th century.

The boatyard

The history of the harbour at North Berwick, as discussed previously, certainly dates back to at least to the 12th cen-tury with the pilgrim ferry. However, according to Graham, none of the present harbour walling suggests a date earlier than the 18th century (Graham 1968–9, 258). Because of its exposed position, the harbour walls were often damaged by storms, and Graham lists repairs required in 1788, 1802 and 1811, though there were undoubtedly other incidents of damage previously and subsequently (*ibid.*). The violent 1811 storm required substantial repairs, and a report and works were commissioned from the engineers Messrs Robert Stevenson and Sons.

Fig. 5.6: Photograph taken c.1880, looking S from the Plattcock. It shows the boatyard, and beyond the higher ground level of the Kirk Green. The north gable of the porch is visible to the right of the flagpole, with its widened doorway. The sandy area in the foreground, and the rocky area to the right, were excavated for the swimming pool in 1899 (© East Lothian Museum Services. Licensor www.scran.ac.uk)

The harbour was improved in the early 1860s, by deepening to the level of the harbour mouth. A drawing from the burgh council in the National Archives of Scotland shows the works in a plan and several sections, and is by 'D. & T. Stevenson, Civil Engineers' (RHP 24754/1). Graham however notes that J. Young of Sunderland carried out the works (Graham 1968–9, 258). Perhaps responding to an increase in boat traffic in the harbour, and an expanding fishing fleet, a small boatyard was established in the area to the north-east of Sir Hew's enclosed land after the 1860s. The area the yard was to occupy appears on the first edition Ordnance Survey map of 1853, with the high water mark drawn on the strata of the bedrock, indicating a tidal inlet. The harbour deepening scheme of 1862 reclaimed this land from the tide, by filling it and another area to the north with the spoil from the harbour excavation. Stevenson's proposal drawing of February 1862 shows the protruding areas of bedrock, and notes a 'Spoil Bank' to the north east of Sir Hew's Kirk Green property (RHP 24754/1). Another drawing from July of the same year, previously referred to, is largely concerned with the layout of herring drying stances. It shows the same area following the completion of the excavation works, with Sir Hew's Kirk Green enclosure in outline (RHP 24766/1). The spoil heap has vanished and a larger flat area has been created, bounded by a north–south line, probably indicating a retaining wall against the sea.

It was on this area that the boatyard was built, probably in the later 1860s or 1870s. Its enclosure was accessed through a pair of gate piers aligned north–south, just north of the tip of the Kirk Green enclosure wall. Its odd shape and the orientation of the entrance are explained by the way it was tucked into the headland, and its necessary proximity to the harbour slipway. A stone building was erected in the eastern corner before the 1893 first revision of the Ordnance Survey, which presumably served as offices or stores. The yard appears in a photograph c.1880, with several boats pulled out of the harbour (Figure 5.6) and again in a later photograph reproduced in Ferrier (1980, 73), showing carts in the yard. It appears on the 1893 first revision of the Ordnance Survey, but vanished by the 1930s, with the building of the Harbour Pavilion. The solitary survivor is one of the circular stone gate piers.

The Rocket Patrol

It was also in the mid-19th century that a coastguard was established in North Berwick. At this time, the coastguard was responsible for both administration of customs and life saving, but was unconnected with the precursor of the Royal National Lifeboat Institution (RNLI). There are numerous newspaper accounts of ships being driven aground on rocks around North Berwick, and it must have been decided that a coastguard lookout station was needed. In the late 1850s, after the 1853 Ordnance Survey, the Coastguard station was built on the ground between Shore Road (Victoria Road) and the porch of the old kirk, this location being particularly good for spotting ships driven ashore in either the east or west bays. It appears, newly built and whitewashed, in Figure 5.6.

Ferrier (1980, 76) notes, 'The Rocket Brigade … used the south porch of the old church at the harbour to house their apparatus'. The Rocket Patrol was a team of men who manned a piece of equipment which used rockets to save people stranded on board ships that had run aground in stormy weather, liable to be destroyed by the sea. Methods had been pioneered from the early 19th century for saving lives where the use of boats was not possible. The method that had been perfected by the 1850s, required a life saving apparatus (LSA) to be taken as near as possible to the grounded vessel, so that rockets could be fired to it, carrying the end of a line of rope. The line was rigged with a pulley system and a *breeches bouy* – a life ring with a canvas seat – which could carry rescued sailors and passengers back to safety, one by one. The system was very effective and continued in use into the 20th century.

Following the 1854 Merchant Shipping Repeal Act, the Board of Trade was made responsible for supplying this equipment to coastguards, and by 1859 there was an LSA stationed in North Berwick when newspapers reported it was used in the attempted rescue of the crew of the schooner *Bubona* (*The Scotsman* reports misnamed the vessel the *Rabona*). It was the loss of life associated with the destruction of this vessel that also caused a lifeboat to be stationed in the town by 1860 (Richardson 1907, 34). The Board of Trade rocket apparatus was carried on a liveried cart, pulled by a single horse or the Rocket Patrol team themselves, which seem to have been supplied in two- and four-wheeled models, a few of which survive in regional museums. However, even the two-wheeled cart would have been too big to fit into the porch of the old kirk.

A fireplace was inserted into the north-west corner of the porch, which makes the storage of explosives or gunpowder in the structure unlikely (see Figure 4.27, above). It is also certain, as described in Chapter 4, that the entrance on the north side of the porch that formerly led into the kirk was widened at about the same time. The impressed maker's mark in the fireback – *BANK PARK . PYROPALITE WORKS . PRESTONPANS* – establishes that it dates from the middle to later decades of the 19th century (the factory works are shown on the first edition Ordnance Survey map of Haddingtonshire in the 1850s but they had disappeared by the time of the 1890s revision). The presence of a fireplace in an open-sided porch seems curious, and it is possible that the widened opening on the north side contained a timberwork infill. It is suggested that the porch was used as a lookout position for ships in distress, with the widened north opening partly glazed, to give a clear view to seaward for a Coastguard lookout.

The porch is shown in a postcard view from the 1880s, with an iron gate, and no evidence of occupation by the coastguard (Jamieson 1992, 15). However, it is probably in this decade that the LSA moved to a purpose-built garage, marked on the 1893 first revision of the Ordnance Survey, at 14 Melbourne Road. There is also a photograph showing the new four-wheeled vehicle with its brigade, presumably shortly after its arrival.

While the Rocket Brigade may not have used the old south porch 'to house their apparatus' the archaeological and historical evidence certainly suggests that the porch was adapted for use by the coastguard in the 1850s, possibly as a lookout station, a function that seems to have been relatively short-lived.

The Biarritz of the north

Between the 1830s and the 1880s, North Berwick was transformed from 'a small and decayed burgh' into an exclusive retreat for the wealthy and, increasingly, into a populous resort with an economy largely based on tourism. A particular catalyst for this change was the building by the North British Railway of a branch line from Drem in 1848 (Groome 1894, 151). Statham compares North Berwick to Gullane and comments that the tourist potential of both towns was about equal in the mid-19th century. However, Gullane had to wait until the 1880s for the railway, and in that time its population had stagnated in comparison to the rapid growth of North Berwick (Statham 2011, 133).

Statham comments that the railway line was built as an attempt by the North British Railway to secure a year-round passenger base of day-trippers and holidaymakers from Edinburgh (*ibid.*, 132). Initially, however, the branch line was something of a commercial failure, and by 1856 provision was downgraded from steam to a horse-drawn service (Ferrier 1980, 68). However, the visit of the Prince of Wales in 1859 by rail, presumably to play golf, seems to have been a turning point in the town's popularity, and it began to flood with visitors. Groome (1894, 151) lists the hotels, banks, post office, gas-works, water-works, and library, built since the 1860s, all evidence of a booming local economy.

When the same Prince of Wales visited North Berwick again, as King Edward VII, in 1902, the backwater he had visited in 1859 was completely changed. The town had become an established seaside resort of the aristocracy and middle classes. The King's hosts were his cousins, the holidaying Prince and Princess Edward of Saxe Weimar, and it was intended that he visit the Prime Minister, Arthur Balfour, at his country house at nearby Whittinghame (Ferrier 1980, 77). Statham (2011, 132) quotes a source of the following year, 1903, presumably a newspaper society column, which noted that playing on the West Links were: 'four MPs, the Speaker of the House of Commons, two bishops and the Prime Minister'. Later they were joined by Lord Kitchener. HMS *Dreadnought*, on passage to Rosyth, fired a ten-gun salute over the course.

By the end of the 19th century the increasingly wealthy middle class, following the fashions of the nobility as their leisure time and disposable income increased, and broadened the social diversity of tourism in North Berwick. Interestingly, this pattern of royalty visiting seaside resorts later populated by middle class holidaymakers, was mirrored in France, where the Empress Eugenie led the fashion for holidays at former fishing towns like Deauville, connected by train to Paris in the mid-19th century.

Bathing in the sea at North Berwick had become very popular at the end of the century. The burgh council regulated the bathing in 1901, with specified hours and locations for gentlemen and lady bathers (Ferrier 1980, 74). A swimming club was formed and, in 1899, the *Haddingtonshire Courier* reported the burgh council's approval of the club's plans to build a pool to improve the safety of swimmers (Addyman 1999). The pool was built in 1900 by Edinburgh architects and engineers Belfrage & Cardrae (see *Dictionary of Scottish Architects*), within the former inlet immediately to the north-east of the harbour and was opened in September. McWilliam (1978, 364) notes that it was one of the earliest outdoor pools in Scotland. The club raised the sum required by public subscription (Statham 2011, 151) and borrowed the rest – initially around £800 – and after this debt had been discharged in 1905, the town assumed ownership (Jamieson 1992, 17).

By the beginning of the 20th century North Berwick's economy was almost totally dependant on the tourist industry, with thousands of visitors every year, particularly in the summer season. In 1907, a tourist guide to the town lists one boarding house, six guest houses, and six hotels, with a seventh being built in 1907 (Statham 2011, 133). One of these was the vast Marine Hotel of more than 160 rooms, rebuilt with astonishing speed after a fire in 1882 (*ibid.*, 141).

The impact of the First World War on this tourist industry was disastrous. In the changes in social habits that followed the war, aristocratic visitors largely forsook North Berwick. This meant that there was greatly reduced demand for large houses to rent, seasonal house staff, and accommodation in the grander hotels. The Royal Hotel, for example, was sold by its owners in 1923 to its tenant manager, probably after declining returns since the war (*ibid.*, 136), and many other hotels never recovered their reputations after they were used for the billeting of troops (Jamieson 2000, 4). Holidays abroad increased in popularity for the wealthy in the 1920s and 1930s, and North Berwick increasingly became a resort of those who could not afford to travel overseas. Successive burgh councils maintained and enhanced the town's pre-war attractions and appearance, and attempted to recapture its former popularity. Two significant projects were on Kirk Ness, namely improvements to the swimming pool and the building of the Harbour Pavilion.

Improvements to the pool were made at various times in the 1920s and '30s, with the changing facilities extended, the pool itself deepened, diving facilities improved, electric lighting installed, and permanent seating for spectators built (see Figure 1.3). The quite extensive works in 1929 were carried out by Edinburgh architects Henry & MacLennan (McWilliam 1978, 364 and *Dictionary of Scottish Architects*). Photographs and postcards of the pool in this period show that it was very popular in the holiday season, and no doubt the improvements made by the burgh council were responding to continued demand. The last major improvement was the installation of a gas system to heat the water in 1960 (North Berwick Corporation 1966, 49), though Statham notes the pool reopened in 1963 (Statham 2011, 152).

The other major investment by the burgh council was the building of the Harbour Pavilion at the end of the 1920s (see Figure 1.3). With the increase in tourism, from about 1900 the area adjacent to the boatyard had been leased by the council to companies of entertainers, but following the First World War, they must have calculated that the revenue could be increased and the attraction enhanced with the construction of a permanent building. Discussions had begun by 1927 (Jamieson 1996, 35) and by spring of 1930 construction was underway, with an advertisement for bricklayers appearing in *The Scotsman* (19 April 1930, 7). The pavilion is mentioned in an advertisement placed by the Town Clerk in winter 1931, as available for rent in the summer of the same year, fitted out to provide entertainments, with tea rooms and a kiosk for sale of sweets and tobacco (*The Scotsman* 14 January 1931, 1). Jamieson (1996, 38) includes a photograph which shows the original arrangement of the façade with an open loggia.

Architecturally, the building had no pretentions to grandeur, and stylistically, belongs to the long enduring Arts and Crafts style. Considering that it was completed only five years before the spectacularly modernist De La Warr Pavilion in Bexhill, England, the pre-war style of this pavilion is distinctly conservative. This choice of style fits the burgh council's attempts to revive the town's old pre-war popularity, based on its established record, rather then striking a modern new tone. There was regular entertainment, particularly during the holiday season, including variety shows, music and dances. By the 1980s however, this kind of entertainment was in a terminal decline in popularity, and in the 1990s the decision was taken to demolish the Pavilion.

Consolidation and presentation of the old kirk site: 1954–6 and 1977

Following the excavation of the old kirk site under the direction of Dr James Richardson in 1951–2, described in the previous chapter, it seems that there was little immediate progress towards the long-term consolidation, improvement and presentation of the site. As discussed, the newly exposed remains had been tidied and temporarily laid out in their excavated state with only rudimentary interpretation (see Figure 4.19).

Richardson wrote in November 1953 complaining about the apparent lack of interest in completing the proposed works (Town Council minutes, 1 December 1953). The letter seems to have sparked the Council into action and there was a site meeting on the 10 December at which Richardson outlined his recommendations. The Town Council constituted a sub-committee to oversee the Auld Kirk Green project and it was agreed that the works as outlined should be carried out by labour from the Burgh Surveyor's department under the supervision of Richardson.

With some adjustments it seems that Richardson's recommendations were carried out during the summer and autumn of 1954 and in the autumn of 1955. On 1 July 1954 (Minutes) it was recorded that he had submitted a further report on requirements for the completion of the work, although this has not been discovered; it was also noted that efforts were then underway to gather together historic stones from the site. Minutes of 1 September itemise in detail the works to be carried out from thereon. There is then a further gap in correspondence of over two years, until November 1956 when the Permanent Secretary of the Ministry of Works expressed his appreciation to the Town Council regarding the presumably completed work at Auld Kirk Green.

The consolidation of the church ruin generally consisted of the capping or reconstruction of the excavated wall footings, the rebuilding work undertaken by Mr Carl Henderson; here a cementitious mortar was employed. The footings were then over-planted with sea pink and wallflower brought in from Tantallon Castle. The porch was provided with a new brick floor and ironwork at the entrances, its roof repaired and its chimney dismantled; a suggestion that the fireplace within be removed was not acted upon. An asphalt path was laid just within the sea wall to the east and the projected course of the church's walls laid out in whin setts across this. Painted cast aluminium signage was provided for the identification of various parts of the site; this very much in the Ministry of Works' ancient monuments tradition. The ground on the north side of the church was 'contoured and turfed', graded down so that the church wall foot was fully revealed.

An important aspect of the works was, at Richardson's behest, the gathering together at the site of a number of important carved stones. Some of these stones were already present on site or recovered during Richardson's excavation. Others, 'collected at some time in the past from the site of the Auld Kirk of St Andrew and also from the site of the Cistercian Monastery at North Berwick', were recovered from a rockery within the St Andrew's Manse garden, this requiring the permission from the Church of Scotland Trustees (Minutes, 1 July

1954). At least one further stone – the cross-incised grave marker described at the end of Chapter 3 was recovered from the Lodge, formerly the major Dalrymple family property in North Berwick. The stones were relocated and arranged for display within a purpose-built iron-railed enclosure at the Old Church site, erected within the north transept area (see Figure 4.65).

With the exception of a later paved interpretation area, (see following section), by the time of the survey in 2000 the site essentially remained as it had been laid out in the mid-1950s. Some of the displayed carved stones, still at site when visited by the RCAHMS in 1975, were subsequently removed to North Berwick Museum (Ferrier 1980, 19), and presently reside in the East Lothian Council's Museums Service stores in Haddington.

Interpretative scheme (1977)

In 1977 the North Berwick and District Round Table, in co-operation with the Community Council, sponsored the installation of new interpretation at the old church site to commemorate both the Silver Jubilee of Queen Elizabeth II and the golden jubilee of the Round Table itself. Three interpretative panels were mounted on vertical stone monoliths in the area of the north aisle and crossing of the church ruin, these were accessed by new-laid paving (shown in Figure 4.62). The monoliths, including one with a dedicatory panel, were reused in the new interpretative scheme of 2003–4.

St Andrew's Kirk and Anchor Green Environmental Improvement Project (2003–4)

By 2000 the decaying state of both the porch and the consolidated wall footings, including displacement of individual stones, had given increasing rise for concern. Similarly there had been long-term wear of the turf protecting the site and in a number of areas localised erosion had exposed archaeological deposits, including burials. The anticipated increase in pedestrian traffic that the proposed Scottish Seabird Centre was likely to generate was regarded as a potential threat to the Scheduled Monument prompting Historic Scotland to commission proposals for the improved management of the remains.

The adopted scheme emphasised the use of traditional, locally-sourced and lime-based materials employed both in a programme of conservative repair to the monument, including the upstanding porch, and new interventions (Figures 5.7 and 5.8). A particular priority was to declutter the interior of the church ruin by the removal of concrete slab paths, an obscuring interpretation installation and other recent interventions.

A low masonry wall of locally sourced rubble stone from the Markle Quarry at East Linton, lime bonded, was erected along side the path between the sea wall to the east and the church ruin to discourage entry to the church site from that side while still permitting a clear view

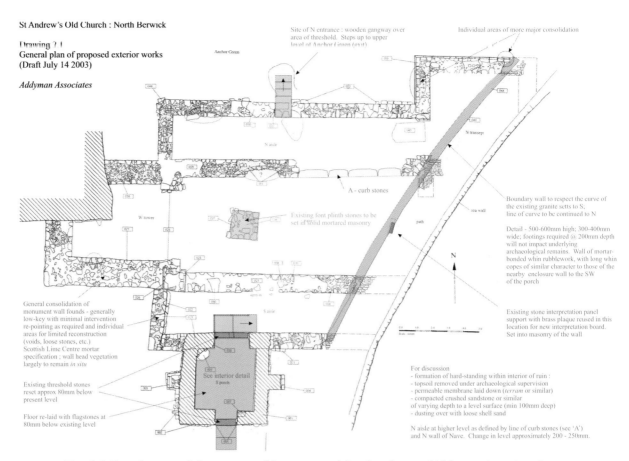

Fig. 5.7: Initial proposal for repair and laying-out of the church ruin (Addyman Associates)

(Figure 5.9). The visiting public, generally arriving at the site from the town to the south, were alternatively encouraged to enter the church by means of its original south porch. Here interpretation boards were mounted within to provide an introduction to the site. The principal access points within the ruin were protected by low-key short walkways to reduce the risk of pedestrian wear of the turf. One of these was placed at the presumed site of the north entrance to the church thereby permitting direct access out to Anchor Green beyond. New woodwork elements were constructed of green oak.

Unstable masonry of the church ruin was rebedded. In a number of areas Richardson's cement-based repairs were unpicked and stones rebedded in lime mortar. Some areas of missing wall footing were 'reinstated' by the addition of new masonry, this of a notably different stone type – this was primarily undertaken for the purpose of improved interpretation.

The porch was comprehensively repaired. 19th and early 20th century photographic images provided evidence that the structure had been limewashed; this finish was reinstated both externally and internally. The ceramic tile floor within was relaid with sandstone flags. A heavily rusted iron lintel above the entrance on the north side of the structure was replaced in green oak. Localised masonry repairs, particularly to the lateral buttresses, were distinguishable from the surrounding fabric, carried out using recycled Scots slates.

To avoid cluttering, the site interpretation was mostly restricted to the interior of the porch. However, two reconstructed views of the site, one of the medieval church interior and one a more distant panorama from the north, were set at appropriate points overlooking the ruin; their pedestals recycled the stone monoliths used for the 1977 scheme of interpretation. To permit easy future maintenance and to improve the legibility of the ruined wall footings narrow borders were introduced, these were infilled with crushed scallop shell from a sustainable source in County Durham.

Historic carved stones from the site were assessed both archaeologically and by a stone conservator. The more sensitive, the red sandstone table tomb and the 13th century recumbent slab, each in a number of pieces, were reassembled and set upon permanent plinths within the porch interior.

The works overall were designed by Thomas Addyman, with Stuart Brown and David Connolly. Tim Meek was the principal contractor for repairs, particularly for masonry and lime works; Alexander Fairfoul undertook new woodwork elements. Stone conservation was undertaken by Nicholas Boyes. Interpretation was designed by David Connolly and artwork, two reconstruction drawings of the medieval site, provided by David Simon. Reinstatement of the interior of the ruin was undertaken by Thomas Addyman and Kenneth Macfadyen.

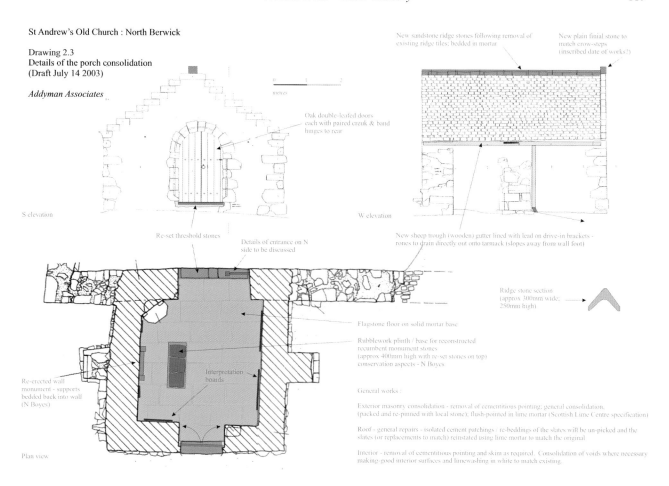

St Andrew's Old Church : North Berwick

Drawing 2.3
Details of the porch consolidation
(Draft July 14 2003)

Addyman Associates

S elevation

W elevation

Oak double-leafed doors
each with paired creuk & band
hinges to rear

New sandstone ridge stones following removal of
existing ridge tiles; bedded in mortar

New plain finial stone to
match crow-steps
(inscribed date of works?)

Re-set threshold stones

Details of entrance on N
side to be discussed

New sheep trough (wooden) gutter lined with lead on drive-in brackets -
rones to drain directly out onto tarmack (slopes away from wall foot)

Ridge stone section
(approx 300mm wide;
250mm high)

Flagstone floor on solid mortar base

Rubblework plinth / base for reconstructed
recumbent monument stones
(approx 400mm high with re-set stones on top)
conservation aspects - N Boyes

Re-erected wall
monument - supports
bedded back into wall
(N Boyes)

Interpretation
boards

General works :

Exterior masonry consolidation - removal of cementitious pointing; general consolidation,
(packed and re-pinned with local stone); flush-pointed in lime mortar (Scottish Lime Centre specification)

Roof - general repairs - isolated cement patchings / re-beddings of the slates will be un-picked and the
slates (or replacements to match) reinstated using lime mortar to match the original

Interior - removal of cementitious pointing and skim as required. Consolidation of voids where necessary
making-good interior surfaces and limewashing in white to match existing.

Plan view

Fig. 5.8: Initial proposal for the repair of the church porch (Addyman Associates)

Fig. 5.9: General view of the church site following completion of repair and interpretation works, looking SW

The building of the Scottish Seabird Centre

Stewart Brown

Around 1993, Simpson & Brown Architects of Edinburgh, were commissioned to design and build a new attraction for the Kirk Ness, for visitors to observe bird life on the outlying islands. The idea was to position cameras on the islands, which would send back live pictures to a central location, so that the public could view the birds without disturbing the colonies. The original proposal was to develop the late 1920s Harbour Pavilion (see previous chapters). However, restoration and conversion were considered impractical and it was agreed that a new purpose-designed building was needed. Funding for the project was from the local authority and private donations, with just over £1,000,000 awarded by the newly announced Millennium Fund.

The exposed position of the new building to the sea and the weather presented challenges to the design team. It is set beside the harbour, on the site of part of the burial ground of the old kirk, and the late 19th century boatyard (see above and previous chapters). It is robustly built with a dry stone weather screen and a copper roof supported on solid, timber trusses. Its unusual 'tear-drop' shape reflects its function, but also expresses the fact that it is a landmark building which must stand alone in an open position and draw people to it. Having such an exposed location, both the shape and the choice of materials was crucial. Simpson & Brown have a long interest in green buildings, and are experienced in working with historic buildings, and these were combined in the development of the design, especially in the use of natural, real and raw materials, sourced locally, wherever possible.

Design concept

The building is the hub of a communications network by which it is linked to discretely located cameras among the seabird colonies on the islands in the Forth, in particular the puffins on Craigleith and Fidra and the gannets on the Bass Rock, one of the largest and most important colonies in the world. Visitors are able to control the cameras and zoom in on the wildlife on large screens, at all times of the year, in real time. At the same time, the birds themselves are protected from disturbance by visitors to the islands. Since the building was completed, additional interactive cameras have been installed on the Isle of May, further out into the Firth of Forth, to enable views of the large colony of breeding seals which arrive on the island just as the seabirds on the Bass Rock and Fidra depart for the winter.

Design

The site itself was a major inspiration for the building, the rocky promontory beside the Old Harbour, with its views of the Bass Rock, the Isle of May, Craigleith and Fidra. This elevated panoramic view generated the concept of a circular building with an extended entrance to draw in visitors across Anchor Green, from the town centre (Figure 5.10).

The driving wind and salt spray were considerable factors in the modelling of the building. Overhanging eaves and ridges were intended to protect the upper walls and windows from spray, and thus they were designed to be sturdy and aerodynamic. Some commentators have likened the roof forms of the building to a bird's wing, but this was coincidental. More conscious influences were aeroplane structures and the desire to create a dramatic, distinctive and visually attractive shape.

The main roof and monopitch entrance roof are very sculptural forms, but their initial form was generated by the shape of the plan (Figure 5.11). This initial form was then made more dramatic, especially the monopitch roof over the entrance, which was designed to make it more dominant, to define the way in. The spinal wall projects along the path to protect visitors from the extremes of the weather and helps to guide them towards the entrance.

The internal planning was intended to be very simple. To make the best of the all-round views out from the site, the shop, reception and restaurant were located on the entrance level, along with a viewing deck. The exhibition and auditorium areas, which as 'black box' spaces did not require natural light, were mostly buried into the ground on the floor below. The different functions of the building, on the upper and lower levels, are reflected in the choice of structure and materials.

Materials and construction

The architects devised a strategy for the building which informed the whole of the detailed design. The strategy prioritised the use of natural materials, ventilation and light. In this way, the design was also intended to exceed minimum standards of energy performance, with as low a demand as possible on the power plant. Full height windows light all the public spaces on the upper floor and a large central cupola allows natural light into the centre of the building, originally penetrating to the lower floor through an oculus. The upper floor, with its reception area, office, shop, restaurant, toilets and viewing gallery, is all naturally ventilated.

The structure

The exposed position and half-buried nature of the building presented several challenges in the choices of materials and construction methods. Because of the seaboard location, the always envisaged semi-basement was to be in concrete, so that it would be waterproof. This is despite the fact that concrete production contributes around 10% of the world's annual industrial production of CO_2 and is the fastest rising industrial producer of

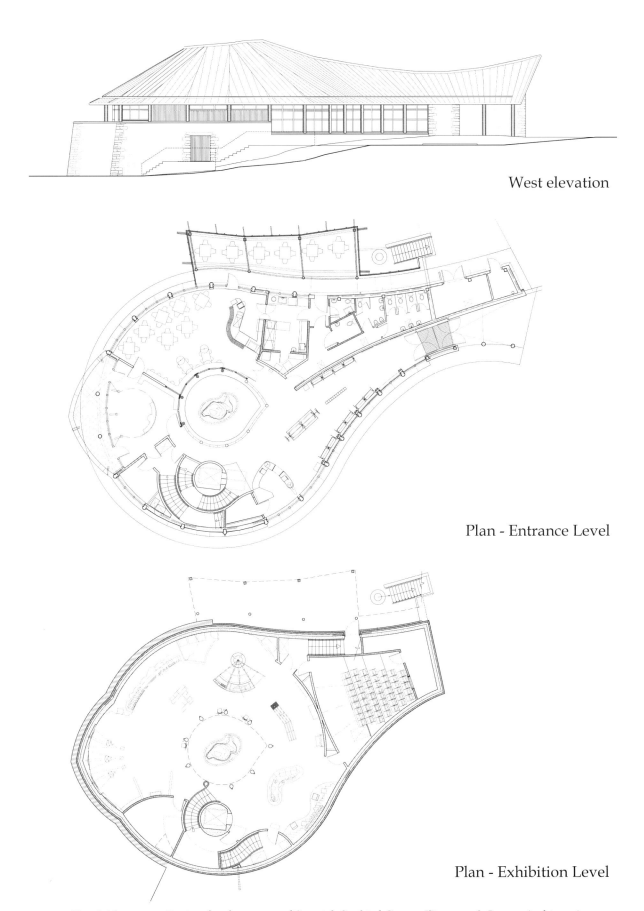

West elevation

Plan - Entrance Level

Plan - Exhibition Level

Fig. 5.10: *Design for the proposed Scottish Seabird Centre (Simpson & Brown Architects)*

Fig. 5.11: The newly completed Scottish Seabird Centre from the beach (Simpson & Brown Architects)

CO_2. By-products also include various heavy metal pollutants, and a dust which is hard to recycle due to its hardness. It is, however, a product reasonably close to its natural origins, as opposed to say a plastic product, and similar to traditional lime in its origin. Its material properties are also unique and it was decided that there was no substitute material for this particular application. The effects on the environment were mitigated by sourcing the concrete from a local cement plant 10 km away at Dunbar. The waterproofing layer outside the basement is of clay mats, these being the greenest waterproofing method available.

Above this concrete and clay basement the first floor and the roof structure are timber. The options for this part of the building were laminated timber, or solid timber in conjunction with steel. The laminations of laminated timber are joined by glue, often incorporating formaldehyde, and at the time of construction this would have had to be manufactured abroad, so not only the wood but also the manufactured members would have been imported. It was decided that solid natural timber should be used structurally as far as possible, but with minimal reliance on steel for stressed points.

This traditional approach made the building technologically Victorian. This is because traditional timber construction in the medieval period utilised local hardwood – oak – without any metal parts, meaning that all the joints, some of which can be quite elaborate, depend entirely on wood to wood contact for all structural per-

formance. This was because metal was, relatively speaking, difficult and expensive to produce. As soon as it became more available, however, it came to be used as part of the structure where its strength immediately gave it a fundamental structural role, rather than just in nails or straps. Eventually it was used for tie rods and flitch beams, which allowed the use of softwoods for structural purposes, replacing oak, and made possible the bigger spans of Georgian and Victorian buildings.

The architects chose to use timber but, as oak was out of the question on cost grounds, they specified a softwood and so the joints rely on steel bolts. The amount and weight of steel used is, however, very low, with metal restricted to simple through-bolts at the joints, and these solely of the locating type with only one per joint. It was intended that the timber would be sourced in Scotland, but in the end it came from northern England, a reasonably local alternative.

The finishes

The use of natural materials in the structure was continued as far as possible in the finishes of the building. The upper floor cladding is in timber, and European Larch heartwood was selected, because it is durable and was available locally. The architects were also keen to use Scottish-made timber windows. However, the closest firm that could provide the necessary quantity and specification was from Yorkshire. Again British-grown

European Larch heartwood was specified for the windows but, unfortunately, this option proved to be unavailable due to production problems and a Scandinavian Redwood with a natural oil-based finish was used instead.

The remaining internal finishes were also natural timber as far as possible, and not processed timbers like MDF. For example, toilet partitions were made of tongue-and-groove boarding, rather than veneered MDF. The insulation above ground is cellulose fibre (wood or paper fibre) to allow the building to breathe, and the insulation levels are well above current minimum standards.

Overall, the architects were satisfied with the extensive use of natural materials, and the way that the design itself has contributed to the success of the Scottish Seabird Centre. The centre has become a vibrant new visitor attraction for North Berwick, drawing visitors to the Kirk Ness once again.

6. Conclusion

The archaeological investigations required at Kirk Ness in relation to the construction of the Scottish Seabird Centre permitted the first systematic examination of the history of the site that forms the setting of St Andrew's Old Kirk, the long-ruined medieval burgh church of North Berwick. Carried out between 1999 and 2006, this fieldwork led to an extensive programme of post-excavation analysis and an important sequence of radiocarbon dates that focused upon the earlier features and deposits encountered at the site. Simultaneously the opportunity was taken to review the wider history of the evolution of Kirk Ness and to draw together knowledge of earlier discoveries at the site, particularly J. S. Richardson's unpublished investigations of 1951 and 1952. Overall this work has transformed the understanding of Kirk Ness as an archaeological site, leading to a better definition of its extent (and former extent), its significance and its archaeological potential.

Since the first Scottish Burgh Survey of North Berwick was produced (Simpson and Stevenson 1981), there have been two substantial updates. A general discussion of the archaeology of the burgh, along with a record of all work in the intervening period, was provided by Hall and Bowler (1997), and an update to the Burgh Survey was undertaken by SUAT the following year (SUAT 1998). Another important expansion of this growing corpus, by Dingwall (2009), considers a further decade of predominantly developer-funded archaeological works that included a major monitoring exercise during pipeline installation throughout the heart of the early burgh. In her wider reappraisal Dingwall reviews the understanding of the morphology of the core area of the medieval burgh in particular and considers its archaeological potential.

The detailed study of the archaeology and development of Kirk Ness embodied in the present report is thus a timely extension to this existing and comparatively recent body of work. Indeed the archaeological works of 1999–2006 have more than borne out Hall and Bowler's observations about the old kirk site (1997, 664):

The church is likely to be the earliest site in the burgh, and a fresh look at the finds assemblage might shed some light on early activity in the area. The site itself is unlikely to experience any major development in future, but could be subject to minor disturbance to consolidate the ruins, or upgrade services such as lighting. Burials, foundations and other evidence are likely to be very near the surface, and even quite fragmentary results might help to date the earliest use of the site.

Extent of the site

An important result of the recent works at Kirk Ness has been a new understanding of the extent and nature of archaeological remains in the vicinity of the ruin of the medieval church of St Andrew and at Anchor Green generally. The boundary defining the area of archaeological survival has now been well established along the eastern, northern and north-western parts of the site, and can be reasonably estimated to the south and south-west (Figure 6.1). This is effectively defined as the area of higher ground enclosed by the existing retaining walls and sea wall respectively to the south-west and south, and to the east; by the existing buildings to the west and north-west; and by the Scottish Seabird Centre site to the north-east. To the south the enclosed ground lies at just less than a metre above the surrounding street level; from there it gently rises up to the north, to some 2.0–2.5m above the lower ground beyond the Scottish Seabird Centre.

As has been well-established the eastern parts of the headland were subject to extensive erosion up to c.1857 when the shore was finally stabilised; perhaps over a third of the site area may have disappeared since the medieval period. The cover illustration by David Simon gives an impression of the former extent suggested at that stage. To the north-east it is unclear to what extent deposits may have been eroded; this area lay between the central and eastern bedrock ridges that define the underlying geology of Kirk Ness and it is clear that, up to its

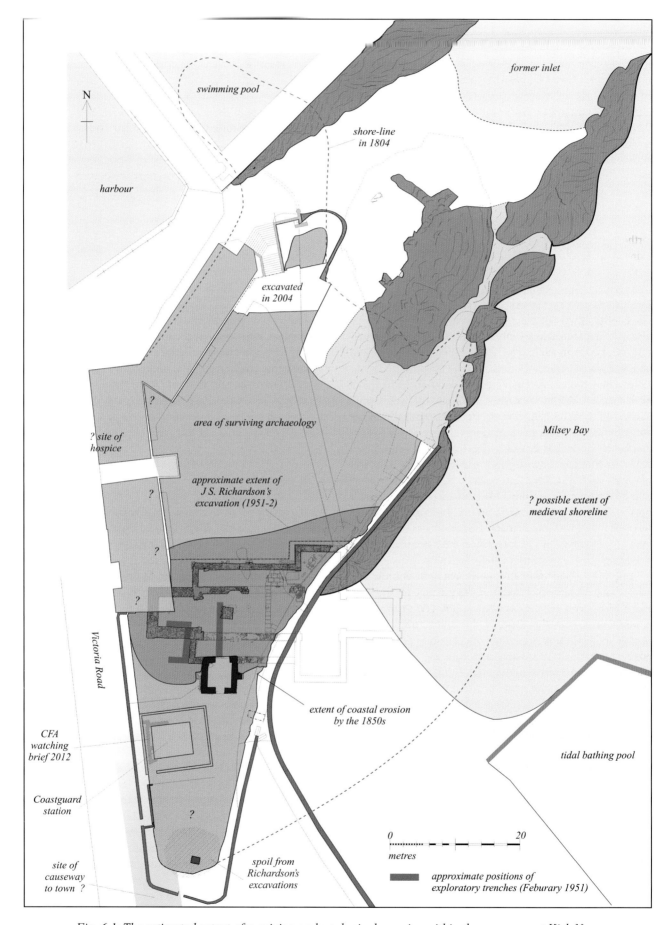

Fig. 6.1: The estimated extent of surviving archaeological remains within the core area at Kirk Ness

infilling in the early 1860s, the land just beyond the boundary of Anchor Green, including the site of the Scottish Seabird Centre itself, had been a sea-washed inlet. Certainly there is evidence that the middle bedrock ridge saw early quarrying activity; stone from this source was employed for the rubble masonry of the medieval church and, possibly, at a later stage for the harbour walls. But whether this triggered attendant erosion at the north-east perimeter (as the quarrying of the red leck stone had done on the foreshore further to the east) is unclear.

The northern extent of *in situ* archaeological remains at Anchor Green closely follows the north-eastern and northern edges of a particular protrusion of the central bedrock ridge; the ground at Anchor Green gently rises up to this point. Where the ridge had extended further to the north it is apparent from the 1804 estate plan by Forrest that there had once existed a further finger of ground that continued to a little beyond the east corner of the harbour; this land was eventually cut away during levelling operations in the early 1860s. Beyond this had lain the foreshore.

The construction of the 19th century coal stores at the north-west perimeter, parts of whose masonry walling are incorporated within the present Scottish Seabird Centre administration building, evidently involved the abrupt cutting-down of any archaeological deposits or remains and even bedrock at the edge of the site in that area. Much may also have been the case on the footprint of the former granary building (now the East Lothian Yacht Club) on the west side of Anchor Green. The possibility that this structure incorporates elements of a medieval hospital building, as already discussed, remains; however, as noted in Chapter 5, a recent evaluation in the vicinity of this building failed to identify any significant archaeology.

The land immediately south of the granary on the west side of the green – the present pend, the site of the Fishermen's Hall, and the associated stables (now Church Cottage) in particular – may yet overlie surviving archaeological levels and features. The exterior walls of the latter will also likely incorporate further carved stones deriving from the church and graveyard monuments (the same is true of the central section of the harbour's north-west wall). Archaeological deposits will doubtless extend to the immediate west, south-west and south of the church ruin. However, with one exception, these areas have not been investigated. The exception was a recent watching brief carried out by CFA Archaeology Ltd within the alley around the former coastguard station to the south-west of the church ruin. Here were encountered discreet deposits of charnel on its west side, these likely representing an impact upon *in situ* cemetery deposits during the construction of the building in the 19th century (McCaig 2012; note – a previous record of a find-spot at this structure was reported in error – Dingwall, 2009, table 1, no. 18).

Archaeological survival

The presence of deeply stratified well-preserved occupation deposits, and the preponderance of major inundations of wind-blown sand, are notable features of the archaeology of the core site area at Kirk Ness, as they are for the archaeology of the burgh of North Berwick more generally (see Hall and Bowler 1997; Dingwall 2009). However, the archaeology of Kirk Ness has also been long subject to direct physical erosion by the sea during major storms, this particularly affecting both the eastern side of the promontory and its connection with the mainland. The core site area was only permanently stabilised within the existing perimeter walling in the late 1850s.

Overall the depth of survival of archaeological remains in the core site area has been demonstrated to be very considerable, this generally between 1m and 2m in many areas. In the area of the church, to its immediate south and south-west, and along the north side of the church ruin (this area relating to the extent of J. S. Richardson's clearance of the church site in 1951–2) archaeological remains including burials survive immediately below the existing laid topsoil, which lies just above the historic floor level of the church. Underlying deposits may extend for a further metre in depth or more. Between the north side of the church ruin and the northern end of Anchor Green archaeological remains lie more deeply buried. Here they are still overlain by a considerable depth of sand that is in part wind-blown accumulation and must, in part, reflect the general formation processes relating to the long use of the cemetery. Further south, where the ground is either paved over (to the east) or grassed, deposits in most areas will lie relatively close to the surface. At the very south end of the enclosed area it is known there had been a more or less extensive dump of spoil from the mid-20th century church excavations.

The significance of excavated remains and further archaeological potential

Within the defined core area of the site at Kirk Ness extensive undisturbed archaeological features and deposits still survive. The present project has demonstrated the extreme sensitivity of the site and in many cases the very ephemeral nature of these highly important remains. While there are no immediate threats, any future interventions within the area must be carefully considered and the preservation of the archaeological resource considered a priority.

Prehistoric

Of the four principal phases of human activity encountered the prehistoric may be a comparatively minor component and one whose potential remains obscure. The solitary fire pit encountered in the south-eastern part of the site provides the only certain evidence from Kirk Ness of a prehistoric presence, of the pre-Roman Iron Age; however, this is unlikely to be an isolated occurrence. It is likely that prehistoric remains concentrated closer to the shore line, with activity focused upon the occasional exploitation of marine resources; much of this may have been lost to the sea.

Early medieval

The principal importance of the recent archaeological works was the firm identification of a multi-phase early medieval component at Kirk Ness. Because of the limited area of exposure and the much-degraded nature of the remains its extent and specific significance are yet to be fully understood but, in both respects, may prove to be very considerable. The site is confirmed as having major potential for the better understanding of this obscure period, one that is poorly represented in the archaeology of south-east Scotland.

That the site and the dedication of its church to St Andrew may have been linked to the flight, in 732, of Bishop Acca of Hexam and the translation of the relics of St Andrew from Hexam to Kilrymont (St Andrews) and had thereafter been a key stop on the pilgrimage route from the south follows the suggestion made in 1860 by Skene: 'It seems to me that Acca's route can be traced by the dedications to St Andrew; for the usual route from Northumbria to the region north of the Forth at that time was by the ferry called Earlsferry'. However, he also noted the ferry route was 'from Gulaneness to Newburn, and the church of Gulane on the south side was likewise dedicated to St Andrew'.

In the 1860s Ferrier discussed a possible foundation of a church at the Kirk Ness by 'St Baldred', as early as the 6th century AD (Ferrier 1869, 16). And in 1911 J. T. Richardson had optimistically proposed that the porch, the only upstanding survivor of the medieval kirk, incorporated an earlier structure, perhaps of 8th or 9th century date. He also suggested the site might be linked to locally established early ecclesiastics – St Baldred inevitably being cited as a possible candidate. Such observations, however erroneous, have coloured secondary commentary ever since.

Earlier suspicions apart, the physical setting of Kirk Ness does nothing to dispel the more general suggestion – its near-island setting providing a clearly-defined 'sanctuary area' not untypical of many early ecclesiastical sites. The relative inconvenience of the site in relation to the medieval burgh might also be reason to suggest that the medieval church was a successor building upon a long-established site; more recent commentators have found no reason to disagree (eg. Hall and Bowler 1997, 664).

The present project has allowed a more careful assessment of the likelihood of an early ecclesiastical origin at the site, based upon the excavated evidence and consideration of this in the light of current historical thinking on the geopolitics of the region between the 5th and 10th centuries. The features and deposits identified in the tunnel excavation area at the north end of Anchor Green may well strengthen the case for an ecclesiastical origin, but the remains themselves and the few associated finds, did not provide definitive evidence. The radiocarbon dates obtained from these deposits also mostly pre-date the possible event of the translation of the relics of St Andrew from Hexam.

Perhaps most suggestive are remnants of the corn-drying kiln, whose scale and constructional details are unusual and, in this report, are judged to be comparable with a sequence of better-preserved 'kiln-barns' of similar date unearthed at the early monastic site of Hoddom in Dumfriesshire. The presence of the kiln structure at Kirk Ness suggests a scale of grain production and processing that was beyond the localised domestic, apparently indicating a higher degree of communal organisation, whether under secular or ecclesiastical auspices.

The cross-incised grave-marker found at the site of the Cistercian nunnery of North Berwick at the end of the 19th century seems likely to pre-date its foundation in the 12th century, and must thereby relate to a predecessor site. If not in the vicinity of the nunnery itself the best candidate may be the church site at nearby Kirk Ness, an important possession of the nunnery that was evidently in existence before its foundation.

In summary while the excavated structural remains, occupation deposits and finds from the site are highly suggestive, and a firm chronology for earlier medieval occupation has been established through radiocarbon dating, there is as yet no definitive confirmation that this was an ecclesiastical site at this period. If the existing church ruin occupies the site of a predecessor then it is perhaps surprising that, even within the very limited sample area where deposits of greater depth were encountered along the east boundary of the site, no evidence for earlier burial activity was recorded. The significance of the site at Kirk Ness lies in the presence of deeply stratified deposits and features preserving evidence for extended episodes of occupation, the variety of types of structure represented, and in the evidence for the exploitation of local resources, both marine and terrestrial. This site is thus an important addition to the limited corpus of recently excavated early medieval sites in East Lothian that includes Eldbotle near Dirleton, Auldhame, and Castle Park at Dunbar.

It is most likely that other significant early medieval remains are preserved at Kirk Ness, within the defined area of probable survival at Anchor Green. The features and deposits found in the tunnel excavation at the northern extent of this area had been extensively affected by erosion, bioturbation and a series of other taphonomic factors that together determined their survival to be very ephemeral. Associated remains further south may well be better preserved, where they were less likely to have been exposed to the elements and where overlying wind-blown sand deposits are more extensive. Thus the potential for the site to further illuminate this obscure period is considerable.

The medieval kirk, cemetery and hospice

J. S. Richardson's excavation of the medieval church site was never published and field records of the work, if they had existed, do not appear to have survived. New conservation repair works provided the opportunity to record and assess the remains fully, to reconstruct the extent and progress of the 1950s investigation, and to better understand the context of a number of recorded discoveries made at the church site both at the time of Richardson's work and historically.

Whilst Richardson had clearly understood the overall sequence of construction of the church it was possible to better define the individual phases and, through various strands of evidence, to understand the process of the building's demise between the mid-17th and early 19th centuries.

While only a small sample, the remains within the excavated parts of the cemetery proved to be of considerable interest, a significant contribution to the study of early Scottish graveyards. Combined dating evidence, stratigraphic relationships and later historical records suggest a chronology for the cemetery beginning in the later 11th or 12th century, this unsurprisingly broadly coeval with the earliest phase of the church ruin, and continuing through to the 17th century. Historical evidence also suggests burial activity persisted, presumably with ever-lessening frequency, to the early 19th century. The principal contrast was between the graves revealed in Trench 6, being earlier in the stratigraphic sequence, and those excavated at higher level in Trench 8. The former were of medieval date and the inhumation burials within had likely been shrouded. Of probable post-Reformation date many of the Trench 8 inhumation burials were notable for the presence of coffins, whose constructional details were preserved as humic stains within the surrounding sand matrix, with associated ironwork. Of outstanding interest was the evidence for the violent death, by stabbing, of one adult male individual dated to the late 12th or early 13th century. The understanding of the cemetery site was complimented by the gathering together of evidence for stone monuments present at the site and the study of grave-goods and other recorded finds made there over the years.

Although much has been lost to the sea to the east, the surviving parts of the cemetery must nonetheless be extensive, probably containing many hundreds of individual inhumation burials or more. Unsurprisingly the density of burial is most concentrated closer to the church, where considerable intercutting was evident. The cemetery may extend to most of the surviving core site area, with the exception of the northern part of Anchor Green where it was striking that almost no cemetery-derived remains were encountered. The northern extent of the cemetery was not confirmed and it is possible that it may have been defined by a boundary feature such as an enclosure wall, bank or ditch. Given the sandy environment the individual burials were notable for the excellent state of preservation of the skeletons and for the unusual survival of coffin details.

Medieval occupation of a more domestic nature was encountered at the northern end of Anchor Green, where prepared surfaces were associated with finds of pottery of 12th–14th century date. Though the remains were difficult to interpret it is clear that they lay out-with the cemetery area and likely that they were associated with the use of a hospice that lay nearby, possibly on the site of the existing granary building. It is probable that the nature of the prepared surfaces encountered may be better understood by investigation of the area immediately to the south, into which they extend; other evidence for domestic occupation may well survive in the vicinity.

At the south end of the site it is perhaps just possible that remains of the causeway or bridge, mostly washed away in the early–mid-17th century may still be identified, this in the area of the Kate Watson Memorial or slightly further to the west.

In summary the nature and extent of the medieval and post-medieval occupation is, by comparison with the earlier periods, much better understood, even though only localised areas were investigated and a very small proportion of the site was sampled. The remains clearly embody a number of important potential research themes, perhaps the most significant of which may be the study of a major medieval and post-medieval cemetery population, its morphology, and evolving burial practice.

Post-medieval and modern

The general assessment of historical sources relating to the later development of the harbour area following the abandonment of the church has led to a clearer understanding of the factors, both natural and man-made, that successively reduced the extent of survival of the earlier archaeological site. The core area will preserve some evidence of comparatively ephemeral post-medieval activities (excluding later burial activity already discussed), these generally· relating to construction of adjacent structures and mostly of 19th century and later date.

In conclusion

The archaeological works at Kirk Ness and Anchor Green constituted a complicated, multi-stage project, but proved a successful collaboration between a supportive and interested client, the archaeologists, and the project architects and contractors. The responsible execution of the project was driven by the Planning Authority, principally East Lothian Council, through their Heritage Service, and by Historic Scotland, who stepped in at a critical juncture to ensure the successful completion of the excavation of remains that were proving to be of great significance. The post-excavation programme of analysis and research and the production of this publication, was made possible by the continuing support of both Historic Scotland and the Scottish Seabird Centre and, through them, the generosity a number of individual trusts.

Fig. 6.2: Memento mori *on the 17th century tomb slab*

Appendices: Specialists Reports

The following presents summary reports of various specialist analyses undertaken on major classes of material recovered from the Kirk Ness excavations. In some cases further detail is provided on the accompanying CD while other classes of material are reported on the CD only.

Abbreviations

In the artefact descriptions below and on the CD, the following abbreviations are used: D = diameter; H = height; L = length; T = thickness; W = width; Wt = weight.

Appendix B: Coarse stone, vitrified material and lead

by Dawn McLaren and Fraser Hunter

A small assemblage of coarse stone tools and vitrified material from the 2006 tunnel excavation was submitted for specialist analysis.

Coarse stone

SF95 (1239): Whetstone

Large, elongated sub-rectangular siltstone; both ends and sides rounded; abrasion marks remaining from manufacture. Unfinished attempts to perforate either end, with deep, concentrated peckmarks on one face (D 8.5 & 7 mm), less-distinct, dispersed peckmarks on other surface. All surfaces smoothed and abraded from use. One face has seen extensive use, being heavily dished along one edge with associated polish. Both ends flattened by later use as pounder (18 × 15mm, 28 × 16 mm). Series of short linear grooves and abrasions on two opposing edges and one face overlie previous polish and abrasion, suggesting tool saw secondary use as a sharpening stone (Figure B.1). L: 215mm, W: 43mm, T: 30mm.

SF100 (1281)/matrix of slab floor [1280]: Burnisher

Flat, sub-rectangular siltstone; rounded corners and edges. One end squared with distinct linear abrasion facet (42 × 6mm) along width of one face. Stone tapers in width and thickness to blunt, irregular rounded end which has been bifacially abraded either as result of use as a grinder or in attempt to shape stone. Both faces and rounded edges smoothed and highly polished through use with dark glossy sheen throughout, particularly along edges (see Figures 3.4 and B.2). L: 133mm, W: 50mm, T: 23mm.

SF153 (1287): possible Pounder

Small, flattened, ovoid sandstone weathered cobble. Indistinct pitted areas present at both rounded ends; due to coarse uneven surface of stone it is unclear whether this is result of use or weathering (see Figure 3.4). L: 85mm, W: 75mm, T: 30mm.

SF157 (1287): Uncertain

Fragment of larger shaped stone of uncertain character. Sub-square block of sandstone; three edges broken. Two opposing flat faces have distinct dispersed peck-marks from shaping (see Figure 3.4). L: 73.5mm, W: 65.5mm, T: 60.5mm.

Vitrified material

A very small quantity (just over 50g) of vitrified material was recovered from throughout the excavated area, from residual contexts. The majority of pieces are small and fragmentary, and thus difficult to classify with any certainty. Most consist of low-density, non-magnetic vesicular glassy vitrified material. Low-density slag is formed when material such as earth, clay, stone or ceramic is subjected to high temperatures. These can be formed during any high temperature pyrotechnic process

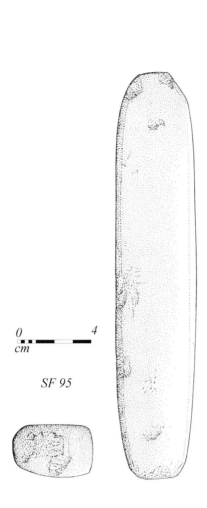

SF 95

Fig. B.1: Whetstone (SF95)

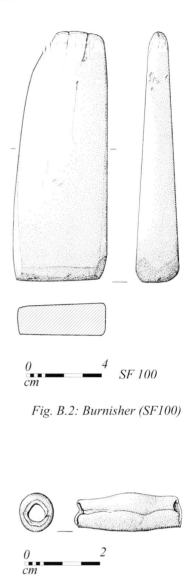

SF 100

Fig. B.2: Burnisher (SF100)

SF 119

Fig. B.3 Lead object (SF119)

and are not necessarily indicative of industrial activity. Three samples are magnetic but need not be residues from iron working; that from context *1178* is so small and fractured it could equally be a corrosion spall from an iron object and, although magnetic, the sample from context *1093* appears to be rounded (?waterworn) gravel with no obvious iron content.

Lead

SF119 (1309): Lead Weight

Barrel-shaped, slightly irregular hollow lead weight or bead; swollen centre; narrowed ends. Formed by rolling thin lead sheet (1 mm thick), edges overlapping, with little attempt to disguise join. Both ends damaged, perhaps through use (Figures B.3 and 3.4). L: 29mm, W (at waist): 10mm (at end): 7mm, T: 1 mm.

General discussion

This small assemblage is not chronologically distinctive, but adds a little information about the site's use. The vitrified material is mostly undiagnostic low-density material; none can be attributed to iron production.

The coarse stone tools and lead object, however, are of more significance. Whetstones and burnishers are commonplace finds on early historic and medieval domestic sites and the possible pounder is similarly consistent with this date. The burnisher (SF100) came from the upper parts of the midden soils *1281*, related to a period of abandonment or collapse of the early structure or possibly associated with the pavement sealing these middens (*1280*). The large whetstone (SF95) was associated with an area of later cobbling, *1239*, contemporary with the mettling for the medieval path, *1069*. Both show extensive wear, with the whetstone showing evidence of additional use for sharpening points, rather than simply sharpening blade edges. Deep peckmarks indicate an abandoned attempt to perforate the object, but it is unclear whether the intention was to suspend it or to alter its function from a whetstone to a weight. A similar large perforated whetstone was recovered from mid-9th century contexts at Whithorn (Nicholson 1997, 454–5). Perforating such large stones for suspension creates a point of weakness and it may have been abandoned for this reason. Whetstones with similar abandoned perforations come from medieval Coppergate and Fishergate, York (Ottaway and Rogers 2002, 2797).

The fragment of a larger shaped stone (SF157), and the possible pounder (SF153) came from a layer of midden, *1281,* which contained material of early medieval date, and it can be inferred that the stone is of similar date.

The lead weight or bead (SF119) is of significance due to its unusual form, but the lack of typological analysis of lead objects makes dating uncertain. Lead was rarely used in prehistoric Britain but was in common use in the Roman and medieval periods, particularly for practical applications rather than ornamental items. The fine barrel-shaped form and fairly careful shaping of the Kirk Ness object could imply a decorative function rather than a simple weight, but the lack of parallels for early historic and medieval lead ornaments suggests it is a weight. The use of lead for small weights is common by the medieval period and can be found in a range of sizes and shapes, from simple rolled-sheet cylinders, such as those from medieval London (Egan 1998, 310), to small cast, perforated discs as recovered from excavations at Perth (Ford 1987, 130, ill. 64, no. 60). In most instances, no further attempt was made to shape the object beyond its initial production. Although lacking the distinctive swollen centre and barrel-shape of the Kirk Ness example, several similar elongated cylindrical weights produced from rolled lead strips come from Fishergate, York: three examples were recovered from contexts associated with the Anglian settlement, four from 11th–12th century deposits (Rogers 1993, 1320, fig. 637, no. 5480, 5482), whilst the majority of such weights came from medieval features (Ottaway and Rogers 2002, 2747–9, fig. 1352, nos 15260–1, 15263–4).

Appendix E: Metal, worked bone and the weapon used to stab SK605

by Julie Franklin

The metal and worked bone assemblage largely relates to the use of the area as a graveyard. Most finds were of post-medieval date, with finds found both within the 16th and 17th century graves and redeposited in layers of 19th century landscaping material overlying them. The exception is a type of early medieval bone pin, though again, this appears to be redeposited in a later grave. Dates given after the context number in finds

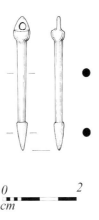

Fig. E.1: Medieval bone pin from inhumation burial SK865

catalogue entries in the report are the apparent date for the deposition of that context, not date of object.

Medieval bone pin

(861) SK865: Bone pin

Hemispherical head; pointed loop on top. Short round-sectioned shaft, distinct hip three-quarters of way down. Well made and polished. Fill of a grave SK865 (15th–17th century). L: 36mm (Figure E.1)

The pin is unusually small and very distinctive, being very well made and polished, with a well defined hipped shaft and a pierced projection rising from the top of the head. This type of bone pin is better known from south-east England. The largest group yet found comprises 19 pins from Castle Acre, Norfolk (Margeson 1982). They were from a well dated phase, between *c.*1085 and the 1140s. Other finds have come from sites scattered across eastern England from London to Yorkshire (*ibid.*; MacGregor 1985, 121; Crummy 1988, 7, fig. 2:5; Margeson 1993, 9, fig. 4:25; MacGregor *et al.* 1999, 1949, fig. 907:6816). Though few have come from such well dated contexts, they do not contradict the post-Norman conquest, late 11th–early 12th century date.

A similar, though cruder version was recently discovered in Aberdeen at St Nicholas church (Alison Cameron, *pers. comm.*), well stratified in a ditch which is known to pre-date the early 12th century. This apparently Norman fashion, then, was not unknown outside of Norman England.

Margeson interprets these pins as hair pins, on the basis that they are too small to be used to fasten items of dress, compared with the larger and unpierced early historic hipped shaft dress pins (Stevenson 1955; MacGregor 1985, 116). Instead, she suggests, they may have fastened veils or been pushed into plaits. The hipped shaft would prevent them slipping out. The heads are sometimes decorated and are clearly meant to be seen while the pierced hole may have held fine ribbons or gold threads.

Given this hypothesis it is tantolizing that the pin was found in the grave of a young (25–35 yrs) woman, in the vicinity of her head (at her collar bone). However, the dating of the grave is some 300–500 years too late for the bone pin. The grave's location both spatially and strati-graphically, the presence of a wooden coffin and the presence in the torso area of a silk and silver thread *passementerie* button (see Appendix G) which has known early post-medieval parallels, all point towards a 16th or 17th century date for the grave; this was corroborated by the radiocarbon dating of the skeleton to AD 1450–1660 (SUERC-28302; 325±40 BP). Accepting that the dating of the burial is secure, the pin must therefore either be redeposited, possibly from an earlier grave, or was worn by the woman as an heirloom.

Copper alloy

Almost all the copper alloy finds came from layers of 19th century landscaping deposits. These include a large collection of wire pins, probably shroud pins, redeposited from disturbed earlier burials. There is also a 17th century coin, again possibly deriving from a grave, although it may possibly represent an accidental loss.

Other finds are largely consistent with the date of the deposit, being of later 18th and 19th century date. Finds such as the dress accessories are the kinds of small objects which are easily lost, though the derivation of the furniture handle must remain a little more mysterious.

SF34 (1073): coin, by Nick Holmes

Charles I turner, 2nd issue (1632–9). 19th century

(817): Thimble

Domed top, covered in grid pattern indentations, sides covered in regular indentations, except for 3mm wide plain band around rim (Figure E.2). H: 21mm, D: 19mm, Wt: 7g. 19th century?

(007): Button No. 4

Flat disc; wire loop at back. Poor condition but appears undecorated. D: 14mm. 18th/19th century?

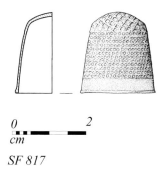

0   2
cm

SF 817

Fig. E.2: Thimble (SF817)

(007): Button No. 5

Flat disc with remains of wire loop at back. Poor condition but appears undecorated. D: 20mm. 18th/19th century?

SF344 (1074): Button

Flat disc; wire loop at back set into conical boss. 19th century

SF196 (1055): Cuff-link

Two discs of copper alloy, joined by short length of wire. Larger disc inlaid with plain bone disc. D: 15mm. 19th/20th century

SF276 (1074): Percussion cap

Top hat shaped; rim divided into four segments. Used. 19th century

(008): Furniture handle/coffin grip

Curving handle; central bulge and out-turned arms. L: 83mm, W: 40mm. 18th century?

General discussion

The thimble (Figure E.2) is a post-medieval type, found in later 18th and early 19th century contexts (Holmes 1991; Johnson 1982; Franklin forthcoming). The buttons are of a long-lived type, but were most common in the 18th and early 19th centuries. Button No. 5 has a silvery appearance which suggests it is made of a copper-zinc alloy, sometimes called 'Tombac', commonly used for buttons in the 18th century. These often have this type of raised cone on the back, present at the Kirk Ness example, into which the loop is set (Bailey 2004, 40). Though earlier examples are known cuff-links did not come into common usage until shirt cuff became plainer in the second half of the 19th century.

The 'exploded top hat' shape of the percussion cap is characteristic of those used to fire Pattern 1853 rifled muskets. These were the best weapons of their type and were supplied to all British land forces seeing action in Britain's colonial wars. Nearly a third of a million were produced between 1858 and 1864 (Peglar 1998).

The handle is of a type used for drawers around the middle of the 18th century (Hume 1976, 229), but its context here might imply that the reuse as a coffin handle or grip is the more likely interpretation. Comparison with contemporary coffin grips shows this is a relatively small example, though not so small as those from child's coffins (Bashford and Sibun 2007, 124–5).

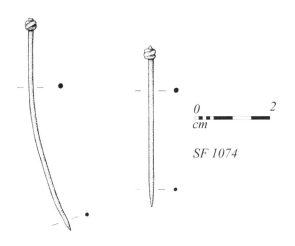

Fig. E.3: Pins (SF1074)

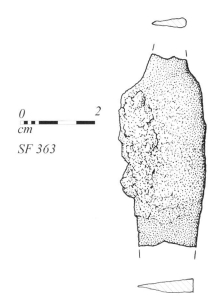

Fig. E.4: Whittle tanged knife (SF363)

Wire pins

There are two types of pins present, based on the morphology of the heads (see Table E.1 on CD). Type A heads (33 examples) are formed from a double coil of wire fixed to the top of the shaft by means of a stamp, giving a characteristic spherical shape. Type B heads (9 examples) are cushion shaped and integral with the shaft. Type A pins have a long history. They are common finds on sites between the 16th and 19th centuries (Caple 1983; Tylecote 1972). Type B pins are essentially the same form as modern stainless steel pins in all but the metal used. The majority of both types of pin show the remains of tinning.

Pins such as these had a variety of uses. They were used in dress to secure items of costume, for sewing purposes and to secure shrouds. This latter obviously accounts for their presence in such large numbers on this site, although none of the pins was found *in situ* in a grave fill. The excavated early post-medieval burials were all made in wooden coffins. Possibly another part of the graveyard, since disturbed, was reserved for less affluent individuals buried wrapped in shrouds.

Most pins were redeposited in 19th century layers with associated graveyard charnel (mainly in *1063* and *1074*). The bends in many of the pins are consistent with strain caused by the weight of the body pulling as it is lifted pulling on these pins. The S-bends in three examples would have occurred if the pin was pushed through the fabric three times rather than the minimum two.

Two pins are considerably larger than the average (Cat Nos 10–11, 42mm and 58mm) and are both probably earlier (Figure E.3). One (Cat No. 10) was stratified in a layer (816) underneath SK871 (16th/17th century, adult, legs only) and is thus the only pin in close association with a grave and the only pin stratified in a layer earlier than the 19th century. The remaining pins are more uniform 22–39mm in length, average 32mm. There is no significant difference between Type A and Type B pins in

term of length.

Lead

There are five small fragments of lead sheet and strips, all from 19th century contexts *1055*, *1063*, *1111*, *1135*, and *1140*. These may be waste from roofing lead or other building works, or possibly the remains of disturbed lead coffin linings.

Iron

Of the 319 iron finds found at the site, the only identifiable objects from secure medieval contexts were one nail SF356 (context *1095*), and a piece of a whittle tanged knife SF363 (*1210*). A hooked fitting SF144A (*1331*), is from a potentially early context, but which seems to have been disturbed in the 20th century.

SF363 (1210): Knife

Part of blade with curving back, shoulder, and stump of whittle tang. L: 51mm, W: 23mm. Medieval (Figure E.4)

SF144A (1331): Hook

Fitting with nail head, double shaft, splayed at end into two hooks, one curving, one tightly folded. L: 64mm, W: 52mm. Modern disturbance (Figure E.5)

General discussion of coffin nails

The majority of the iron assemblage is made up of coffin nails from the early post-medieval graves. Most of the 16th and 17th century burials appear to have been in coffins, whereas there is no evidence for their use in earlier burials. The presence of wooden coffins is confirmed in all cases

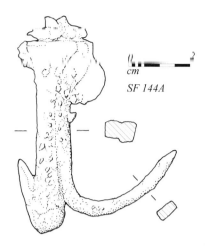

cm

SF 144A

Fig. E.5: Hooked fitting (SF144A)

by the observation during excavation of a 'coffin stain' around the body (see Figure 4.61). The minimum number of nails present in each grave was estimated from the numbers of heads and other sizeable fragments present. Numbers ranged from 3–33 with an average of 16 (see Table E.2 on CD). Typically these are of the form of medium-sized woodworking nails (*cf*. Ford and Walsh 1987, type A).

Burials in wooden coffins, as opposed to the body wrapped in a shroud, became increasingly common during the later medieval period. Coffins are usually accompanied by finds of iron nails, though in widely different quantities. It is difficult to make a coffin using fewer than 12 nails (Boyd 1989), but the use of wooden pegs for some joints is possible and some nails might have been lost to corrosion. The wooden coffins from St Giles Cathedral in Edinburgh used 24–60 nails though, in this case, the burials were within the cathedral and thus both more likely to have been wealthier individual, and to have suffered less from corrosion and decay (Collard *et al.* 2006, 20).

Interestingly, the two coffins using the most nails at North Berwick (SK869 and SK832) were also the only two to hold older adult men. These coffins were apparently better made than others, whether due to the greater weight of the individuals, or greater respect afforded to them.

The exact locations of the nails in relation to the coffin stain were unfortunately not recorded, so it is difficult to determine how the coffins were constructed. For some of the graves, they are recorded as 'upper' and 'lower' nails and, in two cases, there is reference to lines of nails spaced at intervals along the edge, suggesting they were at least used to attach base and lid.

Some nails to secure the corner joints might also be expected. The mineralised wood adhering to the nail shafts suggests the thickness of the wood used ranged from 10mm to 18mm in thickness. Identification of the type of wood was not attempted, but elsewhere, pine has proven the most commonly used, but also oak, spruce and other woods (McCullagh 2006; Boyd 1989).

Later iron finds from the 19th century layers of made up ground seem to be largely of redeposited nature, most likely from the graveyard soil. There were a number of coffin nails, some bearing traces of mineralised wood and some lengths of iron wire, possibly the remains of iron shroud pins.

A chisel, SF23a (*1074*), might have been dropped by a stone mason. A small bracket with a looped ending, SF283 (*1029*), could have possibly been used for suspending a lantern or other fitting from a wall.

Some inferences about the weapon used to stab SK605

with Dave Henderson

SK605 was the skeleton of a young man, dating to the 12th or 13th century, who was fatally stabbed four times in the back, twice in the shoulder (wounds 1 and 2) and twice between the ribs (wounds 3 and 4). There may have been other, undetected injuries as the legs and parts of the right side of the skeleton were cut away by later burials. The man was over 20 years of age, slightly better built than average, with wear to the shoulder suggesting possible archery practice.

From the size, shape and relative positions of the injuries to the bones of SK605 it was possible to infer some facts about the weapon that killed him. It had a symmetrical lozenge-shaped section with very sharp edges (wound 1) and there is no indication that more than one weapon was used. At a point 7.5mm from the tip the blade was 5.2mm wide by 3.5mm thick (wound 1). Where the blade penetrated the scapula (wound 2) the tip embedded in the rib which would have been *c*.20mm below it, thus, at a point *c*.20mm from the tip, the blade was *c*.11mm wide. Wound 1 suggests that the blade was at least 40mm long; the evidence from wound 3 and 4 suggests that the blade was at least 70mm long.

The two most obvious weapons which would fit this description are a sword or a dagger. Arrowheads or spearheads were considered, but seem less likely. Some, though by no means all, arrowheads, from this period have lozenge shaped sections (Jessop 1996), though the edges are not likely to have been as sharp. The location of the wounds also suggests a closer range which would rule out a spearhead. The two wounds between the ribs (wounds 3 and 4) are directed upwards, which, if arrow shots, would have necessitated the body lying face down on the ground. While this is possible, the close spacing and accuracy of both wounds, finding adjacent intercostal spaces, seems unlikely. If caught in a hail of arrows, some more random additional injuries might be expected.

A sword has the correct section and the edge would have been honed to be razor sharp. However, again, the angle and nature of the wounds seems wrong. The wounds have been made by a stabbing point, whereas swords of this period are more effective at slicing. While quite possible to be stabbed by a sword tip, the downward angle of the two scapula injuries (wounds 1 and 2) would have been somewhat difficult to manage with a long sword and again the upward angle of the rib injuries (wounds 3 and 4) would mean the body would probably have had to be lying prone, or the assailant be lying on the ground. A similar negative assessment can be made against the use of a spear with a long shaft.

It seems more likely that a much shorter, more manoeuvrable blade was used. A dagger is therefore the most probable culprit, although daggers with lozenge-shaped sections are relatively new in the late 12th–earlier 13th century, to which the skeleton has been dated (Stuart Campbell *pers. comm.*).

If the dagger as a weapon is accepted, the most likely course of events would seem to be as follows: the two shoulder injuries were inflicted first, over arm and in quick succession, and were enough to bring down the victim. He was then stabbed twice through the ribs at close range, possibly while lying prone, with some accuracy and a knowledge of exactly the right angle needed to reach the heart.

Knives and larger knife-daggers were carried by a large proportion of the general population, both men and women, during the medieval period (de Neergaard 1987). They were a multi-purpose practical tool, for use in hunting, eating, crafts, and self defence. However, these knives had a single edged blade, with a triangular section. Daggers with a lozenge-sectioned blade are a more specialist military weapon and carried mainly by military men (Ward-Perkins 1940, 38). This, combined with the accuracy of the stab wounds, implies a degree of professionalism in the killing and arguably a degree of calculation. It would seem likely, then, that this man was murdered, rather than slain in battle, whether for the purposes of robbery or more complex political or personal reasons, it was perpetrated by someone who was well armed and who knew how to kill.

Appendix F: Small finds from James Richardson's excavation, now held at East Lothian Council Museums Services

by Stuart Campbell and George Haggarty, with Tanja Romankiewicz

Eight finds from Richardson's excavations of the 1950s survive in the East Lothian Museums Service collection, currently held at Haddington, East Lothian (see Figure 4.47)

Bone

Acc No. 1129: Bone domino

A small bone domino, marked with ring and dots to represent the numbers 1 and 4. The surface is divided

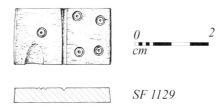

SF 1129

Fig. F.1: Bone domino (SF1129)

into two fields by a single, slightly off-centre, line probably made with the cut of a saw as it is shallower on one side of the cut than the other. L: 26mm; W: 14.5mm; T: 4mm (Figure F.1)

This find is fairly representative of the general class of post-medieval (i.e. 17th–18th century) dominoes and similar examples can be found, for instance, from Plymouth (Fairclough and Barber 1979, 129) and Southampton (Platt and Coleman-Smith, 1975, fig. 249). They were an object made, used and lost in some number.

Copper alloy

Acc No. 1129: Crucifix

Crucifix, crudely engraved; slightly lopsided positioning of cross arms. Made from existing piece of sheet 1mm thick with one polished and prepared surface and other rough and unfinished. Basic design elaborated by cutting decorative terminals at end of arms and central 'X' on front. Some decoration on rear. Top terminal undercut, suggesting crucifix was intended to be suspended from a thong or necklace. L: 32mm; W: 24mm; T: 1mm (see Figure 4.51).

Tellingly, the front of this object is the unfinished surface, suggesting cosmetic appearances were not important. It has been cut using a pair of shears and the angle and impression of the blades can still be seen along the sides of the cross. This would have required excessive force using an unsuitable implement and is likely to have damaged the tool by either bending the blades or the connecting pin. This is an interesting example of a 'home made' artefact, made with a reused piece of metal and with whatever tools were at hand; it is a method of production which an artisan would have certainly eschewed. The purpose and dating are however less clear; in general such crosses could be said to be more likely to be post-medieval in date than earlier (for example, Gilchrist and Sloane, 2005, 92–3) and the slight provision for suspension might suggest it was made for inclusion in a burial rather than for wearing. It might also be said that such objects are likely to represent a cultural adherence to existing customs rather than an overt or doctrinal devotion to Catholic or recusant practices (Tarlow 2003).

Acc No. 1124: Candle snuffer

Conical; spherical finial at top; rounded rim at bottom with annular decorative incision *c*.13mm from base; rivet

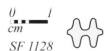

Fig. F.4: Section of lead window came (SF1128)

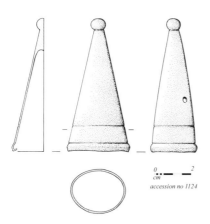

Fig. F.2: Bronze candle snuffer (SF1124)

Fig. F.3: Large copper alloy button (SF1120)

Fig. F.6: Salt-glazed stoneware jug (SF1127)

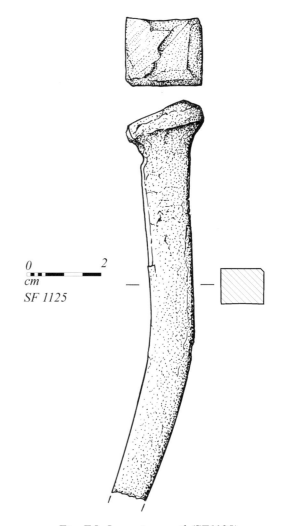

Fig. F.5: Large iron nail (SF1125)

Fig. F.7: Base of drinking cup (SF1127)

hole for staff (lost) at roughly half object height. Some mortar residue inside. H: 70mm; D (bottom): 35.5 × 26mm (deformed); T: 1mm (Figure F.2).

Acc No. 1130: Button

Large, circular; flat disc; wire loop at back; undecorated. Some greenish staining on front where loop is soldered on at back. D: 33.5mm; T: 1mm (Figure F.3).

Lead

Acc No. 1128: Lead window came

Double-grooved, possibly part of medieval lead glazing; twisted and distorted. Total original L (before distortion as surviving): 145mm; D grooves: 1mm; W grooves: 2mm; total H: 6.5mm; total W: 5mm (see Figure 4.46; Figure F.4).

Iron

Acc No. 1125: Nail

Large, square-sectioned (slightly trapezoid at tip); square, hammered out head with squared-off rim. Slightly bend towards tip; original tip missing; diagonal scars across head. Possible use for substantial timber connection; maritime-related? L (as surviving): 105mm; shank section at tip: 10 × 8/7mm (slightly trapezoid); shank section at head: 12.5 × 9.5mm; head: 21 x18mm, 9mm thick (Figure F.5)

Ceramic

Acc No. 1127: Small jug

Salt-glazed stoneware. Raeren, Lower Rhine, *c.*16th century. Small sizes rare in Scotland. H: (inc. base): 83mm; D (base): 43mm; (max.): 64mm; (lower edge rim): 33mm; (top of rim): 29mm; (internal at rim): 20.5mm; T: 1mm (see Figure 4.52; Figure F.6)

Acc No. 1127: base of drinking cup (fragment)

Cream-grey, unglazed, high-fired base; Beckmann-type. Beauvais, northern France or Siegburg, Rhineland, mid-16th century. Most material in Scotland are French imports from Beauvais. D: (as surviving): 69 × 59mm; (base/foot): 45mm; (recess within foot): 21mm; H (as surviving): 9.5mm (Figure F.7)

Appendix G: Textile covering button

by Carol Christiansen, with Lore Troalén

Analysis

The button (Figure G.1) was recovered from grave *861*, inhumation burial SK865 (radiocarbon dated to AD 1450–1660 (SUERC 28302, 325±40 BP). This was the burial of a female in her early 20s. Found *in situ*, the button lay to the left of the body, between the ribs and the arm.

Initial analysis of the object was undertaken in July 2008, using a standard hand lens and stereomicroscope. Analysis by scanning electron microscope was undertaken at the National Museums of Scotland Department of Conservation and Analytical Research in December 2008, in collaboration with Lore Troalén.

The button from Kirk Ness is made from a wooden core (4.5 × 6mm) covered with threads of silk and copper foil. It measures 9 × 11 × 8mm. There is no evidence of a shank. It is in a very fragile state. Some threads have broken, revealing the wooden core in places on the front and most of the button back. The copper wrap is corroded (Figure G.2, on CD) and sections have cracked and broken away, revealing the silk core of the thread

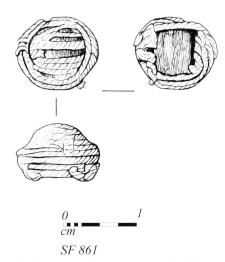

SF 861

Fig. G.1: Textile-covered button, drawn by Marion O'Neill

(Figure G.3, on CD). The fragility and brittleness of the threads meant that conservation was not possible. The button is partially encrusted with soil, making it impossible to examine the underlying fabric structure.

Textile structure

The threads covering the button are made of two strands of Z-spun silk fibre (Figure G.4, on CD), plied together in S-direction. Each double thread was then wrapped, S-direction, with a thin strip of copper foil 500–900μm wide and 25–30μm thick. (Figures G.3 and G.5, on CD). Individual threads measure 500–700μm wide. The threads have become flattened in use or during burial and subsequently are wider than when originally spun.

The thinness of the copper strip used to wrap the silk compares favourably with silver and silver gilt examples that have been measured elsewhere (Hoke and Petrascheck-Heim 1977, 51; Nord and Tronner 2000, 274). The widths of the copper strips (0.5–0.9mm), and whole threads (0.5–0.7mm), are greater than gold, silver and silver gilt threads that have been measured (Christiansen 2009; Crowfoot 1956, 442; Hoke and Petrascheck-Heim 1977, 51; Nord and Tronner 2000, 274). This may suggest that the thread from Kirk Ness, although complex and requiring spinning skill to construct, was of a lower standard of workmanship than silver and silver gilt threads found elsewhere.

The threads were threaded and sewn over the top of the button core first, and then along the sides and are bunched and knotted at both ends (Figure G.6, on CD). The button was probably a self-shank type, i.e. a shank was created with threads and extended from the back. No rigid shank remains and there is no evidence for one (Figure G.7, on CD). It is possible that threads or a layer of fabric which no longer survives (e.g. of linen), existed between the wooden core and the copper and silk threads as on a number of surviving 17th century buttons (Arnold 1985, 81, 89).

Discussion

The Kirk Ness button is a very basic form of passementerie, using decorative thread with a simple wrapping technique. There is no definitive evidence of interlacing or knotting, although a fragment of silk thread running cross-ways on one side may indicate a more complex form of passementerie was originally present (Figure G.8, on CD). Without the possibility of conservation, the remainder of the thread structure remains obscured under soil. The thread covering the Kirk Ness button is unusual in that it is wrapped with copper, rather than gold, silver, or silver-gilt. Using copper foil was a less expensive alternative to silver, certainly less than gold, yet it was a means to achieve a richer look to a garment than plain silk corded buttons. Passementerie buttons, covered in wrapping, interlacing, or knotted thread techniques, were popular in clothing for men and women in the 16th–17th centuries, although they are found in Europe as early as the 10th century (Hedeager Krag 2007, 237–9). A few examples of metal-wrapped threads survive from Scotland (Henshall, *et al.* 1956, 30–3; Henshall 1965, 159–61; Bennett 1987, 166; Christiansen 2009). The published remains are from medieval contexts and are brocades on tablet-woven bands.

A fuller discussion of the button and textile is included on the CD.

Appendix I: The human remains

by David Henderson

The articulated remains from Kirk Ness were analysed to establish the demographic structure of the sample and were examined for pathological data; the non-articulated remains were also analysed, and the limited results obtained are incorporated below. Information previously obtained from the trial-trenching (1998) is included, which concerns context *208.F*, a pit of comingled remains interpreted as the reburial of bones which had been disturbed by an earlier excavation.

In view of the small sample of individuals recovered and the potentially large time-span from which they might derive, any general conclusions about the medieval population of the area must be tentative.

Preservation and taphonomy

In general the preservation of the articulated remains was good. The matrix in which the skeletons were contained was of a shelly beach sand, and much of the bone was hard and well preserved. Due to the erosion of the medieval ground surface, however, many of the remains were at a level just under the turf and the weight of passers-by had caused breakage of some bones. In some very shallow graves, grass roots had etched channels in the surface cortex, possibly masking some pathological lesions.

Over half of the articulated remains comprised basically complete skeletons, although those to the east of the excavated area were truncated by 20th century pipe-trenches and paths, as well as by the erosion of the eastern part of the medieval graveyard by the action of the sea.

The unarticulated remains were recovered from both the matrix layers into which the graves had been dug and from small negative features cut into the layers. These remains seem to represent bones disturbed from the ground when new graves were dug, and possibly others which had eroded out of the eastern side of the graveyard and had been re-interred. Again, preservation was generally good. The exception to this was context *208.F*. The preservation of these remains was markedly worse than the rest of the bone, with extensive root-etching and considerable erosion of the bone surface. Several of the femurs from this context also displayed signs of carnivore gnawing on their distal ends. This finding was confined to the femurs. Given the history of erosion at the eastern edge of the site it is likely that these bones were exposed to the depredations of dogs at some point after burial.

The femur tends to be the bone first chewed for marrow by carnivores, if the full skeleton is available (Lyman 1994, 149) and some nutrition can survive within bones which appear dry and clean on the outer surface. Both these factors suggest that there is no need to assume that the bones were particularly fresh when scavenged.

The feature from which these bones were all recovered is interpreted as the 'charnel pit' into which the disturbed bones from a previous archaeological excavation of the site were re-interred. It may be that the earlier trenches were excavated in an area in which the human bones that had eroded out of the graveyard were reburied. This suggestion is, perhaps, strengthened by the fact that femurs, skulls and humeri were the most commonly occurring elements in this feature. It has been observed that when disturbed bones were reburied in historical times (for example when a new grave had been dug through an older one), the smaller (and perhaps less obviously human) skeletal elements were neglected and disproportionate numbers of skulls and femurs were re-interred. Presumably the smaller bones were left abandoned on the beach, or had been so badly damaged by the action of the dogs than no recognisable fragments remained.

Methods

Age at death of the individuals was determined by examination of dental development and abrasion (Brothwell 1981) and, where appropriate, by examination of the surface of the pubic symphyses and the auricular surfaces of the ilium and sacrum. Gender was assessed by examining the form of the skull and the pelvis, with more weight given to pelvic morphology. In cases where neither of these skeletal areas was diagnostic, or was absent, measurement of limb-bone ends was used to assign a possible gender using comparisons from the same population, where possible.

Stature was reconstructed using the standard regression formulae from long bone lengths of Trotter and Gleser (in Bass 1987). Skeletal measurements were taken as per Cross and Bruce (1989) and indices were calculated using the formulae in Bass (*op. cit.*) Non-metric traits were recorded from those in Brothwell (1981, 93–100).

All bones were examined for pathological lesions and, where possible, these were classified according to cause.

Results

Demography

A total of 24 *in situ* inhumation burials were recovered from the site, representing 18 adults and six individuals under 18 years old. Non-articulated bone deriving from a minimum of a further 33 adults (based on the most common skeletal element, the left femur) and five immature individuals was also recovered.

Age at death

Of the *in situ* individuals, six were classified as young adults (YA, 18–35 years old at death), four were mature adults (MA, 35–55 yrs) and six were of old age (OA, over 55 yrs). Two further individuals (SK 870 and SK871) were represented by their lower legs alone, and consequently classified simply as adult. Some methods of estimating age at death in adults are now thought to be less accurate than previously supposed (Molleson 1995; Mays 1998 49–66). Tooth-wear analysis (as outlined by Brothwell 1981, 72) seems to be reliable for British skeletons at least to medieval times and this method was favoured here, where possible.

Of the six immature *in situ* skeletons, one was a perinatal baby, one an infant of 18 months (± 6months), two children (4.5 yrs ± 6 months and around 6 years old), one a young juvenile (9 yrs) and the last an older juvenile of 13–14 years old. The older of the two children was either advanced in dental development or retarded in skeletal development, as limb length and the state of fusion of the child's bones indicate an age of 4.5–5 years, while the teeth indicate a minimum age of 6.25 years. The individual showed signs of having suffered several severe episodes of bodily stress, as shown by hypoplastic

lines in the enamel of the teeth, with at least three major episodes between the ages of 6 months and 2 years. Tooth eruption appears to be more resistant to being 'set back' by stressful episodes (high fever or malnutrition, for example) than does skeletal development, which may explain the age discrepancy in the present case between teeth and bone development.

In the non-articulated remains, tooth-wear analysis showed 50% young adults, 28.6% mature and 21.4% old aged (out of 14 partial dentitions examined). Figure I.1 shows the survivorship profile of the excavated population.

Although any projection of these data onto the population as a whole must be treated with caution, there appears to be a marked increase in mortality in the young adult category. Mortality profiles in pre-industrial societies more commonly show a high infant mortality with a drop in the death rate in the young adult category (Roberts and Manchester 1997). The excavated area may, by chance, have been an area with a disproportionately high number of young adult burials. Another possibility is that the number of young adult deaths in the population was particularly high, in this age category women are at the peak of their child-bearing years and young men were disproportionately at risk from death in battle in times of strife. At least one of the young adult males had died due to interpersonal violence.

Sex distribution

Of the adult remains *in situ*, seven were male (and one probable male) and nine female (and one probable female). Of the non-articulated remains, 50% were male and 50% female (from eight right innominate bones).

It was not possible to separate the sexes by comparing single dimension measurements of the long bones or teeth, as the sexual dimorphism of the sample was low. It has been suggested that low sexual dimorphism can occur under conditions of growth-inhibiting stress, possibly these individuals had been subject to poor nutrition and/or ill-health in childhood.

A possible difference in the spatial distribution of males and females was observed in the graveyard, with all the burials found in the northern half of the excavated area (furthest from the church) being of women and children. In the small sub-sample of the graveyard excavated, however, this distribution may be more apparent than real.

Stature and body build

Height estimates were obtained for nine adult females and seven adult males. Average female height was 1.57 m (5' 1¾") with a range of 1.51–1.64 m. Male average height was 1.68 m (5'6") with a range of 1.63–1.73 m. The male average is low relative to many other Scottish medieval sites while the female average is towards the

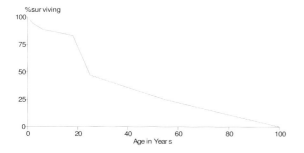

Fig. I.1: Human remains: survivorship profile

top end of the range. Again this may reflect the low sexual dimorphism of the excavated population.

Both sexes showed pronounced muscle insertion points on some bones, evidence of repeated use of particular muscle. Most common in both sexes were muscle scars associated with movements of the shoulder joint, particularly abduction (pulling the elbow away from the side). In two women, pronounced scars were recorded at the pectoralis major attachments on the clavicle, associated with flexion and medial rotation of the shoulder (bringing the elbows forward and towards the midline).

Lower limb shape

Flattening of the femur and tibia (*platymeria* and *platycnemia*) are commonly reported findings from among pre-industrial populations. In both cases it is suggested (Brothwell 1981, 89) that the flattened shape of the bone is a biomechanical response to the stress produced on the leg by a more robust lifestyle (e.g. long-distance walking on rough ground).

It was possible to calculate the meric indices of seven females and six males. All the females were *platymeric*, as were four of the males. One male was *eurymeric* (more rounded femur upper shaft) and another was *stenomeric* (very rounded femur upper shaft). This latter individual (SK829) had peculiarities of the toe joints, possibly relating to an habitually adopted posture (see below) and this may explain his femoral shape.

The *cnemic* indices were calculated for five females and four males. Only one individual of each sex displayed *platycnemia*. Two females were *mesocnemic* (medium broad tibia shape) and two females and three males were *eurycnemic* (broader tibia shape).

In both indices, the females showed greater flattening of the leg bones, reflecting a more robust lifestyle with respect to walking. This is in contrast to many Scottish medieval sites and may reflect the coastal position of North Berwick; many men may have worked in boats rather than been farmers, with less stress being applied to the lower limbs.

Metrical data

Because of the broken nature of much of the material, it was not possible to take measurements of many of the post-cranial bones, and in no case was a full set of measurements available from a single skeleton. As noted above, the excavated sample showed low sexual dimorphism. When an attempt was made to separate the sexes on the basis of single dimension measurements, it was calculated that at least 40% of the individuals of known sex would have been misclassified on this basis, even using usually reliable dimensions such as the maximum humeral head diameter.

From the cranial metrical data, indices were calculated

from ten female and six male skulls (including some material from the non-articulated bones). Some differences between the sexes were observed; female skulls tended to have medium cranial indices (6/9), and have narrow faces and eye-sockets (4/4 and 5/6 respectively). Males tended more to round-headed forms (3/5) with medium–broad faces (3/4) and wide or medium eye-sockets (4/5). Both sexes had narrow nasal apertures and relatively low skulls (breadth-height indices). A full list of measurements is available in the archive.

Non-metric variation

This section concerns traits and developmental anomalies of the skeleton which can be recorded as present or absent. Many of the traits appear to have a purely genetic basis, while the expression of others is influenced by environmental factors.

CRANIAL TRAITS

The most commonly occurring cranial non-metric traits were ossicles in the lambdoid suture (16/21), supra-orbital notch (right-side 12/17, left-side 9/15), posterior condylar canal open (left 13/21, right 7/19) and right-side parietal foramen (12/20, left side 8/17). It has been suggested that the supra-orbital notch and ossicles in the lambdoid suture are both variations which occur more frequently in populations under nutritional stress (Bocquet-Appel 1984). The posterior condylar canal was frequently recorded as open on the left side of the skull, but closed on the right (6/17), while the reverse was true of the parietal foramen (4/15).

Less frequently occurring cranial traits included a double mental foramen at the left side of the mandible (1/18, right 0/18) and an accessory infra-orbital foramen (left 2/14, right 1/12). The metopic suture was present in seven of 30 frontal bones (23.3%). this suture is normally obliterated by the second year of life and rates of its persistence vary greatly between populations. The rate here is towards the high end of the range for Scottish medieval sites.

POST-CRANIAL TRAITS

The most commonly recorded traits for this site occurred in the ankle, where 12 of 18 right tibiae showed lateral squatting facets and six of 18 right calcanei showed discrete anterior facets. Five of 12 right patellae had a vastus notch. It is thought that lateral tibial squatting facets arise in individuals who habitually adopt a squatting posture, and is a frequently occurring variant in Scottish medieval populations. Of less frequently occurring variants, two of 32 left humeri had a septal aperture, two of 18 calcanei had no anterior facets and one of 20 fifth lumbar vertebrae were sacralised. One individual (SK829, young adult ?male) appears to have had six lumbar vertebrae. Because of the condition of the thoracic part of the spinal column it was impossible to determine if the uppermost lumbar vertebra was, in fact, a twelfth thoracic vertebra of a very lumbar form, but the next vertebra in sequence has a very typical twelfth thoracic form (the costal facet is on the pedicle, it has superior and lateral tubercles and both inferior articular facets face nearly to lateral and are slightly curved). The putative first lumbar vertebra has a mamillary process, a transverse process and no costal facet. The sacrum is of five elements.

Pathology

DEGENERATIVE JOINT DISEASE AND SPINAL JOINT DISEASE (DJD AND SJD)

All joint surfaces were examined for degenerative changes. These changes include osteophytes (bony projections) around the joint margins and porosity followed by eburnation ('ivory polish') of the bone of the joint surface. Degeneration was graded following the scheme of Sager (in Brothwell 1981, 150).

Degenerative joint disease (or osteoarthritis) is one of the most common findings reported from archaeological populations. The condition will normally manifest itself in the living as joint pain, although there is often no correlation between the severity of the degenerative changes and the severity of the pain experienced. Its prevalence generally increases with age as one of the contributory factors in its appearance seems to be simple wear and tear. It can also appear following a traumatic injury (Secondary DJD). The spinal form of the disease is even more common than that of the appendicular skeleton, and consists of the same degenerative changes to the spinal joints as well as Schmorl's nodes. These latter are formed by a herniation of the material of the spinal discs into the bodies of the adjacent vertebrae, forming pits or troughs in the joint surface. Schmorl's nodes are formed when the spine is placed under excessive compression loads, such as in a fall onto the feet or in heavy lifting, and occur mostly in younger adults and adolescents, when the spinal discs contain a more fluid material.

Altogether, nine of the 18 *in situ* adults in the excavated population showed degenerative changes to their joints (excluding the spine, discussed below) at Sager's grade II or III. This rose to an incidence in five of six old adults from one of seven young adults. The most severe, grade III, changes (involving eburnation of the bone), were only seen in the old.

The joints most commonly affected with medium or severe degeneration (including bones from the non-articulated material) were at the medial and lateral ends of the clavicles, the hip joints and the knees, especially the left knee. The left elbow was also affected more commonly than the right. Old females were particularly prone to degeneration of the elbows and of the left joint of the mandible and males were more prone to degeneration at the knees. The ankles, shoulders and wrists were seldom affected in both sexes and all age groups. One factor contributing to these gender differences may have been different patterns of labour performed by the different sexes; the degeneration of the joints of the mandible in females may be associated with the high numbers of broken molars found in women (see Trauma, below).

In the case of SK 832 (male, OA), the knees were affected with secondary arthritis following infection with syphilis which had infected the tissues of the tibia. In SK 869 (male OA), the knees were affected with DJD secondary to bowing of the tibiae due to rickets.

In the hands, six individuals (of 15 examined) showed moderate or severe degenerative changes in at least one joint. The joints of the thumb were most commonly affected. Women were less affected (2/8) than men (4/7). The feet of seven individuals were examined (4 male, 3 female) of which only an old male showed moderate or severe degenerative changes (in the little toes of both feet). A young male (SK829) was also affected in the joints of the great toe, apparently due to repeated hyperextension of the joints. No evidence was seen on any joint of the erosive lesions typical of rheumatoid arthritis.

Spinal Joint Disease: Osteoarthritic changes in the spine followed the common pattern seen in most populations; severity and prevalence increased with age, as would be expected of degenerative changes, and most of the affected vertebrae were in the load-bearing areas of the lower thoracic and lumbar spine. The presence of Schmorl's nodes formed the same pattern, with no nodes appearing above the lower surface of the fourth thoracic vertebra. In the lumbar spine, males tended to have Schmorl's nodes on the upper surfaces of vertebrae 3, 4, 5, and the sacrum, while females' lesions were on the lower surface of vertebrae 1, 2 and 3.

Lateral spondylarthrosis, degenerative changes of the articular facets of the vertebrae, was a rare condition in females, but common in males especially in thoracic vertebrae 3–8. More severe stages of lateral spondyl-arthrosis can cause greatly restricted movement of the back. Two individuals (SK840, female MA and an individual from the non-articulated material, context 601/602) had the axis and third cervical vertebrae fused, possibly causing some restricted movement of the head. In SK840 the entire cervical spine showed degeneration, with the fused axis and third vertebrae joined at a slight angle to the side (scoliosis) and the sixth vertebral body wedge shaped (kyphosis); this may be the result of an injury.

DEFICIENCY DISEASES

Evidence of iron-deficiency anaemia is seen in skeletal remains in the form of pitting in the roof of the eye-sockets (*cribra orbitalia*) and/or thickening and pitting of the outer layer of the cranial bones, especially the parietals and the occipital (porotic hyperostosis). Many factors appear to contribute to the condition, the most important being a lack of absorbable iron in the diet and a heavy infestation with gut parasites. The deficiency is most common in childhood, in archaeological populations, but the lesions may remain in evidence on the skull into adulthood.

Of the *in situ* skeletons, nine of 17 individuals (52.9%) showed the lesions of *cribra orbitalia*, a particularly high figure for a medieval Scottish site. In two nearby medieval sites (Isle of May: Roberts and Battley 1998, and Dunbar: Roberts 2001) the prevalence of *cribra orbitalia* was 30% and 8.8%, respectively. At the Seabird Centre site, the condition affected 80% of sub-adult crania and 37.5% of MA and OA individuals (in addition, one male OA cranium displayed porotic hyperostosis) It has been suggested that the high levels of the condition in sub-adults reflects the weakening effect of anaemia on the immune system, making affected individuals more likely to die at a younger age. The high levels of anaemia seen at this site add to the impression of poor nutrition suggested by the low sexual dimorphism.

Another deficiency disease evident in the population under study was vitamin D deficiency (rickets). Vitamin D is essential for the mineralisation of bone tissue and its lack, whether through limited amounts in the diet or particularly through lack of exposure of the skin to sunlight, can cause bowing of the weight-bearing bones of the skeleton.

One of the *in situ* population (SK869, male OA) showed the bowed tibiae typical of the disease, as well as five femur shafts from the non-articulated remains (two adults and three immature). The rate of one adult showing evidence of rickets out of 46 individuals for whom the left femur was recovered (including the non-articulated material) is very low; the broadly contemporary site of St Giles Cathedral in Edinburgh (Henderson 2006) has a prevalence of just under 10% for rickets. This may reflect the difference between life in the dark closes of Edinburgh and the more open-air environment of North Berwick.

CHILDHOOD MORBIDITY

Some evidence of childhood ill-health may be preserved in the adult skeleton in the form of furrows and pits in the enamel of the teeth (Hypoplastic lines), the position of which reflects the state of development of the permanent tooth when the episode of illness or nutritional stress occurred (Figure I.2).

Only four of 17 (23.5%) complete or partial dentitions examined from both the *in situ* and non-articulated material showed no hypoplastic lines. Most affected dentitions showed two or three lines, though the teeth of SK 605 (male, YA) showed seven episodes of illness between the ages of 1 and 13 years, and an isolated upper premolar from context 603 showed eight hypoplastic lines, corresponding to illness or other bodily stress at ages between 4 and 10 years of age. Taken as a whole, the most commonly occurring ages at which hypoplastic lines formed were 1½–2 years of age, with another diffuse peak at 5 and 6 years (Figure I.2).

It is probable that the lines which were formed at 18

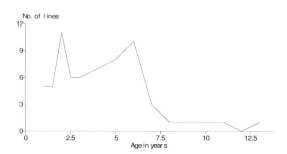

Fig. I.2: Human remains: number of enamel hypoplastic lines recorded against age of occurrence

months to 2 years of age were caused by the nutritional stress which can occur during the switch to solid foods at weaning, while the peak at 5–6 years may reflect the occurrence of 'childhood infectious diseases' passed on from child to child as individuals become more independent of their mothers and begin to interact more with their contemporaries.

TRAUMA

Fractures: Twelve bone fractures were recorded; four well-healed fractures of the clavicle (one was badly aligned), three cases of healed depressed fractures of the skull, two 'clay-shoveller's' fractures of the vertebrae and the remaining cases were healed fractures of the humerus, the calcaneus, and a rib. While the clavicles, humeri and ribs remain among the most common sites for fractures today, often being injured in falls, the other cases are discussed more fully.

Of the cranial depressed fractures, two were on the parietal bone and one on the frontal bone. The individuals were two young males and a female, and in all cases the bone had healed well. While one case (SK829) was adjacent to the lambdoid suture, and this had not been obliterated during the healing process (suggesting that the injury may have occurred in early childhood), the other two injuries are towards the front of the skull and on the left side, conditions which have been suggested as being typical of interpersonal violence, facing a right-handed opponent (Aufderheide and Rodriguez-Martin 1998, 23).

The term 'clay-shoveller's' fracture describes a fracture where the action of the trapezius and rhomboid muscles of the neck and shoulder can avulse (tear off) part of the spines of the seventh cervical and/or the first thoracic vertebrae. Both cases here were seen in individuals of the OA category, a male (SK832) and a female (SK866). In neither case had the avulsed portion of the bone reunited with the vertebra. As the name suggests, the fracture occurs when performing actions that place excessive strain on the upper arms and shoulders.

The calcaneal fracture was of the dorsal anterior edge of the cuboid facet (from the non-articulated remains). A chip of bone had been detached and had subsequently healed slightly misaligned. It is probable that the injury was sustained by dropping a heavy object onto the foot. No degeneration of the joint surface was evident, so it may be that, once healed, the injury presented no further problems of mobility.

Soft-tissue injury: Injury and infection in overlying tissue can sometimes involve an underlying bone; the periosteum (the membrane surrounding a bone) may become involved, laying down additional reactive bone tissue onto the bone surface (periostitis) or the bone itself may become involved, leading to osteomyelitis, a much more serious infection which may lead to pus formation in the marrow cavity and death of the bone tissue. Even today this infection is difficult to treat, and in the past would almost certainly have lead to death. Other signs of soft tissue injury (excluding specific infections, discussed below) are the formation of enthesopathies, where trauma to a muscle causes bleeding into the area where the tendon is inserted into the bone, which later ossifies, and calcification of injured muscle tissue or blood in an overlying bruise. *Osteochondritis dissecans* is the death of small areas of the cartilage of a joint following injury; if the underlying bone is also injured a small 'punched-out' lesion can be observed on the joint surface. The condition usually resolves itself. Schmorl's nodes (see above) is also a traumatic soft tissue injury in origin.

Periostitis is commonly seen on the front of the tibia, where the bone is covered only by the skin of the shin, and so more exposed to injury from knocks and grazes. The incidence of tibial periostitis was surprisingly low from this site; only 10% of tibiae showed evidence of the condition. In the St Giles, Edinburgh, sample (Henderson 2006) the rate of tibial periostitis was 27.3%.

Where possible, the internal surfaces of the maxillary sinuses were examined. In six of 16 crania examined, a periostitic reaction was seen in the sinus, two of these cases were apparently caused by infection from an adjacent tooth abscess; the other four may represent chronic sinusitis.

The pelvic surface of the sacrum of a young man (SK609) showed evidence of osteomyelitis. Unfortunately this part of the skeleton was badly preserved and quite broken, but an ostitic reaction could be seen across the front and upper part of the sacrum which also penetrated the bone around the first and second sacral foramina. The sigmoid colon overlies this area, and some disease of the bowel may have spread to the sacrum; the deep position of the sacrum makes a direct injury to the bone unlikely.

Cranium A from feature 824 (a young female), showed a roughly oval patch of compact bone overlying the sagittal suture, 35 × 28mm with diffuse edges and *c.*5mm thick. This may be the calcified remains of an overlying soft tissue injury, the position and ill-defined borders make the alternative suggestion of a benign osteoma unlikely.

Two cases of osteochondritis dissecans were seen, one on the capitulum of the humerus and one on the condyles of the femur. An enthesopathy of the origin of brachioradialis on the left humerus of an MA male (SK 614) may have been caused by the forearm being accidentally twisted outwards while the elbow was straight.

OCCUPATIONAL AND POSTURAL

Other features were recorded which may have had their origin in occupations or habitually adopted postures. The hands of SK838 (MA female) showed that the second (and probably the third) fingers of both hands were habitually hyperextended, (angled away from the palm) to the extent that the knuckle joint surface was elongated to the backs of the metacarpals. Similarly, the toes of SK 829, a young male, were habitually hyperextended. As all other aspects of the foot and leg bones are normal the condition does not appear to be pathological in origin and may have been caused by adopting a kneeling posture with the toes firmly planted on the ground.

Another finding, probably related to occupation, concerned the teeth, but will be recorded here. Of 19 complete or partial dentitions examined, in seven cases (and two further cases in loose teeth found in the non-articulated material) the first and/or second molars had been chipped, and in some cases the enamel had been completely shattered off. In most of these cases, the edges of the broken enamel were rounded and worn, excluding the possibility of post-mortem damage. Five of the instances were females. It seems likely that some activity was carried out (?mostly by women) involving using the teeth as a vice to hold a hard object. In the case of the MA female SK840, all her upper and lower first molars were broken and her lower left second molar was broken, leading to a gross caries cavity. Probably as a consequence of her damaged teeth, she appears to have eaten only very soft food such as pap or gruel for some time before her death, allowing calculus to form on the biting surfaces of her molars.

BLADE INJURIES

The skeleton of a young male adult (SK605) showed four stabbing wounds from a sharp, narrow, pointed blade, at least 40mm long. The skeleton consisted of the trunk and left arm along with part of the left side of the skull, having been truncated by later grave cuts.

The four wounds observed were:

1: Stabbing the left scapula from above, cutting the angle of the acromial process with the tip of the weapon penetrating the bone of the scapular neck just beside the root of the scapular spine to a depth of 7.5mm. The edge of the blade was extremely sharp and the tip was lozenge shaped, 5.2mm wide and 3.5mm thick at the wound in the scapular neck.

2: Stabbing the left scapula 43mm above the inferior angle and beside the medial margin, with the tip of the blade penetrating the body of the underlying fifth rib. The blade was thrust in at an angle of about 45° downwards, and also removed with a downwards motion. As it passed through the scapula the weapon was about

11.8mm wide, although this may be distorted by the two actions of thrusting and withdrawing.

3: Stabbing through the seventh intercostal space. The blade was driven up below the angle of the seventh rib pointing towards the midline of the body and cutting both the seventh and eighth ribs.

4: Stabbing upwards and towards the midline through the eighth intercostal space, above the angle of the ninth rib and nicking the lower margin of the eighth rib on both the thrust and the withdrawal.

The effect of injury (1) would have almost certainly been to sever the suprascapular artery and nerve, causing some bleeding and partial paralysis of the action of lifting the arm away from the side. Both injuries (3) and (4) would have penetrated the descending aorta if the blade was over about 70mm long, and if it was long enough, injury (3) could have penetrated the heart. It seems certain that either of the last two blows would have been fatal.

Infectious Disease

Skeleton number SK 832, an old male, showed the some of the characteristic skeletal signs of infection with syphilis. The tibiae ('sabre shin') and fibulae and the medial ends of the clavicles were distorted by the osteomyelitis reaction typical of infection with *Treponema pallidum*. A possible healed gumma scar was seen on the right side of the frontal bone, although the nose showed no signs of degeneration.

Neoplastic Disease

Neoplastic diseases are those involving cancerous growths, whether malignant or benign.

A 'button' osteoma (a benign small bone cancer) was recorded on the right parietal bone of SK 832. These osteomas are among the most commonly reported findings in skeletal material, although more usually found on the frontal bone. They tend to be completely asymptomatic.

In a skull from the non-articulated bone (824 A, a young adult female) a very large 'Inca bone' was seen, occupying only the right side of the squamous part of the occipital bone. It is not clear whether this had been the cause of, or had been caused by, an associated bulge in the cranium; in either case it suggests a pathological episode probably before 11 months of age (when the lateral fissures of the occipital fuse). If an external injury occurred, the subsequent disruption to the formation of the lambdoid suture could have caused the Inca bone and its associated bulge to form; if the bulge was caused by a swelling of intra-cranial tissues (such as a benign cancer of the brain or meninges) it could, of itself, disrupt the formation of the lambdoid suture.

Dentition

Aside from the broken teeth mentioned above, the dentitions of the mature and the older individuals were in a particularly poor state. In the old age category, 39% of the upper teeth had been lost ante-mortem (am loss) or were carious, and 36% of the carious lesions had destroyed most of the tooth involved. Of the five old age dentitions recorded, three had caries cavities in lost more than eight teeth. For the adult dentitions as a whole, of 356 teeth examined, 34 (9.6%) were carious. Other medieval Scottish sites consistently report levels of caries at around 6% (Roberts 2001).

Some developmental anomalies were recorded with regard to the dentition:

SK 822 Male YA: the upper right deciduous canine had been retained, with the permanent canine retained in the maxilla.

SK829 ?Male, YA: the upper right third molar was of a much reduced, peg-like form, but another socket (3.8mm diameter) for a single-rooted tooth was present just beside it. This socket gave the appearance of being a normal alveolus for a tooth, rather than, say, the sinus of an abscess, and as the second and first alveoli were both present, appears to have been for an accessory third molar.

SK 833, Female, OA: all the permanent canine teeth had failed to emerge from the jaws at the normal time. This did not appear to have been because of overcrowding of the teeth, as there was an ample gap between the lower second incisors and the first premolars in the lower jaw. Shortly before death, however, the upper canines had started to erupt, and were both nearly in occlusion. This may have been precipitated by the extensive loss of other teeth from the jaws. This individual also exhibited lumbarisation of the first sacral vertebra, which would normally start to become fused to the rest of the sacrum at around 11 or 12 years of age in females, the same age at which the canines normally begin to erupt.

Context 208F: Left mandible fragment with the third molar erupted, but with the deciduous second molar retained and no sign of its replacing permanent second premolar within the jaw.

Conclusions

Although a small sample, the skeletal remains from the Scottish Seabird Centre site at North Berwick provide an insight into some aspects of the life of the medieval inhabitants of the Burgh. Generally shorter and more poorly fed than many Scottish contemporaries, they appear to have suffered from relatively poor nutrition. The higher than usual numbers of young adults in the sample may be a reflection of a high risk of death from interpersonal violence; at least one young man died as the result of a vicious stabbing attack with a stiletto-type blade. Many of the females appear to have been working in occupations which caused them broken teeth, no doubt leading to much pain, and in at least one case to a diet of soft food only.

Full data on the metrical, non-metrical and dental make-up of the sample are held in the site archive.

Charnel material from evaluation phases

by David Henderson and Simon Colebrook

Human bone was recovered from 18 contexts within the area of Anchor Green. None of this material was from articulated, *in situ* inhumation burials; the assemblage was formed by generally incomplete, somewhat weathered bones, with a number etched by the action of plant roots. The contexts yielding human bone were medieval and later, a period when the graveyard to the south was in active use.

Taphonomy

As very little of the material was complete, it seems likely that the assemblage represents charnel from disturbed graves which was unnoticed and so not re-interred. Judging by the weathering and root-etching, in some cases this material may have become incorporated into middens, mixed with domestic refuse, and subsequently reworked into its current contexts (see Chapter 3). Contexts *1073* and *1088* contained less mixed material; in both cases articulating or matching bones were recovered (adult ribs and a partial skeleton of a perinatal infant) indicating that these contexts contained primary deposition of material from disturbed graves. Similarly *1131* contained less weathered material, and may also be primary redeposition. A tibia fragment from context *1140* exhibited possible carnivore tooth-marks (most likely dog). Several femora recovered from the graveyard site (context *208.F*), interpreted as having been reburied from an earlier archaeological excavation, also showed signs of carnivore gnawing. Probably these bones became available to the dogs as a result of having become exposed when the seaward edge of the cemetery eroded.

Demography

Very little information regarding sex or age was recovered from the bones. Most of the material was adult, although immature individuals were well represented. A minimum of one individual was represented from each of the age categories; perinatal (within 2 months of birth), infant (0–2 year old), child (2–6 yrs), young juvenile (6–12 yrs) and older juvenile (12–18 yrs). Both sexes were represented. A minimum of three adults were present (represented by left parietal bones), the most common post-cranial bone was the midshaft portion of the left tibia (2 adult, 1 immature). Both these areas of the skeleton are relatively dense and so may represent items of bone more likely to resist mechanical attrition. Adult teeth exhibited wear typical of all stages of life from youth to old age.

Pathology

One of four upper molars had a caries cavity (at the distal contact facet). An immature tibia shaft exhibited periostitis. No further examples of the *ante-mortem* breakage of molars, seen extensively in the sample from the cemetery area of the excavation, were noted.

Appendix J: The mammal and bird bones

by Catherine Smith

A summary of the animal bone report is presented here, further details may be found on the accompanying CD and in archive.

Methods and measurements

Mammals

The mammalian bones were identified by direct comparison with modern reference material and were allocated to particular bone and species where possible. Where it was not possible to identify bones as far as species, the terms *large ungulate*, *small ungulate* and *indeterminate mammal* were used. Thus all large vertebrae other than the atlas and axis were described as large ungulate, while small vertebrae were described as small ungulate. Ribs were similarly allocated depending on their size. Large ungulate bones were most likely to have come from cattle, but could also have come from horse or red deer. Similarly, small ungulate bones were most likely to have come from sheep, but could possibly have originated from goat, pig or roe deer. All other mammalian fragments for which neither species nor bone could be ascertained were described as indeterminate mammal. Boessneck's (1971) criteria for differentiating between the bones of sheep and goat, which are morphologically very similar, were applied where feasible.

Measurements were made in accordance with the scheme of von den Driesch (1976) and are expressed in millimetres. Additional measurements on the humerus follow Legge and Rowley-Conwy (1988). Mandibular tooth wear and eruption patterns were assessed using Grant's (1982) scheme for cattle, sheep/goats and pigs, as well as Payne's (1973) scheme for sheep/goats. Horn cores were aged using Armitage's (1982) criteria. Withers heights for sheep/goats were estimated using Teichert's (1975) factors.

Birds

Identifications were made by direct comparison with modern comparative material, collected in Scotland. Where two closely related species were present, for example, cormorant and shag (*Phalacrocorax carbo* and *P. aristotelis*), the largest specimens were attributed to

Species	Number of fragments							
	Phase 2a	*Phase 2b*	*Phase 3a*	*Phase 3b*	*Phase 4a*	*Phase 4b*	*Phase 4c*	*Total*
Cattle	89	18	51	–	2	7	2	*169*
Sheep/goat	88	8	98	1	3	7	4	*204*
Pig	7	2	23	–	–	1	3	*36*
Horse	–	–	1	–	–	–	–	*1*
Red deer	3	–	–	–	–	–	–	*3*
Dog	17	1	1	–	–	–	–	*19*
Cat	–	–	–	–	–	–	1	*1*
Seal sp	8	2	–	–	–	–	–	*10*
Rabbit	–	–	–	–	–	1	–	*1*
Vole	2	3	3	–	–	–	–	*8*
Small mammal	–	1	3	1	–	–	–	*5*
Large ungulate	64	12	53	–	3	2	2	*136*
Small ungulate	42	19	42	–	8	4	1	*116*
Indeterminate mammal	385	45	371	–	12	26	10	*849*
Cormorant	5	–	2	–	–	–	–	*7*
Shag	20	2	–	–	–	1	1	*24*
Cormorant/Shag	2	–	2	–	–	–	–	*4*
Goose sp	11	–	15	2	–	2	–	*30*
cf Goose	1	–	6	–	1	–	–	*8*
Duck cf Mallard	–	–	1	–	–	–	–	*1*
Duck cf Eider	1	–	–	–	–	–	–	*1*
Duck sp	1	–	–	–	–	–	–	*1*
Gull cf Herring gull	1	–	–	–	–	–	–	*1*
Guillemot	9	2	2	–	–	1	–	*14*
Razorbill	–	1	–	–	–	–	–	*1*
Guillemot/Razorbill	6	2	–	–	–	–	–	*8*
Raven	–	1	1	–	–	–	–	*2*
Starling	–	–	1	–	–	–	–	*1*
Domestic fowl	10	–	11	1	2	3	–	*27*
cf Fowl	1	–	2	–	–	–	1	*4*
Indeterminate bird	43	–	19	–	1	2	–	*65*
Amphibian		–	1	–	–		–	*1*
Total	*819*	*119*	*704*	*5*	*32*	*57*	*25*	*1758*

Table J.1 Animal bone: number of fragments by phase

cormorant and the smallest to shag. Those which were intermediate between the two could have come from either bird due to size overlap between the species. Similarly, for guillemot and razorbill, the largest bones were attributed to guillemot and the smallest to razorbill.

Bird bones which were not identifiable to species were recorded as *indeterminate bird*. Bones in this category were mainly ribs, vertebrae, foot phalanges and shafts of long bones.

General

All of the material discussed here originates from hand-excavated material. One bag of sampled material extracted from context *1317*, sample number 56, was scrutinised only briefly and is not included in the tables. Other sampled material was not seen or recorded. The descriptions below associate the bones from the redeposited contexts (*1210 / 1097*) as part of the Phase 2a occupation, as indicated by their dating (phase 2a/c).

The assemblage

A summary of bone fragments by phase is presented in Table J.1. A full catalogue of bone fragments, showing species identified in each context and with finds number, is available in the site archive. Minimum numbers of large and medium-sized mammals is shown in Table J.2.

Species	Minimum number of individuals (MNI)			
	Phase 2a/c	2b	3a	3b
Cattle	2	1	2	–
Sheep/goat	3	1	4	1
Pig	1	1	2	–
Horse	–	–	1	–
Dog	1 adult, 1 pup	1	1	–
Red deer	1	–	–	–
Seal (cf grey seal)	1 adult, 1 pup	1 adult, 1 pup	–	–

Table J.2: Animal bone: minimum number of individuals by phase of most common species

Domesticated livestock

A range of domesticated livestock, including cattle, sheep/goat, pig, horse, dog and cat was represented. Cattle and sheep/goat bones were present in all phases from early medieval Phase 2 (early building and agricultural use Phase 2a/2c and corn-drying kiln Phase 2b) to modern 20th century Phase 4c. Pig bones were present in early medieval Phases 2a/2c and 2b, absent from Phases 3b and 4a and present again by the early modern period. The single horse tooth was recovered from an interface context of redeposited early medieval material contemporary with Phase 2a and high medieval material associated with 3a and is most likely of 12th century origin. Cat, represented by a single bone, occurred only in modern Phase 4c, while most of the dog bones came from a single, very young individual in Phase 2a.

Wild mammals

Wild mammals were also present. Seal species, including several fragments referable to grey seal (*Halichoerus grypus*) was present in early medieval Phases 2a/c and 2b. Water vole (*Arvicola terrestris*) occurred in Phases 2a/c and 2b and in high medieval Phase 3a, while rabbit was present only in early modern Phase 4b, in an 18th or 19th century context. Three bones of red deer, from a single individual, were present only in the bone-rich soil outside the early building.

Birds

Bird species included the domestic fowl (*Gallus gallus*), most plentiful in the high medieval Phase 3a, and in context *1097*, apparently representing redeposited material contemporary with the early medieval Phase 2a. The same applies to domestic/greylag goose (*Anser anser*).

Most of the wild birds, not unexpectedly, were seabirds. In the hand-excavated assemblage these included cormorant (*Phalacrocorax carbo*), shag (*Phalacrocorax aristotelis*), probable mallard (*Anas* cf *playrhynchos*) and

eider ducks (*cf. Somateria molissima*), probable herring gull (*Larus* cf *argentatus*), raven (*Corvus corax*) and starling (*Sturnus vulgaris*). One bone of great auk (*Alca impennis*), a distal right humerus, was present in a sieved soil sample, context (*1317*), Sample 56, interpreted as an early floor spread within the entrance area of the early building. This may confirm the early date for this context, 5th–7th centuries, since the species had declined to such an extent by the mid 19th century that it had become extinct.

Somewhat surprisingly, given the proximity of the Bass Rock, gannets (*Morus bassanus*, synonym *Sula bassana*) were entirely absent from the assemblage. Finally, one amphibian bone, from a frog or toad, was retrieved from Phase 3a.

Distribution of bones across the site

The distribution of bones by phase is described in more detail on the accompanying CD. The most substantial assemblages were from the Phase 2a/2c early building and agricultural soils, the phase 2b kiln and the Phase 3 midden-like deposits. The common domestic animals, cattle, sheep/goat, pig and dog, were well represented in all these deposits along with a range of domestic fowl and seabirds and some seal bones.

Age of animals at death

Mammals

Assessment of mandibular tooth eruption and wear is generally accepted as a reliable method of estimating age at death. However, survival of mandibles which still retained teeth was limited to two cattle and five sheep/goat. The cattle mandibles came from Phase 2a while three sheep mandibles were from Phase 2a and two from Phase 3a (Table J.3, on CD).

Two cattle mandibles came from very young individuals, one neonate and one juvenile. Adult teeth were present throughout the assemblage, but none was found *in situ* (in the mandible) and could therefore not be reliably used to estimate age. Of the five sheep/goat mandibles, two came from animals of less than a year old, while two were from older adults of 6–8 years in modern terms.

A less reliable, but necessary, method of assessing age is to determine the state of epiphysial fusion of the long bones. Age categories based on the age range at which the epiphyses (articular ends) ossify and fuse to the shaft of the bones can therefore be assigned, using dates published by Silver (1969). Tables J.4–J.6, on CD, present the age categories by phase for the cattle, sheep/goats and pigs at Kirk Ness.

Despite the small sample sizes it is clear that young as well as mature animals died or were killed. In cattle, an apparent bias in Phase 3b towards animals in the immature or adult category (I/A) is almost entirely due to the survival of a relatively high number of first and second phalanges. These too bones fuse at an intermediate stage and their survival when compared with other, later fusing bone elements is due in part to their relatively dense structure and the fact that their small size prevents them being subjected to intense butchery for marrow. Similarly, in sheep/goats, a commonly preserved bone element is the distal humerus, which also fuses at an intermediate stage. Thus a fused distal humerus, if found in isolation, can be inferred only as having come from an immature or an adult sheep/goat. This accounts for the high proportion of sheep/goats in category I/A, particularly in Phase 3a (Table J.5, on CD).

Very few pig bones provided an age at death, due to butchery of the articular ends. Some of the fragments must have come from older animals, but it was not possibly to quantify them. Of the younger age groups, there is evidence of one very young individual, probably a neonate, in Phase 3a.

Of the dog bones, all were probably adult with the exception of one individual, a very young, possibly neonatal puppy from Phase 2a (context *1287*, SF 152). The seal bones were from both adult and pup seal, possibly indicating hunting had taken place during the breeding season.

Birds

As regards the age of the birds, it was only possible to separate the bones into either 'immature' or 'adult' age groupings, simply because the way in which bird bones mature is slightly different than in mammals. In mammals, long bone growth occurs at the cartilaginous epiphysial plate, which only ossifies after the optimum shaft length has been reached. By contrast, in birds, the route taken to achieve bone growth is slightly different. The entire epiphysis (articular end) is composed of cartilage, and ossifies at an early age, so that no further lengthening of the shafts of the long bones can take place. Growth in birds is thus relatively more rapid than in mammals, and the full bone length is quickly achieved early in life. This means that although the stages of fusion of the mammalian epiphyses are gradual, occurring over a relatively long period of time, in birds, the epiphyses are either not present (because they have been formed in cartilage and have therefore not survived under burial conditions) or they are present as fully developed bone. This process is complete in the domestic fowl, for example, before the age of 6 months, as compared with 3–4 years in larger domesticated mammals such as sheep and cattle (Silver 1969, 285; 300). Thus, the term 'immature' is meant in an osteological sense rather than an ornithological one. In the latter case the term is used to describe birds which have not yet reached the breeding stage, but which may still be several years old. Unfortunately, there would be little to distinguish between the bones of an ornithologically immature bird (that is, non-breeding)

and an osteologically mature one (or individual in which epiphyseal fusion is complete).

Osteologically immature birds were found at Kirk Ness (see Table J.7 on CD). Although it was not possible to distinguish between the bones of young cormorants and shags, it was likely that a higher proportion were of the latter, given that more adult shag bones were present in the assemblage. The figures appear to be biased towards immature birds because only bones bearing articular ends have been counted. However, there is definite evidence that young seabirds were being exploited in the breeding season, not only shags and/or cormorants, but guillemots and/or razorbills, gulls, ducks and geese too.

Butchery

Because of surface abrasion, evidence of butchering implements was fairly scant. However, there was evidence of knife cuts on several long bones of cattle and sheep/goat in Phases 2a/c, 3a, 4a and 4b. These cuts were probably inflicted during removal of the flesh from the bones, and included cuts on the head of a cattle femur (Phase 3a, context *1239*, SF 89), the shaft of a sheep/goat calcaneum (Phase 2c, context *1097*, SF 78) and the proximal articulation of a sheep/goat radius (Phase 3a, context *1092*, SF 47).

Other, heavier implements, which left evidence of hack marks, were also used in butchery at Kirk Ness. These tools were probably axes or cleavers. Examples included two medio-lateral hacks on the lateral process of a large ungulate vertebra (Phase 3a, context *1092*, SF 291) and dorso-ventral hack marks on two fragments of cattle pelvis (Phase 2a, context *1321*, SF104). A similar tool was used to split a pig mandible in two at the symphysis, where the two halves of the jaw unite (Phase 2a, context *1304*, SF 141).

Long bones of cattle and sheep/goat were chopped across in a medio-lateral direction in order to produce manageable joints of meat, the earliest evidence being a cattle femur shaft in Phase 2a (context *1319*, SF 106) which was also split open in a sagittal direction. Sagittal splitting was commonly used to extract marrow from long bones, although another method which was often applied to bones of sheep, was to punch a hole near an articular end and apply suction. A sheep/goat distal tibia with a rough hole punched above the distal articulation is likely to be evidence of marrow extraction (Phase 3a, context *1092/1178*, SF 56).

The general impression of butchery of the cattle, sheep/goats and pigs is that fragments, including articular ends, were chopped to a fairly small size, possibly to fit cooking pots (for example a group of chopped cattle epiphyses in Phase 2a, context *1287*, SF 170). This also implies that there was a desire to use all available foodstuffs, including the bones.

There is evidence of saws having been used on only two fragments. One, a cattle humerus shaft was sawn medio-laterally across the shaft, but its large size implies the bone may have come from a modern animal (Phase 4b, context *1146*, SF 35). A sawn large ungulate rib fragment from Phase 2a (context *1281*, SF158) was also large in contrast to other bones from this site, and may therefore indicate a disturbed context containing modern material.

Although it is suggested that birds too were dismembered, cooked and eaten, there is little evidence of tools having been used. This is possibly because birds may have been cooked whole, before the meat was removed from the bones. Thus there would be no need for sharp knives as cooked flesh is more tender and comes away from the carcass without effort.

Abnormal bone

Joint abnormalities

Where abnormalities were present, these were found to be slight. Several examples of cattle phalanges with small depressions in the articular surfaces, of the type reported by Baker and Brothwell (1981, 109–12) were noted in Phases 3a and 4a/b. These depressions would have had no effect on the health of the live animals.

Arthritic changes, not, however, sufficient to diagnose osteoarthritis, were observed in the glenoid cavity of a cattle scapula, at the articulation with the head of the humerus (Phase 3a, context *1092*, SF 68).

One bird bone, the ulna of a raven, was affected by pathological changes (Phase 3a, context *1080*, SF 63). Osteophytic new bone growth was present on the anterior aspect of the distal articulation and the shaft of the bone was slightly remodelled for about one fifth of its length. The changes could have been due to infection, perhaps as a result of injury.

Size of animals

A summary of anatomical measurements of bones of cattle, sheep/goat, pig, dog, domestic fowl and domestic/greylag goose in the early medieval and medieval Phases 2 and 3 is presented in Table J.8 on CD. Unfortunately the sample sizes were very small for each measurement. However, the dimensions of the bones are not dissimilar to those recorded at sites of medieval date elsewhere in Scotland, for example, Perth High Street (Hodgson *et al.* 2011) or indeed in the Anglian phases of the multi-period site at Castle Park, Dunbar (Smith 2000, 203–12). This tends to suggest that the livestock from North Berwick were of small stature and light build when compared with large modern day breeds of cattle, sheep and pigs.

Discussion

The bone assemblage from the site of the Scottish Seabird Centre at Kirk Ness has shown that both domesticated animals and wild species were exploited for food. A relatively high proportion of the domesticated livestock was killed before reaching full adulthood, although older adult cattle and sheep/goats were present, these latter representing the breeding stock.

The close proximity of the sea with its rocky shores, cliffs and isolated offshore islands provided a variety of habitats for nesting seabirds, which seem to have been a valuable resource for the inhabitants of the site. Collecting seabirds and their eggs from the breeding cliffs would not have been without risk to human life and limb, a factor which had to be balanced against the nutritional and economic value of the food obtained. It is notable that by far the largest assemblage of seabirds, including cormorant/shags, guillemots/razorbills and ducks was recovered from the earlier Phases 2a/c and 2b, and to a lesser extent from Phase 3a. Seabird bones are much less frequent in the later periods. On the one hand this might represent a change in hunting/cooking habits, and possibly tastes, but on the other might simply result from the fact that domestic occupation of the site ceased from the 15th century onwards.

It is interesting to compare the proportions of young seabirds taken. Although young guillemots or razorbills (auks) are present they are nowhere as numerous as young shags/cormorants. This is probably related to the age at which the young of different species leave the breeding ledges, where they are most easily caught. Young guillemots and razorbills take to the sea at the age of only 2–3 weeks, before the chicks have fully fledged. Unable to fly, they form large swimming flocks (Tuck and Heinzel 1978, 125). By contrast, young shags and cormorants leave the nest at about 5–6 weeks, but remain with the colony, only becoming independent at about 10–12 weeks (*ibid.*, 71). This vulnerability possibly puts them at more risk of capture by humans at the nesting site.

Thus there are several factors which would prevent recovery of the bones of young auks in archaeological deposits – first, hunting would have to be timed closely to the period just after hatching, and secondly, the small size of the chicks may not have warranted expending energy on their capture. In the Faroe Islands, however, where the guillemot is one of the most plentiful seabirds, a method of capture was developed which took advantage of the flightless young birds, gathered in swimming flocks. They were herded using a number of boats, driven into an inlet and killed using stones tied to the end of poles (Jackson 1991, 64).

Although only one bone of great auk was found, this was of interest since the species is known to have become extinct in the mid-19th century, due to over-exploitation of this large, flightless species by man. The great auk bone from Kirk Ness was recovered from a soil sample extracted from an early context (*1317*), and dated to the 5th–7th centuries. The last great auk reported off the British coast was an individual killed on Stac an Armin, St Kilda, about 1840 (Fisher and Lockley 1989, 71).

Possibly the latest known example from Scotland was retrieved from excavations on the Isle of May, one of the Forth Islands, recovered from a post-medieval context (Smith 2008a, 94).

Perhaps the most surprising aspect of the seabird culture at Kirk Ness is the lack of gannet bones in the assemblage. Given the proximity of the breeding grounds on the Bass Rock to the site it is most difficult to explain why other seabirds were collected and gannets neglected. Indeed gannets were found at another medieval excavation in North Berwick, at Forth Street (Smith 2008b, 64), and have been recorded in the medieval phases at Castle Park, Dunbar (Smith 2000, 205). They were also present in deposits recovered from excavations on the Isle of May, and may have bred there from the medieval period until the mid-19th century (Smith 2008b; Baxter and Rintoul 1953, 466). Although Serjeantson (1988, 213) has pointed out that, on coastal sites where seabirds have been exploited, gannets are the most frequently recorded species, this does not appear to be true for the site at Kirk Ness. Since it is known that the gannet colony on the Bass Rock was harvested from at least the 16th century until the middle of the 19th century (Nelson 1989, 22) the explanation may be that this was, in part at least, a commercial activity and that the remains of birds sold as complete carcasses, with bones in, were disposed of elsewhere. It may also be possible that the rights to the exploitation of the gannets was controlled or restricted from an early time. In the later medieval period the nunnery controlled the processing of young gannets caught on the Bass Rock for their fat, documented by their complaint to the Pope in the 15th century that their rights were being eroded by Robert Lauder, Lord of the Isle of Bass at the time (*cf.* Ross in Chapter 4).

As well as birds, marine mammals were also exploited. A seal distal metapodial (Phase 2c, context *1095*, SF 9) bore evidence of a knife cut near the articulation, indicating removal of the flesh. This may be evidence of butchery for meat, removal of the skin to be cured as leather, or production of oil. Seal oil was traditionally used in cruisie lamps, for lighting, especially in the Northern Isles (Fenton 1978, 525). Some of the young seals found at Kirk Ness were pups, presumably in their first white coats, which may therefore have been killed for their fur.

Appendix L: Palaeoenvironmental sample assessment

by S J Haston and S Timpany

Seventy-four soil samples were taken during excavations at Kirk Ness and submitted for palaeoenvironmental analysis. The samples relate to four phases of activity discovered at the site and were taken from a number of features including early medieval midden deposits within an early stone-footed structure (Phase 2a) and an early medieval corn-drying kiln of the same general occupation phase (Phase 2b).

Methods

All samples were processed in laboratory conditions using a standard floatation method (cf. Kenward *et al.* 1980). The floating debris (flot) was collected using a 250μm sieve and, once dry, were analysed using a stereomicroscope at magnifications of x10 and up to x100 where necessary to aid identification. Identifications were confirmed using modern reference material and seed atlases including Cappers *et al.* (2006). Any material remaining in the flotation tank (retent) was wet-sieved through a 1mm mesh and air-dried. This was then sorted by eye and any material of archaeological significance removed.

Results

The results for individual features or contexts are presented in Tables L.1 (retent samples) and L.2 (flot samples) and are described on CD where they have been organised by phasing identified for the site. All plant material of archaeological significance was preserved through charring.

Charred cereal grain was present in rare to abundant amounts in 43 samples (see Tables L.1 and L.2). The grain assemblage includes, primarily, barley (Hordeum vulgare) with lesser amounts of oat (Avena species). A small number of grains were in such a poor state of preservation that identification was not possible (cereal indet. in Table L.2). Some lighter chaff elements such as lemma and palea fragments were also recovered in Sample 31 (Table L.2). Weed seeds were generally sparse throughout the samples. The most commonly recovered seeds include fat hen (Chenopodium album), chickweed (Stellaria media), sedges (Carex species) and grasses (Poa species). Florets of heather (Calluna vulgaris) together with a mixture of leaves and stems of the same species were also found.

The most interesting environmental assemblages relate to the early medieval phases of the site, Phase 2a/c and 2b, The palaeoenvironmental material recovered from Phase 2a/c is largely of rare and occasional finds of charred cereal grain of oat and hulled barley. The charred grain can be seen to be scattered across the area during this phase of the site, with no concentration of grain from any of the samples meaning that no areas of (specific cereal) activity can be identified. The presence of the kiln in the above layer (see below Phase 2b), which was seen to cut down into this layer raises the possibility that some of this grain from Phase 2a may be intrusive and is actually related to the kiln activity above. The broken and degraded preservation of some of the grain underpins that these grains had undergone some movement prior to final deposition. However, the domestic character of the associated finds assemblage (including a whet stone and pottery fragments) could suggest that some of this grain relates to domestic activity (e.g. baking) from this level.

The quantities of charred barley grain recovered from the fill of the drain and a cut feature matches the grain assemblage from the kiln and thus is likely to represent grain material from the later kiln. Since it seems that the drain is stratigraphically earlier than the kiln, and in use during Phase 2a, the occurrence of grain within its fill can only relate to the infilling and hence abandonment of the drain while the kiln was in use. Samples from *1291* to *1294* and *1298* and *1299* from the backfill of the stone-lined drain should therefore similarly be associated with the kiln (see below).

Other materials indicative of domestic refuse as part of this earliest occupation of the building are also present, largely in the form of discrete midden deposits (e.g. *1304*, *1306*, *1307* and *1308*). The samples relating to these midden dumps were found to contain abundant marine shell fragments largely of periwinkle shells, with lesser amounts of oyster, limpet and dog whelk. Mammal bone was also abundant within one sample <50>, indicating that terrestrial as well as marine food resources were being utilised by the community. Together with the abundant marine shell in the midden deposits, small amounts of fish bone were recovered from shallow hollows, discrete patches of midden spreads *1309* and *1317*, indicating that fish as well as shell fish were being harvested from the nearby coastline. The abundance of charcoal fragments indicates that charcoal was still the main fuel used during this period.

The kiln and associated destruction deposits were rich in ash and charred cereals. Those associated with the kiln (<30>, <31>, <36>, <70> and <74>) contained abundant quantities of barley followed by lesser numbers of oat grain with few weed seeds and only sample <36> including any potential ruderals, with sedges, grasses and fat hen seeds present.

The grains themselves were relatively clean with the majority of the barley grain having been removed from their hulls. However, oat grains were found to be largely hulled. The absence of embryo growth on the barley and embryo fragments within the samples indicates that the grain had not been malted prior to being dried suggesting an intended use for baking rather than brewing. The large quantity of charred grain recovered indicates some form of accident occurred within the kiln, burning the grain and subsequently putting the kiln out of use.

Another source of abundant grain was sample <27>, which relates to a shell midden deposit overlying the kiln *1227*. The shell from the midden was once more dominated by periwinkle shells, with small quantities of limpet and whelk. The grain assemblage from this sample is the same as that of the kiln suggesting they are related. This together with the presence of abundant periwinkle shells in the kiln base (*1226*) and associated deposit (*1228*) indicates a degree of mixing between the underlying kiln and the overlying midden deposit. It is probable that following the destruction of the kiln the area was used as a dumping ground for domestic refuse. Other potential domestic refuse encountered in the samples include burnt bone, unburnt bone, fish bone and other shellfish such as oyster and mussel (see table L.2).

Samples from *1291* to *1294* and *1298* and *1299* derived from the backfill of the stone-lined drain as mentioned above and in all likelihood represent kiln material that was mixed into the infilling of the drain. These layers were found to contain only rare amounts of grain (all identified as barley), marine shell (periwinkle and limpet), fishbone and charcoal. However, one sample *1299* did contain frequent remains of heather with the presence of charred florets (flower heads), stems and leaves; rare amount of charred florets were also found in samples from *1298*. Charred sedge nutlets were also recovered from samples *1293* and *1298*. The presence of charred heather remains within the drain fill is unclear but it may relate to material used for lighting the kiln.

Appendix M: Analysis of soil thin sections

by Stephen Lancaster

The Kirk Ness site is a complex multi-period accumulation of sediment. In the course of excavating the earliest layers, some of which are of early medieval date, Kubiena tin samples were taken. The samples comprise the soils in the open area to the west, Phase 2c, in front of the early building. Five samples were taken through a sequence of soil deposits in order to elucidate a number of issues concerning the site formation processes. In particular the nature of depositional processes, any changes in composition over the period of deposition and the impact of post-depositional changes on the deposits was to be investigated. The samples were: 1: contexts *1210*, *1094*; 2: context *1097*; 3: contexts *1094*, *1095*; 4 and 5: context *1095*.

Methods

Thin sections were prepared from five soil blocks. Resin impregnation and thin section preparation was undertaken by the Department of Geography, Royal Holloway, University of London, and followed standard procedures (Lee and Kemp 1992). The thin sections were recorded under a variety of lighting techniques using the descriptive scheme and terminology recommended by Bullock *et al.* (1985), as supplemented and modified by *Courty et al.* (1989).

Results

Descriptions of the thin sections are given in Table M.1. Particularly salient points are noted below.

In general most of the samples show traces of extensive biological reworking through the activity of soil fauna and plant roots. As such there are very few traces of the original sedimentary structure of the deposits. The main exception to this is the finely laminated structure of Zone 1 Sample 3 *1094*, discussed below. The sand grains found in all of the samples have a rounded shape.

Sample 1: 1210/1094

These two contexts could be tentatively distinguished in this sample. A lateral concentration of small stones was noted about halfway down the slide, interpreted as an earthworm sorted stone line. Above this feature the fine fraction tends to contain more calcite than the fine fraction below it, but this is not an entirely consistent pattern.

Sample 2: 1097

The apparently two contexts *1210* and *1097* covered by this sample could not be readily distinguished, although there was trend of reducing frequency and size of calcitic concretion with depth. The calcitic concretions incorporated coarse mineral material including quartz grains and fragments of shell and bone. Bone fragments throughout this sample were often heavily weathered.

Sample 3: 1094/1095

The two contexts covered by this sample could be clearly distinguished, with Zone 1 being *1094* and Zone 2 being *1095*. Whereas the rest of the samples did not show traces of sedimentary structure, Zone 1 of Sample 3 had an intermittent laminar structure. The composition of the laminae alternated between pale grey silt sized quartz with abundant phytoliths, reddened silt sized quartz with a small amount of finely comminuted charcoal and areas of finely divided humic material. Both types of mineral laminae contained occasional weakly impregnated pseudomorphs of plant tissue.

Zone 2 was relatively homogenous in both structure and composition, with the exception of a higher proportion of bone and shell in the region immediately below Zone 1.

Samples 4 and 5: 1095

Sample 4 covers the upper part of *1095*, and Sample 5 the lower part. The two slides have relatively homogeneous fabrics, with differences across and between them being slight and gradual rather than discrete changes. The main trends are a reduction with depth of porosity, in the proportion of calcite in the groundmass and of the number of shell fragments.

Discussion

Composition and sediment sources

The high degree of biological reworking of most of the contexts (see below) makes it difficult to be completely certain of all of the sources of the material. Despite this a number of input sources can be identified for the samples. Possible sources are discussed below.

Windblown sand from the nearby beaches and dunes, and/or turf/topsoil from areas where this was a predominant mode of deposition is one of the probable components. Although the local sands are often characterised as shelly, the shell component of the sand was minimal and may not be autochthonous (Macaulay Institute 1982). A similar situation has been observed in samples from Forth Street in North Berwick (Lancaster 2005). The issue of source for this material is inextricably linked to that of process of deposition, which will be discussed further below.

The wide lithological variety of stones noted throughout the samples (with the exception of Zone 1 Sample 3), combined with the preponderance of silt sized quartz in the fine fraction of the samples, indicates the presence of turf/topsoil from soils that had developed on glacial till. Given that the natural subsoil of the site is sand overlying bedrock such soils would not have developed on the site itself, and must have been imported (Addyman and Macfadyen 2008). The soils to the west and south of North Berwick are mapped as having glacial till as their parent material (Macaulay Institute 1982).

The occurrence of charcoal and, in most samples, bone, is generally at low frequency and the state of preservation is often poor, these elements often being fragmentary, crushed and weathered. The exception with respect to bone is Sample 2, *1097*. This contains a much higher proportion of bone. The bone is still highly fragmentary and weathered.

Rare concentrations of almost pure silt grade quartz occur throughout the samples. The main exception to this is Zone 1 of Sample 3, *1094*, which is mostly composed of fine laminae of such material, which in many cases are reddened. Small iron oxide pseudomorphs of plant tissue also occur in this zone. This material is usually interpreted as the mineral ash left after burning peat or turf/topsoil.

Deposition processes

As noted above, the biological reworking of most of the deposits makes the identification of the processes of deposition more difficult, as it disrupts the sedimentary structures that would be indicative of depositional processes. Some aspects may, however, be inferred from other characteristics of the deposits.

The distinctive rounded shape of the sand grains noted above in all the samples indicates that the sand

Sample No.	Zone No.	Context No.	Coarse Mineral Components	Coarse Organic Components	Fine Fraction and Fabric	Microstructure	Pedofeatures
1		1210, 1094	Dominant poorly–moderately sorted sub-rounded–rounded quartz grains, 70–1150μm; rare–occasional frags igneous rock, c. 900μm.	Occasional charcoal frags, <4mm, mostly 200–400μm wide range of sizes & conditions.	Fine material organo-mineral, mineral component: silt grade quartz & calcite. Ubiquitous com-minuted charcoal. Occasional phytoliths, often fragmented. Porphyric to gefuric C/F limit 70μm, C/F ratio 2:1–1:2.	Massive–crumb, channel & chamber, porosity 30–60%. Occasional incorporated aggregates, predominantly mineral fine material.	Many red ferruginous nodules, 50–125μm. Occasional–rare silty & dusty clay coatings. Occasional neoformed calcite accumulations.
2		1097	Dominant poorly–moderately sorted sub-rounded–rounded quartz grains, 70–600μm, occasional–frequent frags shell, 100–1050μm rare frags igneous rock, c. 700μm.	Rare–occasional charcoal frags, 150–600μm wide range of sizes & conditions.	Fine material organo-mineral mineral component: silt grade quartz & calcite. Frequent phytoliths, often fragmented. Porphyric to gefuric C/F limit 70μm, C/F ratio 1:4.	Massive–crumb, channel & chamber, porosity 15–30%.	Rare–occasional orange ferruginous nodules, 50–150μm. Occasional–many calcitic concretions <8.5mm.
3	1	1094, 1095	Occasional–common poorly sorted sub-angular–sub-rounded quartz grains, 50–300μm.	Occasional–common charcoal frags, 50–2500μm, fractured & compressed.	Composition varies between laminae (see text). Phytoliths abundant.	Laminar, packing voids, porosity 20%.	Rare clay coatings
3	2	1094, 1095	Dominant poorly sorted sub-rounded–rounded quartz grains, 50–725μm, rare–occasional frags shell, 360–5500μm, rare frags igneous rock, 300–3250μm, rare sedimentary rock frags, <35mm.	Occasional charcoal frags, <12mm, usually 200–550μm wide range sizes & conditions.	Porphyric to gefuric C/F limit 50μm, C/F ratio 1:3.	Massive–weakly developed crumb structure, channel & chamber, porosity 30–50%.	orange ferruginous nodules, 110–350μm, angular/fragmentary form.
4		1095	Dominant poorly sorted sub-rounded–rounded quartz grains, 50–750μm, rare–occasional frags shell, 250–1600μm, rare frags igneous rock, 300–3250μm, rare limestone frags, <1450μm.	Occasional charcoal frags, 50–3500μm, crushed & fractured.	Fine material organo-mineral, including clay component, frequent phytoliths & occasional diatoms, ubiquitous finely comminuted charcoal. Porphyric to gefuric C/F limit 50μm, C/F ratio 1:2.	Weakly–well developed crumb structure, areas of intergrain aggregate, channel & chamber, porosity 40–65%.	Many orange ferruginous ovoid nodules, 10–70μm, angular/fragmentary form.
5		1095	Dominant poorly sorted sub-rounded–rounded quartz grains, 50–650μm, rare–occasional frags igneous rock, 450μm–20mm, rare limestone frags, <1450μm.	Rare–occasional charcoal frags, 250–3750μm slightly crushed & fractured.	Fine material organo-mineral mineral component: silt grade quartz. Frequent phytoliths, well preserved. Gefuric to porphyric C/F limit 50 μm, C/F ratio 2:1–1:2.	Weakly developed crumb structure, areas of inter-grain aggregate, channel & chamber, porosity 50% (locally 50%). Occasional incorporated aggregates of predominantly mineral or charred fine material.	Occasional–many orange ferruginous ovoid nodules, 50–75μm, angular/fragmentary form.

Table M.1: Thin Section descriptions

component has undergone extensive transport. This may be through water or wind transport, and may be a relict property due to transport in this fashion before deposition in the sampled locations. With respect to *1095*, which overlay sand and has the characteristics of a buried soil, it seems most likely that sand was deposited through natural processes, which subsequently underwent processes such as biological reworking and weathering to form a soil. During the period that this was an active soil burning either occurred on the site or residues of burning were dumped, leading to the occasional ash aggregates and charcoal noted in Samples 4 and 5. Turf/toposil, either in burnt or unburnt form, derived from glacial tills was also deposited during the process of soil formation. The process of soil formation implies that gross deposition was not occurring at the time, e.g. there were no major wind blow events to deposit a thick layer of sand on the site.

The fine laminar structure of *1094* is the result of a series of small depositional events. The particles of the laminae are not well sorted and there is no preferred orientation of the larger elements. This allows the possibility of some form of fluid transport process, either through wind or flowing water, to be ruled out as the type of depositional process. Instead the most likely process is of either dumping or raking out of ash, probably from a nearby fire. The survival of a series of laminae implies a number of burning events rather than a single event.

In *1210* and *1097* the issue of the process of deposition of sand again arises. The two possible mechanisms are the deposition of windblown sand or the accumulation of sandy turf/topsoil as a result of human activity. The presence of bone, charcoal and traces of turf/topsoil derived from glacial till indicates that some cultural inputs were made. The poor state of preservation of the charcoal and bone suggests that this was residual material rather than deposited as primary dumps of refuse. While is not possible to completely resolve the mode of deposition, the rate can be surmised to have been sufficiently rapid to prevent the complete reworking of the underlying laminated sediments in *1094*, but not so rapid or great a quantity as to prevent the reworking of *1210* and *1097*.

Post-deposition processes

There is evidence of biological reworking in all of the sampled contexts. The impact of biological reworking is considerable and, as noted above, has largely destroyed the sedimentary structures that would have demonstrated the nature of the depositional processes. The effect of biological reworking has also been to mostly destroy the traces of other post-depositional processes. Situations where this has not happened are those where other post-depositional processes post-date biological reworking, reworking did not reach the features left by other post-depositional processes or these processes formed features that are robust with regard to biological reworking.

There is also evidence, mainly from the field observations, of gross reworking of *1095*, in the scattered distribution of stones and other clasts throughout the depth of the context (Addyman and Macfadyen 2008). This contrasts with the situation in *1210*, where a stone line could be observed, both in the field and in the thin section sample (Sample 1). A stone line underlying a homogeneous, stone free region is characteristic of developed soils that have undergone complete biological reworking but not more disruptive disturbance such as ploughing or digging. The material represented by *1095* can be characterised as a soil that has been heavily disturbed, in this context most probably as a result of human activity. In comparison *1210* can be characterised as a soil that has developed without such disruption, such as might be found in established pasture or wasteland.

The effects of disturbance in the soil profile can be observed in a different form elsewhere in the profile. Both *1094* and *1210* have occasional dusty clay coatings in their pores. These are formed as a result of soil aggregates being disrupted, releasing fine material such as clay and silt which is transported by water and left as fine coatings within the soil spaces. he causes of aggregate disruption may include digging, ploughing or stripping an area of soil. The survival of such coatings in the heavily reworked *1210* implies that the formation of the clay coatings must post-date the biological activity in that context, and probably relate to groundbreaking activities in the overlying deposit.

Water transport of materials may also include the movement of dissolved minerals. There is considerable evidence of small scale movement of iron, in the form of the small ferrous nodules that have formed throughout the profiles. Significant concretions of calcite have been observed in Sample 2, *1097*. This has probably formed as result of the high bone content of this context, some of which has dissolved and reformed as masses of calcite, causing the deposit to become partially concreted.

Archaeological implications

The accumulation of most of the sampled sequence has been relatively gradual. Although *1095* is a natural soil, it has undergone cultural modification in terms of inputs of charcoal and till-derived turf/topsoil, and physical disruption as a result of a process such as digging or ploughing. The importation of till derived from turf/topsoil may reflect a number of uses: turf as a roofing material, turf or topsoil as a construction material, turf as animal bedding or turf/topsoil as a fuel. The local till-derived topsoils tend to be poorly drained and can be quite peaty. If the occasional occurrence of fragments of peat charcoal in the samples, along with mineral ash, is remembered the use as fuel seems the most likely interpretation.

The deposition of the ash layer which forms *1094* probably represents a change in the function of the immediate area: only ash is deposited and there is no gross disruption of the deposit. As argued above, the ash has probably been dumped or raked out from a nearby hearth. This area was abandoned, and accumulation of material *1210* and *1097* began again, through the deposition of similar waste materials as for *1095*. There may have been an input of windblown sand. At least in the later life of *1210* and *1097* there was no gross disruption of the deposits, allowing the formation of a homogeneous soil with a stone line. The dumping of a considerable quantity of bone must have occurred only a few years before the soil was buried: the bone has not been incorporated into the stone line.

Appendix N: Radiocarbon dating, Marine Reservoir Effect (MRE), and Bayesian modelling

by Nicola Russell and Derek Hamilton

The following reports on the radiocarbon results from material associated with excavated archaeological features from the Scottish Seabird Centre, Kirk Ness, and the use of some of the radiocarbon dates in two studies: 1) a PhD project investigating the Marine Reservoir Effect; and 2) a Bayesian chronological model for the late Roman–early medieval activity on the site. A total of 26 radiocarbon measurements are available on samples recovered from 11 excavated contexts. All the samples were single-entities (Ashmore 1999) of either articulated human bone from graves, short-lived charcoal/charred grain, disarticulated animal bone, or winkle shell. All the samples were submitted to the Scottish Universities Environmental Research Centre to be measured by Accelerator Mass Spectrometry (AMS).

The radiocarbon results are given in Table N.1. These are conventional radiocarbon ages (Stuiver and Polach 1977), quoted according to the international standard set at the Trondheim Convention (Stuiver and Kra 1986), and calibrated with the internationally agreed curve of Reimer *et al.* (2009) using OxCal v4.1 (Bronk Ramsey 1995; 1998; 2001; 2009). The date ranges in Table N.1 have been calculated using the maximum intercept method (Stuiver and Reimer 1986), and quoted in the form recommended by Mook (1986) with the endpoints rounded outward to 10 years. The probability distributions seen in Figures N.3 and N.5 were obtained by the probability method (Stuiver and Reimer 1993).

Radiocarbon dating and the Marine Reservoir Effect (MRE)

The basic principle of radiocarbon (^{14}C) dating is that the ^{14}C activity in a living organism remains constant throughout its life and that this 'living' value has been constant in organisms throughout the applied timescale of the technique (approx. the last 55,000 years). After death, the living value of ^{14}C is no longer sustained and the ^{14}C activity of carbon in the organism decreases exponentially with passing time. Thus, knowing the rate of decrease (i.e. the half-life of ^{14}C) and the ^{14}C activity of the sample carbon, an age can be calculated that reflects the time that has elapsed since death of the organism.

This procedure is valid for the well mixed atmosphere and the terrestrial flora and fauna that atmospheric carbon supports, provided that appropriate corrections are made for any isotopic fractionation that occurs during uptake and metabolic fixation of CO_2 by plants, and subsequently during transport through the food chain. In contrast, the oceans and the life that they support represent a rather heterogeneous reservoir with respect to ^{14}C that is not in equilibrium with the atmosphere. The oceans are not subject to the rapid carbon cycling that occurs in the atmosphere and instead, carbon atoms have extended residence times in oceanic environments. ^{14}C enters the oceans by CO_2 exchange across the air-sea interface. This becomes part of the inorganic carbon equilibrium involving carbonic acid, bicarbonate ions, carbonate ions and CO_2 (Mills and Urey 1940; Mook *et al.* 1974). As surface water currents travel towards the polar regions, the water begins to cool and in so doing becomes denser, sinking to depth within the water column (Broeker 1987; Broecker *et al.* 1991). Thus, water is removed from the point of atmospheric ^{14}C input. During thermohaline circulation, water travels slowly through the deep oceans (during which time ^{14}C decay occurs) before up-welling and mixing with surface waters. Surface water ^{14}C activity is hence somewhat enriched relative to deep waters but depleted relative to the atmosphere and terrestrial biosphere (Broeker 1987; Broeker *et al.* 1991; Gordon and Harkness 1992). This depletion of the ocean ^{14}C content is known as the Marine Radiocarbon Reservoir Effect (MRE). However, local conditions and mixing rates prevent there from being a universal ^{14}C offset from the atmosphere for all oceanic environments (Jones *et al.* 2007; Gomez *et al.* 2008; Harkness 1983). Conditions such as the stratification of water masses, up-welling and residence time all affect the ^{14}C content of water bodies, resulting in a non-uniform ^{14}C concentration (Gordon and Harkness 1992).

The average MRE age offset between contemporary marine and terrestrial material is of the order of 400 ^{14}C years for the global surface oceans in the northern hemisphere (Stuiver and Braziunas 1993) but because of the inherently variable nature of this offset, accurate calibration of radiocarbon ages determined from samples containing marine derived carbon is problematic (Ascough *et al.* 2004). The modelled marine calibration curve (Marine04; Hughen *et al.* 2004), accounts for the global average offset, however, temporal and spatial deviations from this offset, known as ΔR, are evident

Lab ID	Context <Sample ID>	Material	$\delta^{13}C$ (±0.1‰)	$\delta^{15}N$ (±0.1‰)	C:N	Radiocarbon Age (BP)	Calibrated Date (95% confidence)
SUERC-27987	415F: fill of pit [416] that is cut into a deposit of wind-blown sand (417). The fill is charcoal-rich with fire-scorched beach pebbles <420>	charcoal: *Calluna vulgaris* (heather)	-29.2	n/a	n/a	2000 ±30	90 cal BC–cal AD 80
SUERC-28300	612: grave cut to SK611. Earliest grave of the graveyard assemblage <SK611>	human bone: right humerus shaft	-19.2	12.8	3.3	905 ±40	cal AD 1020–1220
SUERC-28301	615: grave fill for SK614, which is associated with cut SK616. <SK618/SK622>	human bone: occipital	-20.1	12.6	3.4	755 ±40	cal AD 1210–1300
SUERC-28299	617: grave fill for SK614, which is associated with cut SK606 <SK605>	human bone: left humerus	-18.0	14.3	3.5	815 ±40	cal AD 1150–1280
SUERC-28302	861: grave fill for SK865, coffin stain (867) <SK865>	human bone: left femur shaft	-20.3	10.6	3.5	325 ±40	cal AD 1450–1660
SUERC-28292	1097: dark brown humic soil that forms part of a substantial build-up of midden material with a very high concentration of animal bone and also early 14th century White Gritty Ware <SF91>	animal bone: pig; right scapula	-21.5	10.1	3.7	1320 ±40	cal AD 640–780
SUERC-28293	1097: dark brown humic soil that forms part of a substantial build-up of midden material with a very high concentration of animal bone and also early 14th century White Gritty Ware <SF175>	animal bone: sheep/goat; right mandible	-22.1	7.5	3.5	1490 ±40	cal AD 430–650
SUERC-29349	1226: silty grey/black clay with much burnt grain that is interpreted as the base of a corn-drying kiln <SBNB08>	shell: *Littorina littorea* (winkle)	1.4	n/a	n/a	1715 ±40	cal AD 230–420
SUERC-29350	1226: silty grey/black clay with much burnt grain that is interpreted as the base of a corn-drying kiln <SBNB08>	shell: *Littorina littorea* (winkle)	1.1	n/a	n/a	1785 ±40	cal AD 120–350
SUERC-29351	1226: silty grey/black clay with much burnt grain that is interpreted as the base of a corn-drying kiln <SBNB08>	shell: *Littorina littorea* (winkle)	0.6	n/a	n/a	1790 ±40	cal AD 120–350
SUERC-29352	1226: silty grey/black clay with much burnt grain that is interpreted as the base of a corn-drying kiln <SBNB08>	shell: *Littorina littorea* (winkle)	1.1	n/a	n/a	1765 ±40	cal AD 130–390
SUERC-29353	1226: silty grey/black clay with much burnt grain that is interpreted as the base of a corn-drying kiln <SBNB08>	charred grain: barley	-23.3	n/a	n/a	1275 ±40	cal AD 650–870
Lab ID	Context <Sample ID>	Material	$\delta^{13}C$ (±0.1‰)	$\delta^{15}N$ (±0.1‰)	C:N	Radiocarbon Age (BP)	Calibrated Date (95% confidence)

Table N.1: Radiocarbon results

Lab ID	Context <Sample ID>	Material	δ13C (±0.1‰)	δ15N (±0.1‰)	C:N	Radiocarbon Age (BP)	Calibrated Date (95% confidence)
SUERC-27987	415F: fill of pit [416] that is cut into a deposit of wind-blown sand (417). The fill is charcoal-rich with fire-scorched beach pebbles <420>	charcoal: *Calluna vulgaris* (heather)	-29.2	n/a	n/a	2000 ±30	90 cal BC–cal AD 80
SUERC-28300	612: grave cut to SK611. Earliest grave of the graveyard assemblage <SK611>	human bone: right humerus shaft	-19.2	12.8	3.3	905 ±40	cal AD 1020–1220
SUERC-28301	615: grave fill for SK614, which is associated with cut SK616. <SK618/SK622>	human bone: occipital	-20.1	12.6	3.4	755 ±40	cal AD 1210–1300
SUERC-28299	617: grave fill for SK614, which is associated with cut SK606 <SK605>	human bone: left humerus	-18.0	14.3	3.5	815 ±40	cal AD 1150–1280
SUERC-28302	861: grave fill for SK865, coffin stain (867) <SK865>	human bone: left femur shaft	-20.3	10.6	3.5	325 ±40	cal AD 1450–1660
SUERC-28292	1097: dark brown humic soil that forms part of a substantial build-up of midden material with a very high concentration of animal bone and also early 14th century White Gritty Ware <SF91>	animal bone: pig; right scapula	-21.5	10.1	3.7	1320 ±40	cal AD 640–780
SUERC-28293	1097: dark brown humic soil that forms part of a substantial build-up of midden material with a very high concentration of animal bone and also early 14th century White Gritty Ware <SF175>	animal bone: sheep/goat; right mandible	-22.1	7.5	3.5	1490 ±40	cal AD 430–650
SUERC-29349	1226: silty grey/black clay with much burnt grain that is interpreted as the base of a corn-drying kiln <SBNB08>	shell: *Littorina littorea* (winkle)	1.4	n/a	n/a	1715 ±40	cal AD 230–420
SUERC-29350	1226: silty grey/black clay with much burnt grain that is interpreted as the base of a corn-drying kiln <SBNB08>	shell: *Littorina littorea* (winkle)	1.1	n/a	n/a	1785 ±40	cal AD 120–350
SUERC-29351	1226: silty grey/black clay with much burnt grain that is interpreted as the base of a corn-drying kiln <SBNB08>	shell: *Littorina littorea* (winkle)	0.6	n/a	n/a	1790 ±40	cal AD 120–350
SUERC-29352	1226: silty grey/black clay with much burnt grain that is interpreted as the base of a corn-drying kiln <SBNB08>	shell: *Littorina littorea* (winkle)	1.1	n/a	n/a	1765 ±40	cal AD 130–390
SUERC-29353	1226: silty grey/black clay with much burnt grain that is interpreted as the base of a corn-drying kiln <SBNB08>	charred grain: barley	-23.3	n/a	n/a	1275 ±40	cal AD 650–870
Lab ID	Context <Sample ID>	Material	δ13C (±0.1‰)	δ15N (±0.1‰)	C:N	Radiocarbon Age (BP)	Calibrated Date (95% confidence)

Table N.1: Radiocarbon results

Lab ID	Context <Sample ID>	Material	$\delta^{13}C$ (±0.1‰)	$\delta^{15}N$ (±0.1‰)	C:N	Radiocarbon Age (BP)	Calibrated Date (95% confidence)
SUERC-27987	415F: fill of pit [416] that is cut into a deposit of wind-blown sand (417). The fill is charcoal-rich with fire-scorched beach pebbles <420>	charcoal: *Calluna vulgaris* (heather)	-29.2	n/a	n/a	2000 ±30	90 cal BC–cal AD 80
SUERC-28300	612: grave cut to SK611. Earliest grave of the graveyard assemblage <SK611>	human bone: right humerus shaft	-19.2	12.8	3.3	905 ±40	cal AD 1020–1220
SUERC-28301	615: grave fill for SK614, which is associated with cut SK616. <SK618/SK622>	human bone: occipital	-20.1	12.6	3.4	755 ±40	cal AD 1210–1300
SUERC-28299	617: grave fill for SK614, which is associated with cut SK606 <SK605>	human bone: left humerus	-18.0	14.3	3.5	815 ±40	cal AD 1150–1280
SUERC-28302	861: grave fill for SK865, coffin stain (867) <SK865>	human bone: left femur shaft	-20.3	10.6	3.5	325 ±40	cal AD 1450–1660
SUERC-28292	1097: dark brown humic soil that forms part of a substantial build-up of midden material with a very high concentration of animal bone and also early 14th century White Gritty Ware <SF91>	animal bone: pig; right scapula	-21.5	10.1	3.7	1320 ±40	cal AD 640–780
SUERC-28293	1097: dark brown humic soil that forms part of a substantial build-up of midden material with a very high concentration of animal bone and also early 14th century White Gritty Ware <SF175>	animal bone: sheep/goat; right mandible	-22.1	7.5	3.5	1490 ±40	cal AD 430–650
SUERC-29349	1226: silty grey/black clay with much burnt grain that is interpreted as the base of a corn-drying kiln <SBNB08>	shell: *Littorina littorea* (winkle)	1.4	n/a	n/a	1715 ±40	cal AD 230–420
SUERC-29350	1226: silty grey/black clay with much burnt grain that is interpreted as the base of a corn-drying kiln <SBNB08>	shell: *Littorina littorea* (winkle)	1.1	n/a	n/a	1785 ±40	cal AD 120–350
SUERC-29351	1226: silty grey/black clay with much burnt grain that is interpreted as the base of a corn-drying kiln <SBNB08>	shell: *Littorina littorea* (winkle)	0.6	n/a	n/a	1790 ±40	cal AD 120–350
SUERC-29352	1226: silty grey/black clay with much burnt grain that is interpreted as the base of a corn-drying kiln <SBNB08>	shell: *Littorina littorea* (winkle)	1.1	n/a	n/a	1765 ±40	cal AD 130–390
SUERC-29353	1226: silty grey/black clay with much burnt grain that is interpreted as the base of a corn-drying kiln <SBNB08>	charred grain: barley	-23.3	n/a	n/a	1275 ±40	cal AD 650–870
Lab ID	Context <Sample ID>	Material	$\delta^{13}C$ (±0.1‰)	$\delta^{15}N$ (±0.1‰)	C:N	Radiocarbon Age (BP)	Calibrated Date (95% confidence)

Table N.1: Radiocarbon results

Lab ID	Context <Sample ID>	Material	δ13C (±0.1‰)	δ15N (±0.1‰)	C:N	Radiocarbon Age (BP)	Calibrated Date (95% confidence)
SUERC-27987	415F: fill of pit [416] that is cut into a deposit of wind-blown sand (417). The fill is charcoal-rich with fire-scorched beach pebbles <420>	charcoal: *Calluna vulgaris* (heather)	-29.2	n/a	n/a	2000 ±30	90 cal BC–cal AD 80
SUERC-28300	612: grave cut to SK611. Earliest grave of the graveyard assemblage <SK611>	human bone: right humerus shaft	-19.2	12.8	3.3	905 ±40	cal AD 1020–1220
SUERC-28301	615: grave fill for SK614, which is associated with cut SK616. <SK618/SK622>	human bone: occipital	-20.1	12.6	3.4	755 ±40	cal AD 1210–1300
SUERC-28299	617: grave fill for SK614, which is associated with cut SK606 <SK605>	human bone: left humerus	-18.0	14.3	3.5	815 ±40	cal AD 1150–1280
SUERC-28302	861: grave fill for SK865, coffin stain (867) <SK865>	human bone: left femur shaft	-20.3	10.6	3.5	325 ±40	cal AD 1450–1660
SUERC-28292	1097: dark brown humic soil that forms part of a substantial build-up of midden material with a very high concentration of animal bone and also early 14th century White Gritty Ware <SF91>	animal bone: pig; right scapula	-21.5	10.1	3.7	1320 ±40	cal AD 640–780
SUERC-28293	1097: dark brown humic soil that forms part of a substantial build-up of midden material with a very high concentration of animal bone and also early 14th century White Gritty Ware <SF175>	animal bone: sheep/goat; right mandible	-22.1	7.5	3.5	1490 ±40	cal AD 430–650
SUERC-29349	1226: silty grey/black clay with much burnt grain that is interpreted as the base of a corn-drying kiln <SBNB08>	shell: *Littorina littorea* (winkle)	1.4	n/a	n/a	1715 ±40	cal AD 230–420
SUERC-29350	1226: silty grey/black clay with much burnt grain that is interpreted as the base of a corn-drying kiln <SBNB08>	shell: *Littorina littorea* (winkle)	1.1	n/a	n/a	1785 ±40	cal AD 120–350
SUERC-29351	1226: silty grey/black clay with much burnt grain that is interpreted as the base of a corn-drying kiln <SBNB08>	shell: *Littorina littorea* (winkle)	0.6	n/a	n/a	1790 ±40	cal AD 120–350
SUERC-29352	1226: silty grey/black clay with much burnt grain that is interpreted as the base of a corn-drying kiln <SBNB08>	shell: *Littorina littorea* (winkle)	1.1	n/a	n/a	1765 ±40	cal AD 130–390
SUERC-29353	1226: silty grey/black clay with much burnt grain that is interpreted as the base of a corn-drying kiln <SBNB08>	charred grain: barley	-23.3	n/a	n/a	1275 ±40	cal AD 650–870
Lab ID	Context <Sample ID>	Material	δ13C (±0.1‰)	δ15N (±0.1‰)	C:N	Radiocarbon Age (BP)	Calibrated Date (95% confidence)

Table N.1: Radiocarbon results

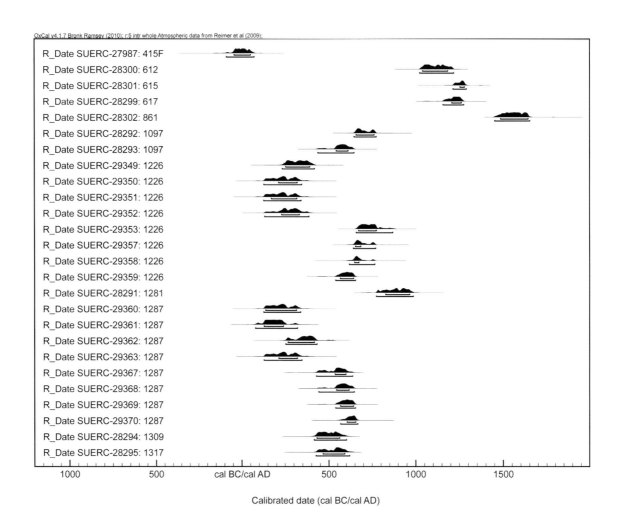

Calibrated date (cal BC/cal AD)

Fig. N.3: Calibrated radiocarbon results of samples

(Stuiver and Braziunas 1993; Ascough *et al.* 2006). Global ΔR values can show significant variation as shown by the data held on the [14]CHRONO Marine Reservoir database at http://intcal.qub.ac.uk/marine/. However, it is important to note that extreme ΔR values such as +2482 ±46 ^{14}C years from Punta Mogotes in Argentina (Gomez *et al.* 2008) are influenced by old dissolved terrestrial carbonate entering the ocean from rivers and groundwater and so are not true marine reservoir effects *per se*. Nevertheless, in the absence of suitable terrestrial material, accurate and precise quantification of ΔR is imperative for accurate calculation of calendar age ranges based on samples containing marine-derived carbon.

Due to the United Kingdom's island setting, and the variety of coastal resources available to archaeological communities, marine material is common within the archaeological record. Therefore, improved accuracy and precision of ^{14}C ages based on such material is desirable. The most direct approach to improving the reliability of marine samples is to quantify ΔR values for the U.K., as shown by previous research in the area (Harkness 1983; Reimer *et al.* 2002; Ascough *et al.* 2004; 2005a; 2005b; 2006; 2007; 2009; Butler *et al.* 2009; Russell *et al.* 2010;

2011a; 2011b). This research has produced ΔR values varying from -155 ^{14}C years off the coast of the Isle of Man (Butler *et al.* 2009) to +94 ^{14}C years off the coast of the Fair Isle (Harkness 1983). These values were determined using a range of methodological approaches and highlight the changing nature of the MRE and the aquatic regimes that drive it. Russell's study (2011) refined the ΔR values on the North Sea coast of Scotland for the post-Roman–late medieval period, producing a mean value of -29 ±51 ^{14}C years.

Methodology and results

Details of the methodology behind the selection and pre-treatment of samples, and the results of the statistical analyses, are provided on the accompanying CD.

Essentially, the methodology emulated the multiple paired sample protocol employed by Ascough *et al.* (2005a; 2006) in previous studies on the Atlantic seaboard of Scotland, with statistical treatment of the data following Russell *et al.* (2011b) in order to calculate a weighted mean ΔR to give a single representative value for each context.

The ΔR values produced from contexts 1226 and 1287

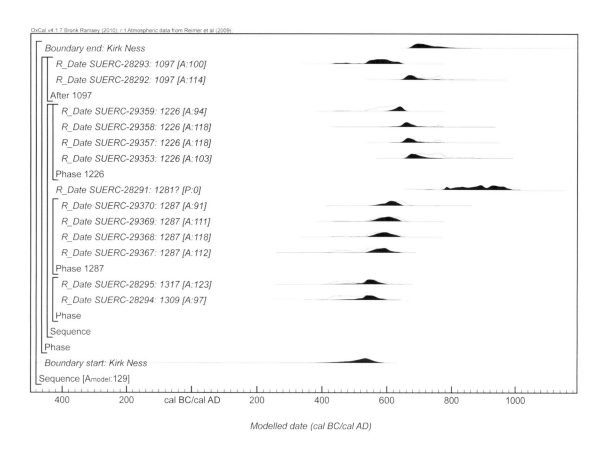

OxCal v4.1.7 Bronk Ramsey (2010): r:1 Atmospheric data from Reimer et al (2009)

Boundary end: Kirk Ness
R_Date SUERC-28293: 1097 [A:100]
R_Date SUERC-28292: 1097 [A:114]
After 1097
R_Date SUERC-29359: 1226 [A:94]
R_Date SUERC-29358: 1226 [A:118]
R_Date SUERC-29357: 1226 [A:118]
R_Date SUERC-29353: 1226 [A:103]
Phase 1226
R_Date SUERC-28291: 1281? [P:0]
R_Date SUERC-29370: 1287 [A:91]
R_Date SUERC-29369: 1287 [A:111]
R_Date SUERC-29368: 1287 [A:118]
R_Date SUERC-29367: 1287 [A:112]
Phase 1287
R_Date SUERC-28295: 1317 [A:123]
R_Date SUERC-28294: 1309 [A:97]
Phase
Sequence
Phase
Boundary start: Kirk Ness
Sequence [Amodel:129]

400   200   cal BC/cal AD   200   400   600   800   1000

Modelled date (cal BC/cal AD)

Fig. N.5: Chronological model

of 39±48 and -21±47 ^{14}C years are statistically indistinguishable from one another as well as indistinguishable from values calculated from 17 other contexts from medieval archaeological sites on the east coast of Scotland (Russell 2011). When all 19 values are χ^2-tested for contemporeity and are combined to give a weighted mean for the entire dataset, they produce a ΔR of -29±51 ^{14}C years (Russell *et al.* 2011b), which is in good agreement with Reimer *et al.* (2002) who quote a value of -33±93 ^{14}C years for the area encompassing western Ireland, Scotland and the Orkney Islands during the mid- to late Holocene (4185–368 BP). The mean value derived for this study is also in good agreement with that determined by Cage *et al.* (2006) of -26±14 ^{14}C years on samples dating back to AD 1850 from fjordic and coastal waters in north-west Scotland. We can confidently suggest using a ΔR of -29 ±51 ^{14}C years for dating medieval marine material from the North Sea coast of Scotland.

Chronological modelling of the ^{14}C results

A Bayesian approach has been adopted for the interpretation of the chronology from this site (Buck *et al.* 1996). Although the simple calibrated dates are accurate estimates of the dates of the samples, this is usually not what archaeologists really wish to know. It is the dates of the archaeological events represented by those samples, which are of interest. In the case of Kirk Ness, it is the

overall chronology of the various levels – when was the structure abandoned; when was the last use of the kiln; for how long was there human activity at this location – that is under consideration, not necessarily the dates of any individual samples. The dates of this activity can be estimated not only using the absolute dating information from the radiocarbon measurements on the samples, but also by using the stratigraphic relationships between samples.

The Bayesian approach allows the combination of these different types of information explicitly, to produce realistic estimates of the dates of archaeological interest. It should be emphasised that the *posterior density estimates* produced by this modelling are not absolute. They are interpretative *estimates*, which can and will change as further data become available and as other researchers choose to model the existing data from different perspectives. Details of the Bayesian modelling are provided on the accompanying CD.

Bayesian-modelled results

The model (Figure N.5) shows good agreement between the radiocarbon dates and the recorded stratigraphic positions of the samples (A_{model}=129).

The model suggests that the modelled late Roman–early medieval activity on the site began in *cal AD 410–590* (*95% probability*; Figure N.5; *start: Kirk Ness*) and

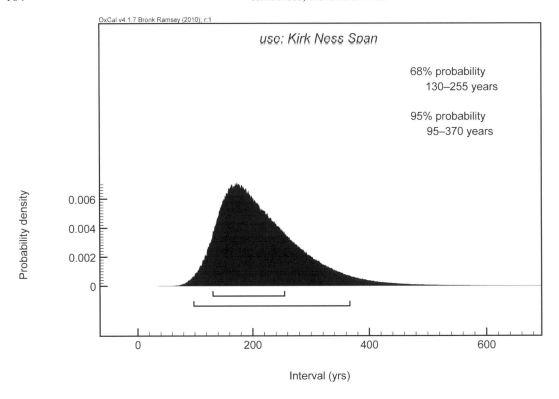

Fig. N.6: Probability distribution for the overall span of time that the late Roman–early medieval activity took place on site

probably in *cal AD 485–565* (*68% probability*). The activity continued for *95–370 years* (*95% probability*; Figure N.6; *use: Kirk Ness*) and probably for *130–255 years* (*68% probability*). This dated activity ended in *cal AD 665–810* (*95% probability*; Figure N.5; *end: Kirk Ness*) and probably in *cal AD 675–745* (*68% probability*).

Discussion

The Bayesian chronological model provides robust estimates for the start, end, and overall duration of activity associated with the dated and modelled contexts. Although there are a substantial number of radiocarbon dates available from the site as a whole, only a small subset could be used in the chronological model. The eight results are from winkle shell and are not entirely appropriate given their marine reservoir offset. Although this can be accounted for to some degree, given the availability of other samples from the same context, they were not deemed ideal and so not included. Furthermore, the four results from the medieval graveyard were not included as that material is more recent than the period under consideration, just as the isolated pit feature [416] was older. This left a total of 13 radiocarbon results from six contexts. So, while the modelling provides a robust estimate, the low number of results produces results that are less precise than possible (Steier and Rom 2000) and the 68% probability ranges provided by the modeling are likely to provide more realistic estimates for the occurrence of the modelled events.

Bibliography

General

Acts and Proceedings, 1575, August, 1839, *Acts & Proceedings of the General Assemblies of the Kirk of Scotland, 1560–1618*, 331–347.
http://www.british-history.ac.uk/report.aspx?compid=58954

Adamson, A. B. 1980, *In the Wind's Eye: North Berwick Golf Club*. Loanhead: Macdonald

Addyman, T., 1999a, *The Scottish Seabird Centre: archaeology (Phase 1): interim report and data structure report*. Unpublished report, Addyman & Kay.

Addyman, T. and Kay, W., 1999b, *The Scottish Seabird Centre, North Berwick, East Lothian: archaeology (Phase 1) – desk-based assessment*. Unpublished report, Addyman & Kay.

Addyman, T., 2000a, *St Andrew's Old Church: archaeological Survey*. Unpublished report, Addyman Archaeology.

Addyman, T., 2000b, 'St Andrew's Old Church and Kirkyard, North Berwick', *Discovery & Excavation in Scotland* 1, 27–8.

Addyman, T., Macfadyen K., 2008, *Excavations at Anchor Green: November 2004–February 2005. Data Structure Report*. Unpublished report, Addyman Archaeology.

Addyman, T., Macfadyen K. and Terry J., 2003 (revised 2011), *The Scottish Seabird Centre, North Berwick, East Lothian: archaeology (Phases 2–5) – data structure report* Unpublished report, Addyman Archaeology.

Anderson, A.O., 1908, *Scottish Annals from English Chroniclers A.D. 500 to 1286*. London: D. N. Nutt.

Anderson, A.O., 1922, *Early sources of Scottish History, A.D. 500 to 1286* (2 vols). Edinburgh: Oliver & Boyd.

Archaeologia Scotia, 1890, Volume 5, Appendix, 59, List of Donations presented to the Society of Antiquaries of Scotland.

Armitage, P. L., 1982, A system for ageing and sexing the horn cores from British post-medieval sites (17th to early 18th century) with special reference to British Longhorn cattle, in *Ageing and Sexing Animal Bones from Archaeological Sites*, Wilson, B., Grigson, C. and Payne, S. (eds). Oxford: British Archaeological Report 109, 255–61.

Arnold, J., 1985, *Patterns of Fashion: the cut and construction of clothes for men and women c 1560–1620*. London: Macmillan.

Arnold, T. (ed.), 1882–5, *Symeonis monachi opera omnia* 2 vols, London: Rolls Series.

Ascough, P. L., Cook, G. T., Dugmore A. J., Barber J., Higney E. and Scott E. M. 2004, Holocene variations in the Scottish marine radiocarbon reservoir effect, *Radiocarbon* 46(2), 611–20.

Ascough, P. L., Cook, G. T. and Dugmore, A. J., 2005a, Methodological approaches to determining the marine radiocarbon reservoir effect. *Progress in Physical Geography* 29, 532–47.

Ascough, P. L., Cook, G. T., Dugmore, A. J., Scott, E. M. and Freeman, S. P. H. T., 2005b, Influence of mollusc species on marine DELTA R determinations. *Radiocarbon* 47(3), 433–40.

Ascough, P. L., Cook, G. T., Church, M. J., Dugmore, A. J., Arge, S. V. and McGovern, T. H. 2006, Variability in North Atlantic marine radiocarbon reservoir effects at c.1000 AD, *The Holocene* 16(1), 131–6.

Ascough, P. L., Cook, G. T., Dugmore, A. J. and Scott, E. M., 2007. The North Atlantic Marine Reservoir Effect in the Early Holocene: implications for defining and understanding MRE values', *Nuclear Instruments and Methods in Physics B* 259(1), 438–47.

Ascough, P. L., Cook, G. T. and Dugmore, A. J., 2009, North Atlantic Marine 14C Reservoir Effects: implications for late-Holocene chronological studies. *Quaternary Geochronology* 4(3), 171–80.

Ashmore, P. J., 1999, Radiocarbon dating: avoiding errors by avoiding mixed samples, *Antiquity* 73, 124–30.

Aufderheide, A. C. and Rodriguez-Martin, C., 1998, *The Cambridge Encyclopedia of Human Palaeopathology*. Cambridge: Cambridge University Press.

Bailey, G., 2004, *Buttons & Fasteners 500BC–AD1840*. Witham: Greenlight.

Bailey, M., 1988, The rabbit and the medieval East Anglian economy. *Agricultural History Review* 36(1), 1–20.

Baker, J. and Brothwell, D., 1980, *Animal Diseases in Archaeology*. London: Academic.

Balasse, M., Tresset, A. and Ambrose, S. H., 2005, Stable isotope evidence ($\delta 13C$, $\delta 18O$) for winter feeding on seaweed by Neolithic sheep of Scotland, *Journal of Zoology* 270(1), 170–6.

Barrow, G. W. S., 1952–3, The earls of Fife in the 12th century. *Proceedings of the Society of Antiquaries of Scotland* 87, 51–62.

Barrow, G. W. S. (ed.), 1960, *Regesta Regum Scottorum i: The Acts of Malcolm IV*, Edinburgh: Edinburgh University Press.

Barrow, G. W. S. 1973, *The Kingdom of the Scots*. London: Edward Arnold.

Barrow, G. W. S. (ed.), 1999, *The Charters of David I*. Woodbridge: Boydell.

Barrow, G. W. S. (ed.), with W.W. Scott, 1971, *Regesta Regum Scottorum ii: The Acts of William I*, Edinburgh: University Press.

Bashford L. and Sibun, L., 2007, Excavations at the Quaker Burial Ground, Kingston-upon-Thames, London, *Post-medieval Archaeology* 41(1), 100–54.

Bass, W. M., 1987, *Human Osteology: a laboratory and field manual*, 3rd ed. Columbia: Missouri Archaeological Society.

Battiscombe, C. F., 1956, *The Relics of Saint Cuthbert*. Oxford: University Press.

Baxter, E. V. and Rintoul, L. J., 1953, *The Birds of Scotland*, vol 2. Edinburgh: Oliver & Boyd.

Bennett, H., 1987, The textiles, in *Excavations in the Medieval Burgh of Perth 1979–1981*, Holdsworth, P. (ed.). Edinburgh: Society of Antiquaries of Scotland Monograph 5, 159–74.

Blackwell, A., 2010, Anglo-Saxon Dunbar, East Lothian: a brief reassessment of the archaeological evidence and some chronological implications, in: *Medieval Archaeology* 54, 361–371.

Blair, J. 2005, *The Church in Anglo–Saxon Society*. Oxford: Oxford University Press

Boardman, S., 1996, *The Early Stewart Kings: Robert II and Robert III, 1371–1406*. East Linton: Tuckwell.

Bocquet-Appel, J.-P., 1984, Biological evolution and history in 19th century Portugal, in: *Multivariate Statistical Techniques in Physical Anthropology*, Vark, G. N. van and Howells W. W. (eds). Groningen: Reidel.

Boessneck, J., 1971, Osteological differences between sheep (Ovis aries Linné) and goat (Capra hircus Linné), in: *Science in Archaeology*, Brothwell, D. and Higgs, E. S. (eds), 2nd ed. London: Thames & Hudson, 1–58.

Bourke, C. (ed.), 1995, *From the Isles of the North, Early Medieval Art in Ireland and Britain*. Belfast: HMSO

Boyd, W. E., 1989, Perth: the wooden coffins, in: *Three Scottish Carmelite Friaries: excavations at Aberdeen, Linlithgow & Perth 1980–86*, Stones, J. A. (ed). Edinburgh: Society of Antiquaries of Scotland Monograph

6, 117–18.

Branch, G. M., 1985, Limpets: their role in littoral and sublittoral community dynamics, in: *The Ecology of Rocky Coasts*, Moore, P. G. and Seed, R. (eds). London: Hodder and Stoughton.

Brereton, G. (ed.), 1968, *Froissart Chronicles* Harmondsworth: Penguin.

Broecker, W., 1987, The great ocean conveyor. *Natural History Magazine* 97, 74–82.

Broecker, W. S., Klas, M,. Clark, E., Bonani, G., Ivy, S. and Wolfli, W., 1991, The influence of $CaCO_3$ dissolution on core top radiocarbon ages for deep sea sediments. *Paleoceanography* 6(5), 593–608.

Bronk Ramsey, C., 1995, Radiocarbon calibration and analysis of stratigraphy: the OxCal program. *Radiocarbon* 37, 425–30.

Bronk Ramsey, C., 1998, Probability and dating. *Radiocarbon* 40(1), 461–74.

Bronk Ramsey, C., 2001, Development of the radiocarbon calibration program. *Radiocarbon* 43, 355–63.

Bronk Ramsey, C., 2009, Bayesian analysis of radiocarbon dates. *Radiocarbon* 51(1), 337–60.

Brothwell, D. R., 1981, *Digging Up Bones*. Oxford: British Museum (Natural History) and Oxford University Press.

Brothwell 1981 appx I

Brown, M., 2007, *The Black Douglases*, John Donald, Edinburgh

Buck, C. E., Cavanagh, W. G. and Litton, C. D., 1996, *Bayesian Approach to Interpreting Archaeological Data*. Chichester: Wiley.

Bullock, P., Federoff, N., Jongerius, A., Stoops, G. and Tursina, T., 1985, *Handbook for Soil Thin Section Description*. Wolverhampton: Waine Research Publications.

Burr, G. S., Beck, J. W., Corrège, T., Cabioch, G., Taylor, F. W., Donahue, D. J., 2009, Modern and Pleistocene reservoir ages inferred from South Pacific corals. *Radiocarbon* 51(1), 319–35.

Burton, J.H. and Masson, D. (eds), 1877–98, *The Register of the Privy Council of Scotland*. Edinburgh: Lords Commissioners of H. M. Treasury.

Butler, P. G., Scourse, J. D., Richardson, C. A., Wanamaker, A. D., Bryant, C. L. and Bennell, J. D., 2009, Continuous marine radiocarbon reservoir calibration and the 13C Suess effect in the Irish Sea: results from the first multi-centennial shell-based marine master chronology. *Earth and Planetary Science Letters* 279, 230–41.

Cage, A. G., Heinemeier, J. and Austin, W. E. N., 2006, Marine radiocarbon reservoir ages in Scottish coastal and fjordic waters. *Radiocarbon* 48(1), 31–43.

Campbell, A. C. and Nicholls, J., 1989, *Seashores and Shallow Seas of Britain and Europe*. London: Hamlyn Guides.

Caple, C., 1983, Pins and wires, in: *Sandal Castle Excavations 1964–1973*, Mayes, P. and Butler, L. A. S. Leeds: Wakefield Historical Publications, 269–78.

Cappers, R. T. J., Bekker, R. M. and Jans, J. E. A., 2006, *Digital Seed Atlas of the Netherlands*. Groningen: Barkhuis & Groningen University Library.

Cachart, R., Hall, D. W., and Middleton, M. (1999), *Gazetteer of Medieval Hospital Sites in Scottish Borders and Fife Council Areas*, held at the RCAHMS

Cardonnel, A. de, 1788, *The Picturesque Antiquities of Scotland*, London.

Ceron-Carrasco, R., 2005, *The fish and marine-shell remains from the excavation at 33 Forth Street, North Berwick*. Unpublished report.

Ceron-Carrasco, R., 2007a, Fish Remains, in: The transformation of an early post-medieval town into a major modern city: excavation and survey of the Waverly Vaults, New Street, Edinburgh, Scotland, Toolis, R. and Sproat, D. *Post-medieval Archaeology* 41(1). 155–79.

Ceron-Carrasco, R., 2007b, *The marine shell remains recovered at Auldhame*. Unpublished report for AOC Archaeology, see Crone in prep.

Ceron-Carrasco, R., 2008a, *Report on the analysis of the fish remains from the excavations at Blackfriars Street, Edinburgh*. Unpublished report for GUARD.

Ceron-Carrasco, R., 2008b, *The fish remains from Archerfield'*. Unpublished report for AOC Archaeology.

Ceron-Carrasco, R., 2008c, *The marine shell remains from the excavation at Archerfield*. Unpublished report for AOC Archaeology.

Chisholm, B. S., Nelson, D. E. and Schwarcz, H. P., 1982. Stable carbon ratios as a measure of marine versus terrestrial protein in ancient diets. *Science* 216, 1131–2.

Christiansen, C., 2009, Textiles, silver-gilt spangles and glass bead, in: *'Clothing for the soul divine': burials at the tomb of St Ninian: excavations at Whithorn Priory 1957–1967*. Lowe, C. Edinburgh: Historic Scotland.

Christiansen forthcoming appx g

Colgrave, B. (ed.), 1985, *The Life of bishop Wilfrid by Eddius Stephanus: Vita Sancti Wilfridi Episcopi Eboracensis – text, translation and notes*. Cambridge: Cambridge University Press.

Collard, M., Lawson, J. A. and Holmes, N., 2006, *Archaeological Excavations in St Giles' Cathedral, Edinburgh, 1981–93*. Scottish Archaeological Internet Report (SAIR) 22.

Constable, A., (ed.), 1892, *A History of Greater Britain as Well England as Scotland by John Major (1469–1550)*. Edinburgh: Edinburgh University Press for the Scottish History Society.

Cooper, J., 1906, Stone mould for casting pilgrims' signs found at North Berwick, shewing designs for crucifix and badge of Saint Andrew. *Transactions of the Scottish Ecclesiastical Society* 1, 191.

Coull, J. R., 1996, *The Sea Fisheries of Scotland*. Edinburgh: John Donald.

Courty, M. A., Goldberg, P. and Macphail, R., 1989, *Soils and Micromorphology in Archaeology*. Cambridge: Cambridge University Press.

Cowan, I. B., 1967, *The Parishes of Medieval Scotland*. Edinburgh: Scottish Record Society Series 93.

Cowan, I. B. and Easson, D. E., 1976, *Medieval Religious Houses: Scotland; with an appendix on the houses in the Isle of Man* (2nd edn). London: Longman.

Cox, A., 1996, Post-medieval dress accessories from recent urban excavations in Scotland. *Tayside & Fife Archaeological Journal* 2, 52–9.

Cox, A., 1998, Grave consequences: a consideration of the artefact evidence from four post-medieval graveyard excavations. *Tayside & Fife Archaeological Journal* 4, 289–99.

Craig, H., 1953, The geochemistry of the stable carbon isotopes. *Geochimica et Cosmochimica Acta* 3, 53–92.

Cramp, R., 1980, *The Background to St Cuthbert's Life*. Durham: Dean and Chapter

Cramp, R., 1984, *Corpus of Anglo-Saxon Stone Sculpture, Volume 1, County Durham and Northumberland*. Oxford: Oxford University Press for the British Academy.

Cramp, R., 1989, The artistic influence of Lindisfarne within Northumbria, in: *St Cuthbert, His Cult and His Community to AD1200*, Bonner, G., Rollason, D. and Stancliff, C. (eds). Woodbridge: Boydell Press, 213–8.

Crone, A., in preparation, *Living and Dying at Auldhame, East Lothian; the excavation of an Anglian monastic settlement & medieval parish church*. Edinburgh: AOC/STAR monograph.

Cross, J. F. and Bruce, M. F., 1989, The skeletal remains, in: *Three Scottish Carmelite Friaries: excavations at Aberdeen, Linlithgow and Perth 1980–1986*, Stones, J. A. (ed.). Edinburgh: Society of Antiquaries of Scotland Monograph 6.

Crowfoot, G. M., 1956, The braids, in: *The Relics of Saint Cuthbert*, Battiscombe, C. F. (ed.). Oxford: Oxford University Press, 433–63.

Crowfoot, E. and Hawkes, S. C., 1967, Early Anglo-Saxon gold braids. *Medieval Archaeology* 11, 42–88.

Crowfoot, E., Pritchard, F. and Staniland, K., 2001, *Textiles and Clothing c.1150–c.1450* (2nd edn). Woodbridge: Boydell Press/Museum of London: Medieval Finds from Excavations in London 4

Cruft, K., Dunbar, J. and Fawcett, R. 2006, *The Buildings of Scotland: Borders*. Princeton: Yale University Press.

Crummy, N., 1988, *The Post-Roman Small Finds from Excavations in Colchester 1971–85*. Colchester: Colchester Archaeological Report 5.

Curran, K. A., 2005, *Religious Women and their Communities in Late Medieval Scotland*. Unpublished PhD Thesis, University of Glasgow.

Dalland, M., 2006, Statistical analysis of the radiocarbon dates, in: Lowe C, 2006, 00–00.

DES 2000 chap 1

DeNiro, M. J. and Epstein, S., 1978, Influence of diet on the distribution of carbon isotopes in animals.

Geochimica et Cosmochimica Acta 42, 495–506.

Dickson, T., and Balfour Paul, J. (eds), 1877–1916, *Accounts of the Lord High Treasurer of Scotland*. Edinburgh: Scottish Record Office.

Dingwall, K., 2004, *Water Mains Renewal, North Berwick, East Lothian: Data Structure Report of an Archaeological Watching Brief*. Unpublished report, Headland Archaeology.

Dingwall, K., 2009, *The Archaeology of the Streets of North Berwick and Implications for the Development of the Burgh*. Edinburgh: Scottish Archaeological Internet Report (SAIR) 37.

Douglas, G. J. 1985, *A Survey of Scottish Brickmarks*. Glasgow: Scottish Industrial Archaeology Survey.

Driesch, A., von den, 1976, *A Guide to the Measurement of Animal Bones from Archaeological Sites*. Cambridge, Mass.: Peabody Museum Bulletin 1,

Duncan, A. A. M., 1975, *Scotland: The Making of the Kingdom*. Edinburgh: Oliver & Boyd.

Duncan, A. A. M. (ed.), 1988, *Regesta Regum Scottorum v: The Acts of Robert I*. Edinburgh: University Press.

Dunlop, A. I. (ed.), 1930, *Bagimond's Roll: statement of Tenths of the Kingdom of Scotland*, Miscellany of the Scottish History Society 6.

Dunlop, A. I. (ed.), 1956, *Calendar of Scottish Supplications to Rome, 1423–28*. Edinburgh: Scottish History Society

Egan, G., 1998, *The Medieval Household. Daily Living c.1150–c.1450*. London: Medieval Finds from Excavations in London 6.

Everson P. et al.,1999, *Corpus of Anglo-Saxon Stone Sculpture, Volume 5: Lincolnshire*, Oxford University Press for the British Academy, Oxford.

Ewing, T., 2008, *Viking Clothing*. Stroud: Tempus.

Fairclough, G. J., Barber, J., 1979, Plymouth excavations, *St Andrews Street 1976*. Plymouth Museum Archaeological Series 2, Plymouth City Museum and Art Gallery, Plymouth.

Farmer, D. H. (ed.), 1990, *Ecclesiastic History of the English People*. Harmondsworth: Penguin.

Fenton, A., 1978, *The Northern Isles: Orkney and Shetland*. East Linton: Tuckwell.

Fenton 1984 fish appx

Ferrier, G., 1869, *Descriptive Account of North Berwick, The Bass, Tantallon, and the Surrounding Vicinity*. Edinburgh: A. Henderson & Co.

Ferrier, G., 1881, *North Berwick and its Vicinity, with Descriptive and Historical Notices of the Bass Rock, Tantallon Castle and other Interesting Objects and Localities*. Edinburgh: Oliphant, Anderson & Ferrier.

Ferrier, Rev. W. M., 1980, *The North Berwick Story*. North Berwick: Tantallon Press.

Ferrier, Rev. W. M., 1991, *The North Berwick Story* (2nd edn). North Berwick: Tantallon Press.

Fisher, I., 2001, *Early Medieval Sculpture in the West Highlands and Islands*. Edinburgh: Society of Anti-

quaries of Scotland Monograph 1

Fisher, J. and Lockley, Rm., 1989, *Seabirds*, Bloomsbury, London.

Fontugne, M., Carré, M., Bentaleb, I., Julien, M. and Lavallée, D., 2004, Radiocarbon reservoir age variations in the South Peruvian upwelling during the Holocene. *Radiocarbon* 46(2), 531–7.

Ford, B., 1987, The lead alloy objects, in: *Excavations in the medieval Burgh of Perth 1979–1981*, Holdsworth, P. (ed.). Edinburgh: Society of Antiquaries of Scotland Monograph 5, 130.

Ford, B. and Walsh, A., 1987, Iron nails, in: *Excavations in the Medieval Burgh of Perth 1979–1981*, Holdsworth, P. (ed.). Edinburgh: Society Antiquaries of Scotland Monograph 5, 138–9.

Forsyth, K., 2000, Evidence of a lost Pictish source in the Historia Regum Anglorum of Symeon of Durham, in: *Kings, Clerics and Chronicles in Scotland, 500–1297: essays in honour of Marjorie Ogilvie Anderson on the occasion of her ninetieth birthday*. Dublin: Medieval Studies, 19–34.

Fraser, J. E., 2009, *From Caledonia to Pictland: Scotland to 795*. Edinburgh: New Edinburgh History of Scotland 1.

Fraser, Sir W., 1885, *The Douglas Book*. Edinburgh: Edinburgh University Press.

Gibson, A. J. S. and Smout, T. C., 1995, *Prices, Food and Wages in Scotland 1550–1780*. Cambridge: Cambridge University Press.

Gilchrist, R. and Sloane, B. 2005, *Requiem; the medieval monastic cemetery in Britain*. London: Museum of London Archaeology Service.

Ginsburg, M., 1984, Women's dress before 1900, in: *Four Hundred Years of Fashion*, Rothstein, N. (ed.). London: Victoria & Albert Museum, 13–47.

Goggin, J. M., 1960, *The Spanish olive jar: an introductory study*. Yale University Publications in Anthropology 62, 1–37.

Gomez, E. A., Borel, C. M., Aguirre, M. L. and Martinez, D. E., 2008, Radiocarbon reservoir ages and hardwater effect for the northeastern coastal waters of Argentina. *Radiocarbon* 50(1), 119–29.

Good, G. L. and Tabraham, C. J., 1988, Excavations at Smailholm Tower, Roxburghshire. *Proceedings of the Society of Antiquaries of Scotland* 118, 231–66.

Gordon, J. E. and Harkness, D. D., 1992, Magnitude and geographic variation of the radiocarbon content in Antarctic marine life: Implications for reservoir corrections in radiocarbon dating. *Quaternary Science Reviews* 11(7–8), 697–708.

Graham 1907 chap 6

Graham, A., 1960–1, Graveyard monuments in East Lothian. *Proceedings of the Society of Antiquaries of Scotland* 94, 211–71.

Graham, A., 1968–9, Archaeological notes on some harbours in eastern Scotland. *Proceedings of the Society of Antiquaries of Scotland* 101, 257–9.

Grant, A., 1982, The use of tooth wear as a guide to the

age of domestic ungulates, in: *Ageing and Sexing Animal Bones from Archaeological Sites*, Wilson, B., Grigson, C. and Payne, S. (eds), Oxford: British Archaeological Report 109, 55–71.

Gray, M., 1978, *The Fishing Industry of Scotland 1790–1914. A Study of Regional Variation*. Aberdeen: University of Aberdeen Press Studies Series 15.

Griffith, D. and Ashmore. P., 2004, *Aeolian Archaeology: the archaeology of sand landscapes in Scotland*. Edinburgh: Scottish Archaeological Internet Report (SAIR) 48.

Groome, F. H., 1894, *Ordnance Gazetteer of Scotland: a survey of Scottish topography, statistical, biographical, and historical*. New Edition 2. London: HMSO.

Grose, F., 1789–91, *The Antiquities of Scotland*, 2 vols. London.

Haggarty, G., 2005, Newbigging Pottery Musselburgh, Scotland: Ceramic Resource Disk. *Northern Ceramic Society Journal* 21.

Haggarty, G., 2006, A gazetteer and summary of French pottery imported into Scotland c 1150 to c 1650, a ceramic contribution to Scotland's economic history. CD Rom in *Tayside and Fife Archaeological Journal* 12, 117–8, + CD Ceramic Resource Disk.

Haggarty, G., 2008, Portobello Potteries Ceramic Resource Disk. *The Northern Ceramic Society Journal* 24

Hall, D. and Bowler, D., 1997, North Berwick, East Lothian: its archaeology revisited. *Proceedings of the Society of Antiquaries of Scotland* 127, 659–75.

Hall, D. W., 2000, The pottery, in: Perry 2000, 00–00.

Hall, M. A. 2007, Crossing the pilgrimage landscape: some thoughts on a Holy Rood Reliquary from the River Tay at Carpow Perth and Kinross, Scotland, in: *Beyond Pilgrim Souvenirs and Secular Badges: essays in honour of Brian Spencer*, Blick, S. (ed.). Oxford: Oxbow Books, 75–91.

Hall, D. and Bowler, D., 1997, North Berwick, East Lothian: its archaeology revisited. *Proceedings of the Society of Antiquaries of Scotland* 127, 659–75.

Hall, D., 2006, 'Unto yone hospitall at the tounis end': the Scottish medieval hospital. *Tayside & Fife Archaeological Journal* 12, 89–105

Hamilton, N. (ed.), 1870, *Willelmi Malmesbiriensis monachi gesta pontificum Anglorum*. London.

Hannay, R. K., 1915, *Rentale Dunkeldense*. Edinburgh: Scottish History Society.

Harkness, D. D., 1983, The extent of the natural 14C deficiency in the coastal environment of the United Kingdom. *Journal of the European Study Group on Physical, Chemical and Mathematical Techniques Applied to Archaeology* 8(IV.9), 351–64.

Harman, M., 1979, An incised cross on Hirta, Harris. *Proceedings of the Society of Antiquaries of Scotland* 108, 254–8.

Hart, A. and North, S., 2009, *Seventeenth and Eighteenth-Century Fashion in Detail*. London: Victoria & Albert Museum.

Hartigan, J. A. and Wigdor, A. K. (eds), 1989, *Fairness in Employment Testing: validity generalization, minority issues and the general aptitude test battery*. Washington: National Research Council (U.S.), Committee on the General Aptitude Test Battery and commission on behavioural and social sciences and education, 179.

Harvey C. C. H. and Macleod, J. (eds), 1930, *Calendar of Writs Preserved at Yester House, 1166–1625*. Edinburgh: Scottish Records Society.

Hedeager Krag, A., 2007, Christian influences and symbols of power in textiles from Viking Age Denmark. Christian influence from the Continent, in: *Ancient Textiles: production, craft and society*, Gillis, C. and Nosch, M.-L. B. (eds). Oxford: Oxbow, 237–43

Henderson, D., 2006, The human bones, in: *Archaeological Excavations in St Giles' Cathedral Edinburgh, 1981–93*, Collard, M., Lawson, J. A., Holmes, N. Edinburgh: Scottish Archaeological Internet Report (SAIR) 22, 27–42.

Henshall, A. S., 1965, Five tablet-woven seal-tags. *Archaeological Journal* 121, 154–62.

Henshall, A. S., Crowfoot, G. M. and Beckwith, J., 1956, Early textiles found in Scotland, part II: medieval imports. *Proceedings of the Society of Antiquaries of Scotland* 88, 22–39.

Hines, J., 1994, The becoming of the English: identity, material culture and language in early Anglo-Saxon England, in: *Anglo-Saxon Studies in Archaeology and History 7*, 49–59.

Hodgson, G. W. I., Smith, C. and Jones, A., 2011, The mammal bone, in: *The Perth High Street Excavation. The Environmental Evidence*, Bogdan, N. Q., Hodgson, G. W. I., Smith, C., Jones, A., Fraser, M., Heppel, D., Clarke, A. S., Jones, A. K. G., Smart, I. H. M., Longmore, R. B., Cerón-Carrasco, R, and McKay, D. Edinburgh: Perth High Street Archaeological Excavation Fasciscule 9.

Hoke, E. and Petrascheck-Heim, I., 1977, Microprobe analysis of gilded silver threads from mediaeval textiles. *Studies in Conservation* 22, 49–62.

Holden, T., 2006a, The corn-drying kilns at Hoddom, in: Lowe, C. (ed.) 2006, 100–13.

Holden, T., 2006b, The botanical evidence, in: Lowe, C. (ed.) 2006, 150–5.

Holmes, E. F., 1991, *Sewing Thimbles*. London: Finds Research Group 700–1700, Datasheet 9.

Holmes, N. M. McQ., 1985, Excavations south of Bernard Street, Leith, 1980. *Proceedings of the Society of Antiquaries of Scotland* 115, 401–28.

Houart, V., 1977, *Buttons: a collector's Guide*. London: Souvenir Press.

House of Commons, 1832, *Great Reform Act Report*: 'Report on the Burgh of North Berwick'. London.

Hughen, K. A., Baillie, M. G. L., Bard, E., Beck, J. W., Bertrand, C. J. H., Blackwell, P. G. Buck, C. E., Burr, G. S., Cutler, K. B., Damon, P. E., Edwards, R. L., Fairbanks, R. G., Friedrich, M., Guilderson, T. P.,

Kromer, B., McCormac, G., Manning, S., Bronk Ramsey, C., Reimer, P. J., Reimer, R. W., Remmele, S., Southon, J. R., Stuiver, M., Talamo, S., Taylor, F. W., van der Plicht, J. and Weyenmeyer, C. E., 2004, MARINE04 Marine radiocarbon age calibration, 0–26 cal kyr BP. *Radiocarbon* 46(3), 1059–86.

Hume, I. N., 1976, *A Guide to the Artifacts of Colonial America*. Philadelphia: University of Philidelphia Press.

Imrie, J. and Dunbar. J. G., (eds), 1982, *Accounts of the Masters of Works for Building and Repairing Royal Palaces and Castles, 1616–1649*. Edinburgh: HMSO.

Innes, C. Cosmo (ed.), 1847, *Carte Monialium De Northberwic Prioratus Cisterciensis B. Marie de Northberwic Munimenta Vetusta Que Supersunt*. Edinburgh.

Jackson, A., 1991, *The Faroes. The Faraway Islands*. London: Robert Hale.

Jamieson, B. A., 1985, *North Berwick in Old Postcards* (3rd edn). East Lothian Council.

Jamieson, B. A., 1992, *North Berwick: the Biarritz of the north*. East Lothian Council.

Jamieson, B. A,. 1996, *North Berwick Between the Wars*. East Lothian Council.

Jamieson, B. A., 2000, *Old North Berwick*. Ochiltree: Stenlake

Janaway, R. C., 1993, The textiles, in: *The Spitalfields Project, volume 1: the archaeology, across the Styx*, Reeve, J and Adams, M.. (eds). York: Council for British Archaeology Research Report 85, 93–119.

Jessop, O., 1996, A new artefact typology for the study of medieval arrowheads. *Medieval Archaeology* 40, 192–205.

Johnson, E., 1982, *Thimble and Thimble Cases*. Prnces Risboro': Shire.

Johnson, M., 2002, East Lothian Yacht Club, North Berwick, East Lothian (North Berwick parish), evaluation. *Discovery & Excavation Scotland* 3, 40.

Johnson South, T. (ed.), 2002, *Historia De Sancto Cuthberto*. Cambridge: Brewer.

Jones, K. B., Hodgkins, G. W. L., Dettman, D. L., Andrus, C. F. T., Nelson, A. and Etayo-Cadavid, M. F., 2007, Seasonal variations in Peruvian marine reservoir age from pre-bomb Argopecten purpuratus shell carbonate. *Radiocarbon* 49(2), 877–88.

Kemp, D. W., 1887, *Tours in Scotland, 1747, 1750, 1760 by Richard Pococke, Bishop of Meath* Edinburgh: Scottish History Society.

Kennett, D. J., Ingram, L., Erlandson, J. M. and Walker, P., 1997, Evidence for temporal fluctuations in Marine Radiocarbon Reservoir ages in the Santa Barbara Channel, southern California. *Journal of Archaeological Science* 24, 1051–9.

Kenward, H. K., Hall, A. R. and Jones, A. K. G., 1980. A tested set of techniques for the extraction of plant and animal macrofossils from waterlogged archaeological deposits. *Science and Archaeology* 22, 3–15.

Kirk, J., 1977, *The Records of the Synod of Lothian and Tweeddale, 1589 1596, 1640 1649*. Edinburgh: Stair Society.

Koch, J. T., 1997, *The Gododdin of Aneirin, Text and Context from Dark-Age North Britain*. Cardiff: University of Wales Press.

Köhler, C., 1963, *A History of Costume*. (trans. Dallas, A.K). New York: Dover.

Kovanen, D. J. and Easterbrook, D. J, 2002, Paleodeviations of radiocarbon marine reservoir values for the northeast Pacific. *Geology* 30(3), 243–6.

Laing, H., 1850, *Ancient Scottish Seals*, Vol. 1. Edinburgh.

Lancaster, S., 2005, *Analysis of Soil Thin Sections from 33 Forth Street, North Berwick*. Headland Archaeology, Specialist report for CFA.

Law, G., 1905, The Earl's Ferry. *Scottish Historical Review* 2, 14–29.

Lee, J. A. and Kemp, R. A., 1992, *Thin Sections of Unconsolidated Sediments and Soils: a recipe*. London: Royal Holloway, University of London, CEAM Report 2, 1–32.

Legge, A. J and Rowley-Conwy, P. A., 1988, *Star Carr Revisited. A Re-analysis of the Large Mammals*. London: University of London, Birkbeck College.

Liddy, C. D., 2008, *The Bishopric of Durham in the Late Middle Ages, Lordship, Community*. Woodbridge: Boydell Press.

Lindsay, E. R. and Cameron, A. I. (eds), 1934, *Calendar of Scottish Supplications to Rome, 1418–22*. Edinburgh: Scottish History Society.

Lindsay, W. A., Dowden, J., and Thomson, J. M. (eds), 1908, *Charters, Bulls and other Documents Relating to the Abbey of Inchaffray, Chiefly from the Originals in the Charter Chest of the Earl of Kinnoul*. Edinburgh: Scottish History Society.

Livingstone, D., 1999, *A Practical Guide to Scientific Data Analysis*. Chichester: Wiley.

Lockhart, G. W., 1997, *The Scots and their Fish*. Edinburgh: Birlinn.

Longin, R., 1971, New method of collagen extraction for radiocarbon dating. *Nature* 230, 241–2.

Lowe, C., 1999, *Angles, Fools and Tyrants. Britons and Anglo-Saxons in Southern Scotland*. Canongate Books with Historic Scotland, Edinburgh.

Lowe, C., 2006, *Excavations at Hoddom, Dumfriesshire – An Early Ecclesiastical Site in South-west Scotland*. Edinburgh: Society of Antiquaries of Scotland.

Lyman, R.L., 1994, *Vertebrate Taphonomy*, Cambridge University Press, Cambridge

Macaulay Institute for Soil Research, 1982, *South Eastern Scotland 1:250 000 Map*. Aberdeen.

MacDonald, W. R., 1904, *Scottish Armorial Seals*. Edinburgh: William Green.

Macquarrie, A., 1997, *The Saints of Scotland, Essays in Scottish church history: AD 450–1093*. Edinburgh: John Donald.

Mac Airt, S. and Mac Niocaill, G. (eds), 1983, *The An-*

nals of Ulster (To AD 1131). Dublin: Dublin Institute for Advanced Studies.

Macdonald 1904 chap 4

Macfadyen, K., 2004a, *Scottish Seabird Centre, North Berwick, East Lothian: archaeological evaluation*, November 2004, Unpublished client report, Addyman Associates.

Macfadyen, K., 2004b, St Andrew's Old Kirk, North Berwick. *Discovery & Excavation in Scotland* 5, 45.

Macfadyen, K., 2004c, Scottish Seabird Centre, North Berwick. *Discovery & Excavation in Scotland* 5, 45.

Macfadyen, K., 2006, *Memorial at Anchor Green, North Berwick, East Lothian: archaeological evaluation and watching brief, December 2006*. Unpublished report, Addyman Archaeology.

MacGregor, A., 1985, *Bone Antler Ivory and Horn: the technology of skeletal materials since the Roman period*. London: Taylor and Francis.

MacGregor, A., Mainman, A. J. and Rogers, N. S. H., 1999, *Craft, Industry and Everyday Life: bone, antler, ivory and horn from Anglo-Scandinavian and medieval York*, York: Archaeology of York: Fasc. 17/12.

Mackinlay, J.M. 1893–4, Some notes on St Baldred's Country. *Proceedings of the Society of Antiquaries of Scotland* 28, 78–83.

MacSween, A., 1995, Pottery, in: The excavation of Neolithic, Bronze Age and early historic features near Ratho, Edinburgh, Smith, A. N. *Proceedings of the Society of Antiquaries of Scotland* 125(1), 108.

Margeson, S., 1982, Worked bone, in: 'Excavations at Castle Acre Castle, Norfolk 1972–1977, Coad, J. G. and Streeten, A. D. F., *Archaeological Journal* 139, 241–55.

Margeson, S., 1993, *Norwich Households: the medieval and post-medieval finds from Norwich Survey Excavations 1971–1978*. Norwich, East Anglian Archaeology 58.

Markem, W. M., 1994, *Pottery from Spanish Shipwrecks 1500–1800*. Gainesville: University Press of Florida.

Mays, S., 1998, *The Archaeology of Human Bones*. London: Routledge.

McAdam, A. D., 2004, *Saint Andrew Church, Anchor Green: Geological Report*. Unpublished.

McCaig, A., 2012, *Former Coastguard Station, Victoria Road, North Berwick East Lothian Archaeological Watching Brief: Report No. 2029*. CFA Archaeology Ltd, client report.

McCullagh, R. P., 2006, The coffin wood, in: Collard et al. (eds) 2006.

McGowran, T., 1985, *New Heaven-on-Forth. Port of Grace*. Edinburgh: John Donald.

McNeill, P. G. B. and MacQueen, H. L. (eds), 1996, *Atlas of Scottish History to 1707*. Edinburgh: Scottish Medievalists and Dept of Geography, University of Edinburgh.

McWilliam, C. E., 2003, *Lothian Except Edinburgh*. New Haven & London: Buildings of Scotland Series, 364.

Miller, J., 1824, *St Baldred of the Bass, a Pictish Legend; The Siege of Berwick, a tragedy; with other poems and Ballads, founded on the Local Traditions of East Lothian and Berwickshire*. Edinburgh.

Mills, G. A. and Urey, H. C., 1940, The kinetics of isotopic exchange between carbon dioxide, bicarbonate ion, carbonate ion and water. *Journal of the American Chemical Society* 62, 1019–26.

Mitchell, A. (ed.), 1906, *Geographical Collections relating to Scotland made by Walter Macfarlane*. 3 vols. Edinburgh: Scottish History Society.

Molleson, T., 1995, Rates of ageing in the eighteenth century', in: *Grave Reflections: portraying the past through cemetery studies*, Saunders, S. R. and Herring. A. (eds). Toronto: Canadian Scholars' Press.

Moloney, C. and Baker, L., 2001, *Appendix B3, Archerfield Environmental Appraisal*. Unpublished report, Headland Archaeology.

Mook, W. G., Bommerson, J. C. and Staverman, W. H., 1974, Carbon isotope fractionation between dissolved bicarbonate and gaseous carbon dioxide. *Earth and Planetary Science Letters* 22(2), 169–76.

Mook, W. G., 1986, Business meeting: recommendations/resolutions adopted by the Twelfth International Radiocarbon Conference, *Radiocarbon* 28, 799.

Moore, H. and Wilson, G. 1999, Food for thought: a survey of burnt mounds of Shetland and excavations at Tangwick. *Proceedings of the Society of Antiquaries of Scotland* 129, 203–37.

Moreno-Nuño, M. R., 1994a, *Arqueomalacologia: Identificación de moluscos*. Informe No. 1994/18. Laboratorio de Arqueozoologia. Informe técnico. Madrid: Universidad Autónoma.

Moreno-Nuño, M. R., 1994b, *Arqueomalacologia: Cuantificación de moluscos*. Informe No. 1994/19. Laboratorio de Arqueozoologia. Informe técnico. Madrid: Universidad Autónoma.

Morrison, J., Oram, R. and Oliver, F., 2008, Ancient Edlbottle unearthed: archaeological and historical evidence for a long-lost early medieval East Lothian village. *Transactions of the East Lothian Antiquarian and Field Naturalists' Society* 27, 21–45.

Nash-Williams, V.E., 1950, *The early Christian monuments of Wales*. University of Wales Press, Cardiff.

Neergaard, M. de, 1987, The use of knives, shears and scabbards, in: *Knives and Scabbards*, Cowgill, J., Neergaard, M. de and Griffiths N. London: Medieval Finds from Excavations in London 1, 51–61.

Nelson, B., 1989, *The Gannet*. Berkhamstead: Poyser.

Nevinson, J. L., 1977, Buttons and buttonholes in the fourteenth century. *Costume* 11, 38–44.

Nicholson, A., 1997, The stone artefacts, in: *Whithorn and St Ninian. The Excavation of a Monastic Town 1984–91*, Hill, P. Stroud: Sutton, 447–64.

Nicholson, R. A., 1991, *An investigation into variability within archaeologically recovered assemblages of faunal remains: The influence of pre-depositional ta-*

phonemic processes. Unpublished D. Phil. Thesis, University of York.

Nisbet, A., 1816, *A System of Heraldry*, (ed. 1816, i), William Blackwood, Edinburgh.

Nord, A. G. and Tronner, K., 2000, A note on the analysis of gilded metal embroidery threads. *Studies in Conservation* 45, 274–9.

North Berwick Corporation, 1966, *North Berwick: the official publication of the corporation*. North Berwick Corporation

NSO, 1845, *New Statistical Account of Scotland*, Vol. 2. Linlithgow, Haddington, Berwick.

O'Leary, M. H., 1981, Carbon isotope fractionation in plants. *Phytochemistry* 20, 553–67.

Oram, R. 2001, *The Lordship of Galloway.* Edinburgh: John Donald

OSA 1791–1799 chap 4

Ottaway, P. and Rogers, N., 2002, *Craft, Industry and Everyday Life: finds from medieval York.* York: The Archaeology of York Fasc. 17

Paton, H. M. (ed.), 1957, *Accounts of the Masters of Works for Building and Repairing Royal Palaces and Castles, 1529–1615.* Edinburgh: HMSO.

Payne, S., 1973, Kill-off patterns in sheep and goats – the mandibles from Aşvan Kale. *Journal of Anatolian Studies* 23, 281–303.

Peglar, M., 1998, *Powder and Ball Small Arms.* Marlborough: Crowood Press.

Perry, D. R., 2000, *Castle Park Dunbar: two thousand years on a fortified headland.* Edinburgh: Society of Antiquaries of Scotland Monograph 16.

Petersen, B. J. and Fry, B., 1987, Stable isotopes in ecosystem studies. *Annual Review of Ecology and Systematics* 18, 293–320.

Petts, D., 2009, Coastal landscapes and early Christianity in Anglo-Saxon Northumbria. *Estonian Journal of Archaeology* 13(2), 79–95.

Phillimore R. P., 1913, *Guide to North Berwick, Gullane, Aberlady, East Lothian & District.* North Berwick

Phillimore, R. P., 1929, *North Berwick and District* (4th edn). North Berwick.

Piper, A. J., 1989, The first generations of Durham monks and the cult of St Cuthbert, in: *St Cuthbert, His Cult and His Community to AD1200*, Bonner, G., Rollason, D. and Stancliff C. (eds). Woodbridge: Boydell Press, 437–46.

Platt, C. and Coleman-Smith, R., 1975, *Excavations in Medieval Southampton, 1953–69, vol. 2. The Finds.* Leicester: Leicester University Press.

Post, D. M., 2002, Using stable isotopes to estimate trophic position: models, methods, and assumptions. *Ecology* 83, 703–18.

Pope, R., 2007, Ritual and the roundhouse: a critique of recent ideas on the use of domestic space in later British prehistory, in: *The Earlier Iron Age in Britain and the near Continent.* Haselgrove, C., Pope, R. (eds). Oxbow, Oxford, 204–228.

Pryde, G. S., 1965, *The Burghs of Scotland.* London: Oxford University press for University of Glasgow.

Raine, J. (ed.), 1841, *The Correspondence, Inventories, Account Rolls, and Law Proceedings, of the Priory of Coldingham*, Edinburgh.

Raithby, J. (ed.), 1819, *Statutes of the Realm: volume 5: 1628–80.* London: History of Parliament Trust.

Reid, J. J., 1885–6, Early motices of the Bass rock and its owners. *Proceedings of the Society of Antiquaries of Scotland* 20, 54–74.

Reimer, P. J., McCormac, F. G., Moore, J., McCormick, F. and Murray, E. V., 2002, Marine radiocarbon reservoir corrections for the mid- to late Holocene in the eastern subpolar North Atlantic. *The Holocene* 12(2), 129–35.

Reimer, P. J., Baillie, M. G. L., Bard, E., Bayliss, A., Beck, J. W., Bertrand, C. J. H., Blackwell, P. G., Buck, C. E., Burr, G. S., Cutler, K. B., Damon, P. E., Edwards, R. L., Fairbanks, R. G., Friedrich, M., Guilderson, T. P., Hogg, A. G., Hughen, K. A., Kromer, B., McCormac, G., Manning, S., Bronk Ramsey, C., Reimer, R. W., Remmele, S., Southon, J. R., Stuiver, M, Talamo, S., Taylor, F. W., van der Plicht, J. and Weyhenmeyer, C. E., 2004, INTCAL04 Terrestrial radiocarbon age calibration, 0–26 cal kyr BP. *Radiocarbon* 46(3), 1029–1058.

Reimer, P. J., Baillie, M. G. .L., Bard, E., Bayliss, A., Beck, J. W., Blackwell, P. G., Bronk Ramsey, C., Buck, C. E. , Burr, G. S., Edwards, R. L., Friedrich, M., Grootes, P. M., Guilderson, T. P., Hajdas, I., Heaton, T. J., Hogg, A. G., Hughen, K. A., Kaiser, K. F., Kromer, B., McCormac, F. G., Manning, S. W., Reimer, R. W., Richards, D. A., Southon, J. R., Talamo, S., Turney, C. S. M., van der Plicht, J. and Weyhenmeyer, C. E., 2009, INTCAL09 and MARINE09 radiocarbon age calibration curves, 0–50,000 years cal BP. *Radiocarbon* 51(4), 1111–50.

Richardson, J. S., 1906–7a, III. Notice of portion of a stone mould for casting Pilgrims' Signacula and ring brooches. *Proceedings of the Society of Antiquaries of Scotland* 41, 431.

Richardson, J. S., 1906–7b, IV. Note on an undescribed erect slab, with incised crosses on both faces, North Berwick. *Proceedings of the Society of Antiquaries of Scotland* 41, 432–3.

Richardson, J. S., 1928–9, A thirteenth-century tile kiln at North Berwick, East Lothian, and Scottish mediaeval ornamented floor tiles *Proceedings of the Society of Antiquaries of Scotland* 63, 281–310.

Richardson, J. S., 1961, *Traditional Characteristics of Buildings in North Berwick.* Unpublished typescript, held at the RCAHMS, ref. D5/EL(P)

Richardson, J. T., 1911, *A Guide to North Berwick and Central East Lothian.* North Bewrick.

Roberts, J., 2001, Human bone, in: New evidence for the origins and evolution of Dunbar: excavations at the Captain's Cabin, Castle Park, Dunbar, East Lothian,

Moloney, C. *Proceedings of the Society of Antiquaries of Scotland* 131, 293–303.

Roberts, J. and Battley, N., 1998, *Skeletal Remains from the Isle of May excavations 1995–1997*. Unpublished GUARD Report.

Roberts, C. A. and Manchester, K., 1997, *The Archaeology of Disease*, Cornell University Press, New York

Robertson, A. S., 1960–1, Roman coins found in Scotland 1951–60 *Proceedings of the Society of Antiquaries of Scotland* 94, 133–83.

Rogers, N. S. H., 1993, *Anglian and Other Finds from 46–54 Fishergate*. York: The Archaeology of York. Fasc. 17/9.

Rollason, D. W., 1987, *Cuthbert Saint and Patron*. Durham: Dean & Chapter of Durham Cathedral.

Rollason, D. (ed.), 1998, *Symeon of Durham, Historian of Durham and the North*. Stamford: Shaun Tyas.

Rollason, D.W., 2003, *Northumbria, 500–1100: creation and destruction of a kingdom*. Cambridge University Press, Cambridge.

Ross, A., 2006, The Bannatyne Club and the publication of Scottish ecclesiastical cartularies. *Scottish Historical Review* 85(2), 202–33.

Rounick, J. S. and Winterbourn, M. J., 1986, Stable carbon isotopes and carbon flow in ecosystems. *BioScience* 36(3), 171–7.

RCAHMS, 1924, *Eighth Report and Inventory of Monuments and Constructions in the County of East Lothian*. Edinburgh: HMSO.

Russell, N., 2011, *Marine Radiocarbon Reservoir Effects (MRE) in archaeology: Temporal and spatial changes through the Holocene within the UK coastal environment*. Unpublished PhD thesis, University of Glasgow.

Russell, N., Cook, G. T., Ascough, P. L. and Dugmore, A. J., 2010, Spatial variation in the Marine Radiocarbon Reservoir Effect throughout the Scottish post-Roman to late medieval period: North Sea values (500–1350BP.). *Radiocarbon* 52(3), 1166–82.

Russell, N., Cook, G. T., Ascough, P. L., Barrett, J. H. and Dugmore, A. J., 2011a, Species specific marine radiocarbon reservoir effect: a comparison of ΔR values between Patella vulgata (limpet) shell carbonate and Gadus morhua (Atlantic cod) bone collagen. *Journal of Archaeological Science* 38(5), 1008–15.

Russell, N., Cook, G. T., Ascough, P. L., Scott, E. M. and Dugmore, A. J., 2011b, Examining the inherent variability in ΔR: new methods of presenting ΔR values and implications for MRE studies. *Radiocarbon* 53(2), 277–88.

Schoeninger, M. J., DeNiro, M. J., 1984, Nitrogen and carbon isotopic composition of bone collagen from marine and terrestrial animals. *Geochimica et Cosmochimca Acta* 48, 625–39.

Scott, E. M., 2003, The third International Radiocarbon Intercomparison (TIRI) and the fourth International Radiocarbon Intercomparison (FIRI) 1990–2002: results, analysis, and conclusions. *Radiocarbon* 45(2), 135–408.

Scottish History Society, 1926, *Miscellany of the Scottish History Society* Vol. iv. Edinburgh: Scottish History Society

Serjeantson, D., 1988, Archaeological and ethnographic evidence for seabird exploitation in Scotland. *Archaeozoologia* 2, 209–24.

Silver, I. A., 1969, The ageing of domestic mammals, in: *Science in Archaeology*, Brothwell, D. and Higgs, E. S. (eds), 2nd edn. London: Thames & Hudson, 283–302.

Simpson, A. T. and Stevenson, S., 1981, *Historic North Berwick: the archaeological implications of development. Scottish Burgh Survey*. Glasgow: Department of Archaeology, University of Glasgow.

Skene, W. F., 1860, Notice of the early ecclesiastical settlements at St Andrews. *Proceedings of the Society of Antiquaries of Scotland* 4(4), 300–21.

Smith, A. N., 1995, The excavation of Neolithic, Bronze Age and Early Historic features near Ratho, Edinburgh. *Proceedings of the Society of Antiquaries of Scotland* 125(1), 69–138.

Smith, C., 2000, The animal bone, in: *Castle Park, Dunbar. Two Thousand Years on a Fortified Headland*, Perry, D. R. Edinburgh: Society of Antiquaries of Scotland Monograph 16, 194–97.

Smith, C., 2008a, The bird bone, in: *Excavations at St Ethernan's Monastery, Isle of May, Fife 1992–7*, James, H. F. and Yeoman, P. Perth: Tayside Fife Archaeological Monograph 6, 93–7.

Smith, C., 2008b, Animal bone, in: Medieval North Berwick revealed: excavations in Forth Street, Mitchell, S. *Transactions East Lothian Antiquarian and Field Naturalists' Society* 27, 47–71.

Smith, C., Hodgson, G. W. I. and Jones, A., 2011, The mammal bone, in: *The Perth High Street archaeological excavation 1975–1977. Living and working in a medieval Scottish burgh. Environmental remains and miscellaneous finds*, Smith, C., Hodgson, G. W. I. and Jones, A. (eds). Perth: Transactions of the Tayside and Fife Archaeological Committee Fasc. 4, 5–44.

Smyth, A. P., 1984, *Warlords and Holy Men: Scotland AD 80–1000*. Edinburgh: Edinburgh University Press.

Spearman, R. M. and Higgitt, J. (eds), 1993, *The Age of Migrating Ideas, Early Medieval Art in Northern Britain and Ireland*. Edinburgh: National Museums Scotland

Statham, C., 2011, *Lost East Lothian*, Birlinn, Edinburgh

Steier, P. and Rom, W., 2000, The use of Bayesian statistics for 14C dates of chronologically ordered samples: a critical analysis. *Radiocarbon* 42, 183–98.

Stenhouse, M. J. and Baxter, M. S., 1983, 14C dating reproducibility: evidence from routine dating of archaeological samples. *PACT* 8, 147–61.

Stevenson R. B. K., 1955, Pins and the chronology of brochs. *Proceedings of the Prehistoric Society* 21, 282–94.

Stuart, J. et al. (eds), 1878–1908, *The Exchequer Rolls of*

Scotland 23 vols. Edinburgh: Records Commission.

Stuiver, M. and Braziunas, T. F., 1993. Modelling atmospheric 14C influences and 14C ages of marine samples to 10,000 BC. *Radiocarbon* 35(1), 137–89.

Stuiver, M. and Kra, R. S., 1986, Editorial comment. *Radiocarbon* 28(2B), ii.

Stuiver, M. and Polach, H. A., 1977, Reporting of 14C data. *Radiocarbon* 19(3), 355–63.

Stuiver, M. and Reimer, P. J., 1986. A computer program for radiocarbon age calibration. *Radiocarbon* 28(2B), 1022–30.

Stuiver, M. and Reimer, P. J., 1993, Extended 14C data base and revised CALIB 3.0 14C calibration program. *Radiocarbon* 35(1), 215–30.

SUAT, 1998, *Historic North Berwick: the archaeological implications of development: a Scottish burgh survey update*. Edinburgh: Scottish Urban Archaeological Trust, Historic Scotland.

Swan D. B., 1910, *North Berwick and its Antiquities*.

Swan D. B., 1926–7, The Monastery of North Berwick. *TELAS*, 1(2), 55–69. FULL JOURNAL NAME PLEASE

Swan, D. B. n.d., *North Berwick Records of the Sixteenth Century.*

Tarlow, S., 2003, Reformation and transformation; what happened to Catholic things in a Protestant world? in: *The Archaeology of the Reformation 1480–1580*, Gaimster, D. and Gilchrist, R. (eds). Leeds: Maney, 108–21.

Teichert, M., 1975, Osteometrische Untersuchungen zur Berechnung der Widerristhöhe bei Schafen, in: *Archaeozoological studies*, Clason, A. T. (ed.). Amsterdam: Elsevier, 51–69.

Thacker, A., 1989, Lindisfarne and the Origins of the Cult of St Cuthbert, in: *St Cuthbert, His Cult and His Community to AD1200*, Bonner, G., Rollason, D. and Stancliff, C. (eds). Woodbridge: Boydell Press, 103–22.

Thomson, J. M. et al. (eds), 1814–1914, *Registrum Magni Sigilli Regum Scotorum in Archivis Publicis Asservatum* 11 vols. Edinburgh.

Thomson, T. (ed.), 1841, *Liber Cartarum Prioratus Sancti Andree in Scotia E Registro Ipso In Archivis Baronum De Panmure Hodie Asservato*. Edinburgh.

Todd, T. D., n.d., *Syllabus of Scottish Cartularies – North Berwick*. Manuscript

Tuck, G. and Heinzel, H., 1978, *A Field Guide to the Seabirds of Britain and the World*. London: Collins.

Tylecote, R. F., 1972, A contribution to the metallurgy of 18th- and 19th-century brass pins. *Post-medieval Archaeology* 6, 183–90.

Vandeputte, K., Moens, L. and Dams, R., 1996, Improved sealed tube combustion of organic samples to CO_2 for stable isotope analysis, radiocarbon dating and percent carbon determinations. *Analytical Letters* 29(15), 2761–73.

Vince, A., Ixer, R. and Young, J., 2008, *Pottery and society in northern Britain, c 450 AD to c 1100: the Northumbrian Kingdom Anglo-Saxon pottery survey*. Report submitted to English Heritage.

Ward, G. K. and Wilson, S. R., 1978, Procedures for comparing and combining radiocarbon age determinations: a critique. *Archaeometry* 20, 19–32.

Ward-Perkins, J. B., 1940, *London Museum Medieval Catalogue*. London: HMSO

Watson, W.J., 1926, *The History of the Gaelic Place-Names of Scotland*. Edinburgh: Blackwood.

Watt, D. E. R. (gen. ed.), 1987–98, *Scotichronicon* 9 vols. Aberdeen.

Watt, D. E. R. and Shead, N. F. (eds), 2001, *The Heads of Religious Houses in Scotland from Twelfth to Sixteenth Centuries*. Edinburgh: Scottish Record Society, New Series 24

Watt, D. E. R. and Murray A. L. (eds), 2003, *Fasti Ecclesiae Scoticanae Medii Aevi Ad Annum 1638*. Edinburgh: Scottish Records Society.

Watt, J., Pierce, G. and Boyle, P., 1997, *Guide to the Identification of North Sea Fish using Premaxilla and Vertebra*. Denmark: ICES Cooperative Research Report 220.

Webster, B., 1982, *Regesta Regum Scottorum vi: The Acts of David II*. Edinburgh: Scottish Record Society

Weir, M., 1988, *Ferries in Scotland*. Edinburgh: John Donald

Wheeler, A. and Jones, A. K. J., 1989, *Fishes*. Cambridge: Cambridge Manuals in Archaeology.

Will, R. S., 1997, The pottery, in: *Excavations within Edinburgh Castle in 1988–91*, Driscoll, S. T. and Yeoman, P. A. Edinburgh: Society of Antiquaries of Scotland Monograph 12, 140–6.

Williamson, A., 1908, *North Berwick*.

Wilson, D., 1851, *Prehistoric Annals of Scotland*, London.

Woolf, A., 2006, Dun Nechtain, Fortriu and the Geography of the Picts. *Scottish Historical Review* 85(2), 182–201.

Woolf, A., 2007, *From Pictland to Alba, 789–1070*. Edinburgh: New Edinburgh History of Scotland 2.

Xu, S., Anderson, R., Bryant, C., Cook, G. T., Dougans, A., Freeman, S., Naysmith, P., Schnabel, C. and Scott, E. M., 2004, Capabilities of the new SUERC 5MV AMS facility for 14C dating. *Radiocarbon* 46(1), 59–64.

Yeoman, P., 1999, *Pilgrimage in Medieval Scotland*. London: Batsford.

Web References

14 CHRONO Marine Reservoir database: http://intcal.qub.ac.uk/marine/.

British Geological Survey, Geology of Britain: http://mapapps.bgs.ac.uk/geologyofbritain/home.html

www.lib.ed.ac.uk/resources/collections/specdivision/ch200803.shtml

www.nottingham.ac.uk/english/ins/kepn/

www.rcahms.gov.uk/pls/portal/canmore.newcandig_details_gis?inumlink=56610

National Library of Scotland http://geo.nls.uk/roy-lowlands/

www.nls.uk/maps/index.html

www.rps.ac.uk/

www.shc.ed.ac.uk/Research/saints/Project.htm

www.scran.ac.uk/database/record.php?usi=000-000-578-377-C&scache=1ntoy6km6e&searchdb=scran (drawn reconstruction of old kirk)

www.scran.ac.uk/database/record.php?usi=000-000-578-376-C&scache=1ntoy6km6e&searchdb=scran (1816 Morton drawing of the old kirk)

www.stat-acc-scot.edina.ac.uk/link/1791-99/Haddington/North%20Berwick/

www.stat-acc-scot.edina.ac.uk/link/1834-45/Haddington/North%20Berwick/

Manuscript Sources

National Archives of Scotland:

B56	North Berwick Burgh Records
GD1/1386	Charters Relating to North Berwick
GD110	Papers of the Hamilton-Dalrymple Family of North Berwick
CH2/285/1	North Berwick Kirk Session Minutes

Index